POLICE, PROVOCATION, POLITICS

Counterinsurgency in Istanbul

Deniz Yonucu

CORNELL UNIVERSITY PRESS **ITHACA AND LONDON**

First published 2022 by Cornell University Press

Library of Congress Cataloging-in-Publication Data

Names: Yonucu, Deniz, 1979- author.
Title: Police, provocation, politics : counterinsurgency in Istanbul /
    Deniz Yonucu.
Description: Ithaca [New York] : Cornell University Press, 2022. | Series:
    Police/worlds : studies in security, crime, and governance | Includes
    bibliographical references and index.
Identifiers: LCCN 2021041154 (print) | LCCN 2021041155 (ebook) | ISBN
    9781501762154 (hardcover) | ISBN 9781501762161 (paperback) | ISBN
    9781501762178 (pdf) | ISBN 9781501762185 (epub)
Subjects: LCSH: Law enforcement—Political aspects—Turkey—Istanbul. |
    Counterinsurgency—Turkey—Istanbul. | Internal security—Political
    aspects—Turkey—Istanbul. | Political violence—Turkey—Istanbul. |
    Government, Resistance to—Turkey—Istanbul. | Turkey—Politics and
    government—1980–
Classification: LCC HV8241.93.I88 Y66 2022 (print) | LCC HV8241.93.I88
    (ebook) | DDC 363.2/3095694—dc23
LC record available at https://lccn.loc.gov/2021041154
LC ebook record available at https://lccn.loc.gov/2021041155

For the spirits of solidarity and resistance
To Rauf

Agir berda komê, bera xwe da zomê.
They set the community on fire and then went up to the highlands.
—Kurdish proverb

Contents

Preface ix

Acknowledgments xiii

List of Abbreviations xvii

Introduction: Population, Provocative
Counterorganization, and the War on Politics 1

1. The Possibility of Politics: People's Committees,
Sanctuary Spaces, and Dissensus 28

2. "Gazas of Istanbul": Threatening Alliances
and Militarized Spatial Control 53

3. Provocative Counterorganization: Violent
Interpellation, Low-Intensity Conflict,
Ethnosectarian Enclaves 72

4. Good Vigilantism, Bad Vigilantism: Crime,
Community Justice, Mimetic Policing,
and the Antiterror Laws 96

5. Inspirational Hauntings: Undercover Police
and the Spirits of Solidarity and Resistance 116

6. Gezi Uprisings: The Long Summer of Solidarity
and Resistance, and the Great Divide 138

Epilogue: Policing as the Generation of (Dis)Order 158

Notes 163

References 177

Index 191

Growing up in a working-class neighborhood of Istanbul in the 1980s, I often heard stories about the socialist movement of the 1970s; about the strikes organized in the factories near us; and, just before the coup of 1980, about the clashes on our streets between revolutionaries and Turkish nationalists. These stories were told quietly and behind closed doors as tales from a very distant past, as if all the neighborhood workers who had organized mass strikes and factory occupations, taken part in demonstrations, and filled up the ranks of the revolutionary organizations had nothing to do with our current neighbors. Those must have been different people living in the neighborhood in the 1970s, I thought; they must all have moved away. As a child I could feel the fear in the air whenever adults would speak of those years. Later, when I became a teenager, I heard frequent minilectures from adults in the neighborhood about the dangers of politics. For them, even talk of politics could put one in danger—best stay clear of it altogether.

When in 1994 I began attending high school in another neighborhood, I was surprised to discover that there were people in Turkey who believed that the revolutionary struggle was still alive, and they considered themselves to be part of the struggle. These were my Alevi schoolmates and their university student sisters and brothers, from predominately Alevi-populated working-class neighborhoods. My friends described for me the barricades, the checkpoints, the house raids, and the armored military vehicles patrolling their neighborhoods. Listening to their stories, I understood that the urban experience in these areas was radically different from the one I had witnessed in my own predominantly Sunni Turkish-populated working-class neighborhood.

In the winter of 1995, a high school Alevi friend took me to her neighborhood. Like my own neighborhood, the streets were muddy, and the houses were either makeshift cement block shanties (*gecekondu*) or incomplete apartment buildings. The main difference was that in her neighborhood, every single wall was spray-painted with slogans: "Long live the united struggle of the Turkish and Kurdish peoples," "Long live the revolution and socialism," "The murderous state will pay the price," "The people's justice will call [the government] to account." My friend took me to a café where she hung out regularly with her friends. While drinking tea together that day, I listened to high school students debating the possible paths to revolution. In my subsequent visits to my friend's neighborhood, I often found myself listening to and participating in heated conversations on the difference between democratic revolution and socialist revolution, the disputes between Rosa Luxemburg and Vladimir Ilyich Lenin, the possibility of the establishment of a free and socialist Kurdistan, and philosophical debates on Marxism, historical materialism, and dialectics. We were listening to popular Turkish and Kurdish revolutionary music bands of the time, such as Grup Yorum, Grup Kızılırmak, Grup Özgürlük Türküsü, or Koma Dengê Azadî, whose lyrics promised that the victory of the working classes and the Kurdish liberation was at hand. At the time, my Sunni Turk working-class peers were listening to apolitical American music from MTV—Vanilla Ice, Meat Loaf, New Kids on the Block—or to Turkish pop and sad Turkish *arabesk* songs that depicted the misery of life in working-class neighborhoods. Some were developing an interest in religion, others in drugs.

Although my high school friends and I were optimistic about the future in those years, the 1990s, like the present, were dark times in Turkey. Kidnappings of revolutionary leftist and pro-Kurdish activists, disappearances, torture, and deaths in custody were common both in Northern Kurdistan (also known as southeast Turkey) and Istanbul.[1] When we were still in high school, some of my friends were imprisoned, others were forced to leave the country, and many experienced firsthand various forms of police violence. Yet, such intimidating methods were not effective in suppressing the dissent. I remember how shocked and fearful I was in June 1995 when I learned that a number of my friends from high school had joined thousands of others at the funeral of Sibel Yalçın, an eighteen-year-old revolutionary militant killed by the police after taking part in an armed action that resulted in the killing of a policeman. I also cannot forget my shock that year when I saw hundreds of young people dancing and chanting *Rojbaş, gerîla rojbaş* (Good days, guerrilla good days) in Kurmanji Kurdish, during a concert I attended with my high school friends at Abdi Ipekçi Sport Hall, a large Istanbul stadium near my own neighborhood. While the people in my neighborhood were afraid to discuss the old revolutionary days of the 1970s in public, thousands at that stadium that night were listening to dissident music bands and chanting their support for Kurdish guerrillas fighting against the Turkish state. The enormous gulf between the attitudes of the people in my neighborhood who, once upon a time had played an active role in the leftist working-class movement, and the Kurdish and Alevi working classes who filled that concert hall with exuberant revolutionary fervor was beyond my comprehension.

After my visits to my Alevi high school friend's neighborhood in the early to mid-1990s, the next time I went to another such neighborhood was in March 1998, when I went to the Gazi neighborhood to participate in an anniversary demonstration organized to protest the killings of twenty-two people by state security forces three years earlier. A friend from Gazi told me that the entrance to the neighborhood would be closed during the day of the protest and that I should go there the night before the event. I remember asking myself, "How could the entrance to a neighborhood be closed? It's not as though it has gates." Following the suggestion of my friend, I went there the night before the protest and stayed with his family. I still remember the dinner conversation about what the police would do the next day. Listening to his family members talk about the police as a violent enemy ready to attack the people, I realized that the next day would be an exceptional one for me.

I will never forget what I saw when I stepped out of the house the next morning. Large numbers of masked policemen from special operation units were standing on the rooftops of the buildings, pointing their rifles downward toward the streets. Masked policemen with heavy weapons were standing at the street entrances. The presence of these faceless black figures told us that the only law in Gazi that day was the law of the Police—the untouchable, godlike side of the law that has the right to decide to kill or let live. I was full of fear and thought I might easily die that day. The police were there at that anniversary protest of the killing of Gazi residents to remind us that death was never far away; instead, it was an imminent possibility. I overheard that there had already been clashes between the police and people who had wanted to enter the neighborhood. Watching a military vehicle chasing a group of youth, I understood how the entrance of a neighborhood could be closed. I saw the gates of the neighborhood and witnessed its armed gatekeepers. I wanted to run away, to get out of the neighborhood as fast as I could. But there were thousands in the streets, walking calmly despite the threatening presence of the state security forces. I felt embarrassed by my fear.

Two years later, in 2000, I traveled to Mardin, a city in Northern Kurdistan, to conduct research for my bachelor's thesis in sociology. The entrances and exits to the Mardin streets inhabited by dispossessed Kurds were guarded by black-masked and armed policemen from the special operation units. I spent hours and days with Kurdish women talking about their lives and various forms of violence that they had experienced. Listening to the stories of these Kurdish women while those threating men were outside, I again felt both afraid and embarrassed by my fear. I remembered what I had witnessed in Gazi in 1998 and how I had felt there. I was convinced that the Turkish ruling elites were actively and relentlessly waging war against Turkey's dispossessed and racialized Alevi and Kurdish populations.

What I witnessed more than two decades ago in the Alevi working-class neighborhoods of Istanbul and in Northern Kurdistan has haunted me ever since. It is that story of the systematic police repression and fearless political resistance of Turkey's Alevis and Kurds that I now feel obliged to write.

Acknowledgments

I wrote this book in difficult times when we are witnessing a right-wing, nationalist, racist backlash that exacerbated the already difficult conditions of racialized, Indigenous, immigrant, and working-class populations across the globe. Over the course of my research and writing of this book, many of my interlocutors, friends, and acquaintances were incarcerated, had to leave Turkey, or worse, lost their lives to state security violence or the deadly attacks of the Islamic State. Despite this daunting political landscape, the courage, determination, and ethical aspirations of my interlocutors and friends from Istanbul's racialized and dissident working-class neighborhoods serve as a continuous source of inspiration, which made it possible for me to write this book. I owe an enormous debt of gratitude to those inspiring people who shared their lives and experiences with me and who admirably try to keep the spirit of solidarity and resistance alive under challenging conditions in extremely trying times.

This book started as a dissertation at Cornell University. At Cornell, I was very fortunate to be surrounded by scholars and an intellectual environment that profoundly shaped my intellectual formation. I would particularly like to thank to the members of my dissertation committee Steven Sangren, Shelley Feldman, Magnus Fiskesjo, and Vilma Santiago-Irizarry, for their engagement in my work and for their detailed and helpful comments on the earliest draft of this project.

I am grateful to Cornell University Press's Policing/World series editors Sameena Mulla, William Garriott, Ilana Feldman, and, especially, Kevin Karpiak, who believed in this book and who offered me invaluable suggestions that improved its content. The nuanced and detailed comments of two anonymous reviewers and two anonymous in-house editors were also very helpful during the revision process. The acquisition editor Jim Lance had been very encouraging from the beginning. I thank him for his support and encouragement. I am also grateful to the rest of the editorial team at Cornell University Press, including Clare Jones, for their meticulous work. The copyediting efforts of Gail Chalew and Mary Gendron are also much appreciated.

I am grateful to several individuals who read and commented on chapter drafts at various stages. Thank you to Brandy Doyle, Danayt Yosef, Delal Aydin, Deniz Cosan Eke, Dilek Kurban, Erol Saglam, Esra Sarioglu, Jean Comaroff, Martin Sökefeld, Orkide Izci, Talin Suciyan, Ümit Cetin, and Zeteny Bartos. My warmest gratitude is also due to Theresa Truax-Gischler, whose keen editorial eye greatly improved the final version of this manuscript and whose always-refreshing support kept me writing and motivated.

Over the past several years, I have had the opportunity to present my research at numerous conferences, workshops, and seminars. These occasions helped me to sharpen my ideas and improve the main arguments of the book. I am grateful to those friends and colleagues who invited me to talk about various parts of this book at their universities, including Heike Drotbohm (Johannes Gutenberg University Mainz), Maaike Voorhoeve (University of Amsterdam), Cristiana Strava (Leiden University), Caglar Dölek (Carleton University), Kader Konuk (University of Duisburg-Essen), Martin Sökefeld (Ludwig Maximilian University of Munich), Insa Koch (London School of Economics), Gökçe Yurdakul (Humboldt University), Ayse Öncü (Sabanci University), Sevim Budak (Istanbul Universiyt), and Victor Collet (Université Paris Ouest Nanterre).

After my doctoral studies, I spent a semester at the European Institute at the London School of Economics and Political Science (LSE). I am thankful to Esra Özyürek for encouraging me to apply for a fellowship for a visiting scholar position at the LSE and supporting my application. I would also like to thank Georges Khalili and Nora Lafi for hosting me at the Forum Transregionale Studien and the Leibniz-Zentrum Moderner Orient (ZMO) in Berlin as a postdoctoral fellow. These fellowships allowed me to concentrate full-time on research and writing and provided invaluable opportunities to discuss my project with scholars from across the disciplines. Warm thanks to fellows at the ZMO and Europe in the Middle East–The Middle East in Europe (EUME) Programme of the Forum Transregionale Studien for thought-provoking and stimulating discussions.

I am truly indebted to Martin Sökefeld for offering me an academic shelter in the Department of Social and Cultural Anthropology at Ludwig Maximilian University of Munich during challenging times. I will never forget his camaraderie. Many thanks also to Kader Konuk for providing me another academic refuge at the Critical Residency Program at Free University, Berlin. Despite the pandemic, at the Center for Technology and Society at the Technische Uniersität Berlin, Gabriele Wendorf, Martina Schäfer, and Judith Vey created a collegial atmosphere, and for that I am thankful to them.

I took up a new position at Newcastle University after I finished writing this book. I would like to thank my new colleagues for their warm welcome. Thanks are also owed to Anna Secor, Ebru Soytemel, Sertac Sehlikoglu, Murat Keyder, and Zeynep Kezer, who helped me begin my new academic journey.

Research, writing, and editing stages of this book were made possible by grants from the Wenner-Gren Foundation, Middle East Research Competition of the Ford Foundation, Cornell University's Graduate School and the Institute for European Studies, SALT Research, Türkiye Özgür Eğitim Kültür ve Sanat Vakfı (Free Education, Culture and Art Association of Turkey), Newton Fund of the British Council, Alexander Von Humboldt Foundation, the DAAD, and Einstein Foundation, Berlin. I am thankful for their support.

I would also like to thank Sebnem Korur Fincanci and Hurriyet Sener for allowing me to conduct archival research at the Human Rights Association of Turkey.

Portions of the following are previously published: chapters 2 and 3, in "Counterinsurgency in Istanbul: Provocative Counterorganization, Violent Interpellation and Sectarian Fears," *British Journal of Middle Eastern Studies*; chapter 4, in "Urban Vigilantism: A study of Anti-terror Law, Politics, and Policing in Istanbul," *International Journal of Urban and Regional Research* 42 (3): 408–22; and chapter 5, "Inspirational Hauntings and a Fearless Spirit of Resistance: Negotiating the Undercover Police Surveillance of Racialized Spaces in Istanbul," *Current Anthropology*, 2022. I thank the publishers of these journals for permission to include these works in this book.

Being a working-class academic is not an easy task. For racialized and working-class academics, academia's paths are filled with countless obstacles that are often invisible to others. My special gratitude goes to Yiğit Ekmekçi for helping me continue to try to find my way in those difficult paths.

Last but not least, my deepest thanks go to my partner Mehmet Rauf Kesici. This book would have been impossible without his calming spirit, radical optimism, endless care, and love. I thank him for believing in this book even at the times when I lost faith in it and for the life we share.

Abbreviations

AKP	Justice and Development Party (*Adalet ve Kalkınma Partisi*)
BDP	Peace and Democracy Party (*Barış ve Demokrasi Partisi*)
Dev-Sol	Revolutionary Left (*Devrimci Sol*)
DHKP-C	Revolutionary People's Liberation Party Front (*Devrimci Halk Kurtuluş Partisi-Cephesi*)
DYP	True Path Party (*Doğru Yol Partisi*)
HDP	People's Democracy Party (*Halkın Demokrasi Partisi*)
HEP	People's Labor Party (*Halkın Emek Partisi*)
IHD	The Human Rights Association (*İnsan Hakları Derneği*)
IRA	Irish Republican Army
KCK	Kurdistan Communities Union (*Koma Civakên Kurdistan*)
MHP	Nationalist Action Party (*Milliyetçi Hareket Partisi*)
MLKP	Marxist-Leninist Communist Party (*Marksist-Leninist Komünist Partisi*)
NA	Neighborhood Association
OHAL	State of Emergency Region (*Olağanüstü Hal Bölgesi*)
ÖHD	Special Warfare Department (*Özel Harp Dairesi*)
PKK	Kurdistan Workers' Party (*Partiya Karkerên Kurdistan*)
para.	Paragraph
SHP	Social Democratic Populist Party (*Sosyal Demokrat Halkçı Parti*)

POLICE, PROVOCATION, POLITICS

INTRODUCTION

Population, Provocative Counterorganization, and the War on Politics

On September 29, 2013, Hasan Ferit Gedik, a twenty-one-year-old revolutionary, was shot to death by drug gangs while walking in a march in the Gülsuyu neighborhood of Istanbul. The march had been organized to protest the neighborhood's escalating gang violence and the police's reluctance to prevent it. Populated predominantly by working-class Alevis, a stigmatized and ethnically heterogeneous belief group in Turkey, Gülsuyu, like other neighborhoods of its kind, had been known since the 1970s to be a hub for revolutionary organizations. Hasan Ferit had been an active participant in the large-scale Gezi uprising that had mobilized millions of people from diverse ethnosectarian and class backgrounds in dissent against the Justice and Development Party (Adalet ve Kalkınma Partisi; AKP) government in the summer of 2013.[1] He was also an active participant in the Etiler Forum, one of several neighborhood public forums that emerged during the Gezi uprising. Located in the upper-middle-class Etiler district of Istanbul, the forum also attracted people from surrounding areas, including the Alevi working-class neighborhood of Küçük Armutlu, where Hasan Ferit lived with his family.

Due in part perhaps to Hasan Ferit's connections to affluent Etiler residents, his talks at the Etiler Forum were widely circulated on social media. His wide smile, kind voice, and patience in explaining social problems made an impression on those who had never met him personally. The power of his words and the spirit of solidarity created by the shared experience of the uprising inspired hundreds of Turkish middle-class Gezi protesters to attend Hasan Ferit's funeral in Gazi—another predominantly Alevi working-class neighborhood of Istanbul.

Held a few days after he was murdered, his funeral became a fateful encounter as two worlds steeped in vastly different histories, experiences, and realities came into contact (see figure I.1). The presence of red-masked young revolutionaries with rifles, who were at the funeral to provide security, was a stark illustration of the radical difference between the world of Hasan Ferit Gedik and that of the middle-class Turkish attendees. I remember the shock I saw in the face of one of my upper-middle-class artist acquaintances when I ran into her after the funeral. She was frozen, eyes staring out into the space above my head. The only word she could come up with to describe what she had witnessed was one in English: "uncanny."

The mainstream media were quick to sensationalize the "uncanniness" of the funeral. Images of the young, masked men armed with their weapons circulated in the media for days and served as proof of the allegedly "criminal" and "terrorist" activities going on in these dissident working-class neighborhoods. Clashes between the police and neighborhood youth activated by the concentration of police violence in these neighborhoods toward the end of the Gezi uprising were featured frequently in the press. Images of makeshift barricades made from market stalls or garbage cans, flying Molotov cocktails, and teenagers throwing

FIGURE I.1. A scene from the funeral of Şirin Öter, a member of the Marxist-Leninist Communist Party (MLKP), who was killed by state security forces on December 22, 2015. Image has been modified to protect identities of those pictured.

Photo by Sinan Targay.

stones at armored military vehicles from in front of their shanty-like homes or humble apartment buildings served to present the neighborhoods as "terror dens" (see figure I.2). Government officials and pro-government journalists were already accusing Alevis of having organized the uprising, claiming that they were being manipulated by foreign forces (*dış mihraklar*) and "leftist extremists" who sought to sow chaos in the country. Such media representations of the neighborhoods helped paint the Alevi population as a whole with the same brush: as "unruly" people who acted against the interests of the nation-state.

What appeared to the Turkish middle classes as uncanny was for the residents of Istanbul's predominantly Alevi-populated working-class neighborhoods a regular part of their everyday familiar. Throughout the history of Turkey, the successor state to the multiethnic and multireligious Ottoman Empire, Alevis have been subjected to assimilationist policies that sought to turn them into docile Turkish subjects and discriminatory policies that condemn them as internal enemies. They were also persecuted both during the Ottoman era and in modern Turkey.[2] Because of the racialized stigma attached to the word "Alevi"—they have been branded as heretics, infidels, sexual deviants, and atheists—many Alevis tend to hide their identity.[3] It is therefore difficult to know the exact size of the Alevi population in Turkey (Karakaya-Stump 2017). Researchers estimate that approximately 20 percent of Turkey's population is Alevi (Cetin 2016, 251);

FIGURE I.2. Neighborhood youths throw stones at the police.

Photo by Sinan Targay.

at Turkey's current population of 82 million, that means there are about 16.4 million Alevis. Alevis are an ethnically heterogeneous group: the majority of Alevis identify ethnically as Turks, followed by Alevi Kurds who make up approximately 20 percent of the Alevi population of Turkey, there are also sizable populations of Alevi Arabs and Zazas (251). Since the 1960s, Alevis have been among the main constituents of left-wing political organizations, with adherents active in center-left to radical leftist groups. During the Cold War, the Turkish ruling elites stigmatized them, along with the Kurds, who too make up approximately 20 percent of the population in Turkey (Koc et al. 2008), and communists as the three internal threats to Turkish national security (Lord 2017). Thus Kurdish Alevis experience a double racialization due to their intersecting Kurdish and Alevi identities.[4]

Turkey's three designated Cold War "internal enemies"—sometimes embodied in the same person, as in the case of a communist Alevi Kurd—often lived together in Istanbul's dissident working-class neighborhoods. Within leftist circles, many of these neighborhoods—Gazi Mahallesi, Gülsuyu, Okmeydanı, Bir Mayıs Mahallesi, Çayan Mahallesi, and Armutlu—are referred to as revolutionary neighborhoods (*devrimci mahalleler*) or dissident neighborhoods (*muhalif mahalleler*). These neighborhoods were constructed informally as sanctuaries for Alevi workers with the help of revolutionaries in the 1960s and 1970s. Nicknamed by residents the "Gazas of Istanbul," thereby highlighting the extensive police surveillance, violence, and spatial control over these neighborhoods, these urban spaces have been under militarized control since the 1990s. Constant military vehicle street patrols known locally as scorpions (*akrep*), the pervasive undercover police presence, surveillance cameras located on every street corner, and semi-routine antiterror operations that take place with the participation of thousands of police cadres accompanied by helicopters are manifestations of the "endocolonization" (Feldman 1991, 85) of these areas.[5] For the last two decades these urban spaces have also been sites of petty crime involving theft, drugs, and gambling: clashes often erupt between small-scale drug gangs and revolutionary vigilantes, between revolutionary youth and the police, and in and among various revolutionary and pro-Kurdish groups. Widespread police surveillance and militarized control of these areas coexist both with revolutionary violence that is at times turned inward and with counterviolence directed outward against state security forces. The puzzle addressed by this book explores the coexistence since the mid-2000s in these Istanbul neighborhoods of intense police surveillance and militarized spatial control alongside armed and masked revolutionary vigilante activities and gang activities. What are the conditions of possibility of this conflictual and yet long-enduring coexistence?

I argue that this seemingly paradoxical coexistence can only be understood within the context of the Turkish state's policing and counterinsurgency strategies, which are informed by Cold War counterinsurgencies and the colonial school of warfare and which have worked not merely to violently repress the Alevi and Kurdish Left but also to violently refashion a population's dissent against the state. This book combines archival work and oral history narratives with more than four years of ethnographic research in a predominantly Alevi-populated working-class neighborhood of Istanbul of an estimated 100,000 residents that I call "Devrimova"; I also made frequent visits to several other similar Istanbul neighborhoods. The following chapters illustrate the complex and mutually constitutive relationship between the maintenance of social order, which as the Comraroffs (2016, 41) argue a primary task of contemporary policing, and, in defense of that social order, the creation of conditions for perpetual conflict, disorder, and criminal activity.[6] They thus present a counterintuitive analysis of contemporary policing practices, focusing on the incitement of counterviolence and perpetual conflict by state security apparatus. I suggest that provocations of counterviolence and conflict and their containment in the places where racialized and dissident populations live cannot be considered disruptions of social order. In contrast, they can only be conceptualized as forms of governance and policing designed to control and manage dissent. Police attempts to maintain capitalist, racist, colonial, and patriarchal nation-state order by generating and managing violence and conflict are, in fact, an enduring legacy of the Cold War counterinsurgency doctrine of low-intensity conflict, itself informed by colonial warfare. In this book, I situate Turkish counterinsurgent policing within a global context and show how the Turkish counterinsurgency has been informed by global counterinsurgencies—including British counterinsurgencies in Malaya and Northern Ireland, the French counterinsurgency in Algeria, and US counterinsurgencies at home and abroad.

For many decades now, vigilantes, militarized police, and large- and small-scale drug gangs have been major elements in urban spaces inhabited by the racialized and dispossessed urban poor, both in the Global North and South.[7] But in our capitalist present, the revolutionary, one of the main protagonists of this book, is an unusual figure—a remainder of the Cold War and decolonial eras when together revolutionary socialist movements and anticolonial struggles shook the world. In Turkey, however, it must be remembered, the Kurdish liberation movement, which includes the Kurdistan Workers' Party (Partiya Karkerên Kurdistan; PKK) and legal pro-Kurdish political parties and NGOs, is continuing to wage an anticolonial struggle.[8] In 1984, the left-wing PKK initiated a guerrilla war against the Turkish state. For the last several decades, several revolutionary organizations, much smaller in size and impact than the PKK, have been cooperating with the Kurdish liberation movement. In this book, rather than approaching the revolutionary as an anomaly or an irrelevant remnant of a past long gone, I place this figure at the center of my analysis of contemporary policing practices and their complex links to Cold War and decolonial-era counterinsurgencies. Illustrating how the figure of the revolutionary in Istanbul's dissident working-class neighborhoods has since the 1970s been transformed from a protector whose presence was seen as integral to the community's survival to a figure who stands at the threshold of security provision and security threat, I demonstrate how Cold War and decolonial-era counterinsurgency strategies continue to inform urban policing in Turkey. Rather than focusing on the counterinsurgency's strategies for producing docile and compliant citizens,[9] I highlight their provocative, affect-and-emotion-generating divisive techniques and urban dimensions.

Population as Target, Alliance as Threat

Counterinsurgency strategies developed during the United States' imperial war in Vietnam, France's colonial wars in Algeria and Indochina, and Britain's colonial wars in Malaya, Kenya, Northern Ireland, and Palestine were directed against "internal enemies" domestically and later exported to ally countries such as Israel, Germany, South Africa, and Turkey.[10] During and after the Cold War, Latin American military and police officers, as well as officers from other oppressive countries waging wars against dissident portions of their citizenry such as Iran, Sri Lanka, the Philippines, and Pakistan, received counterinsurgency training in the United Kingdom and the United States (Barber and Ronning 1966; Gordon 1987). Turkey was no exception. Despite the Turkish military's ostensible anti-imperialist discourses, Turkey is a NATO member state, which has given the Turkish counterinsurgency access to global counterinsurgencies and made it a "home to a Central Intelligence Agency (CIA) backed counter-insurgency 'Gladio' unit" (Jacoby 2010, 100).[11] In fact, NATO's 2011 *Allied Joint Doctrine of Counterinsurgency* (COIN), which I cite many times throughout this book, was published under the signature of a Turkish major general, then director of the NATO Standardization Agency.[12] To aid them in their fight against left-wing and pro-Kurdish mobilizations, Turkish military and police officers received training in irregular and low-intensity warfare in the United Kingdom and the United States (Gordon 1987; Babül 2017b). Turkish police also received training in Turkey from US security officers as part of US military efforts to reorganize foreign police forces during the Cold War era (Huggins 1987; Schrader 2019).[13]

Developed in the era when major imperial powers were being defeated by left-wing and anticolonial mass mobilizations against unjust and oppressive rule, engineers of counterinsurgency acknowledge the impossibility of suppressing resistance by military force alone. Although it was crafted by military officers, David Galula (2002, 119), a French lieutenant colonel who played a key role in the development of modern counterinsurgency theory and practice, argues that counterinsurgency is police work (see also Schrader 2019). Like policing, counterinsurgency is an art of governance, "a more general problem—or tool—of sociability" (Karpiak 2010, 23) designed to intervene in everyday social relations and subjectivities by informing and transforming them. Or, like policing as defined by Ilana Feldman (2015, 3), counterinsurgency is "a space of both constraint and possibility, of control and action." Unlike conventional military practices that are aimed mainly at the destruction of the enemy, counterinsurgency is both a "war of destruction" and a war of "counterorganization" (McCuen 1966). It is concerned with "a bottom-up reorganization of the political forces" (Haysom 1989) and their relationship to society.

As with Michel Foucault's (2007) notion of the exercise of power in governmentality, counterinsurgency has entire populations as its target. Or, to put it in Galula's (2002, 246) words, in counterinsurgency warfare "the population is . . . the real terrain of the war." Counterinsurgency theory divides populations—"originally colonial populations but now all populations"—into three categories: "a small active minority of insurgents, a small group that is opposed to the insurgency, and a large passive majority who can be swayed one way or the other" (Harcourt 2018, 8). Although the primary aim is "divorcing the rebels from the population" (Galula 2002, 64), counterinsurgents consider all colonized, racialized, and oppressed populations as "rebel allies" (72). Informed by a segregationist colonial logic, counterinsurgency aims to achieve a radical separation of the "active minority of insurgents" who belong primarily to colonized, racialized, and dispossessed populations from one another and from docile noncolonized, nonracialized, advantaged populations. As I illustrate throughout this book, other objectives are destroying existing or emerging alliances and preventing future alliances among and between actually or potentially rebellious populations and between them and the "passive majority."

In Turkey, "the passive majority" and the "small group that is opposed to the insurgency" have come chiefly from Sunni Turkish populations. Turkey was *made into* a Sunni-Turkish–majority country by the Armenian Genocide of 1915 and the systematic persecution, displacement, and assimilation of its non-Turkish and non-Muslim Indigenous populations—such as Alevis, Assyrians, Arabs, Greeks, Jews, Zazas, and Kurds—beginning in the late Ottoman era.[14] Turkey's second president Ismet Inonu's words highlight the Turkish supremacism of the founders of Turkey: "We are frankly nationalists, and nationalism is our only factor of cohesion. In the face of a Turkish majority, other elements have no kind of influence. Our duty is to Turkify non-Turks in the Turkish homeland no matter what happens. We will *destroy* those elements that oppose Turks or Turkism" (cited in Zeydanlioğlu 2010, 5; emphasis added). As Nazan Maksudyan (2005, 313) illustrates Turkish supremacism and nationalism cannot be thought independent of a Turkish racism which is so clearly manifest in the words of Mahmut Esat Bozkurt who served as a Justice Minister from 1924 to 1930: "the master of this country is the Turk. Those who are not genuine Turks can have only one right in the Turkish fatherland and that is to be a servant, to be a slave."

This founding nationalist and racist ideology that went hand in hand with Sunni supremacism[15] has made Turkey's non-Turkish and non-Sunni citizens easy targets of both state and civilian violence. Since the founding of the Turkish Republic in 1923, there have been large-scale Kurdish and Kurdish Alevi massacres; anti-Alevi, anti-Jewish, and anti-Christian pogroms, as well as the massive deportation of Christian populations.[16] However, despite ongoing state violence and systematic nationalist and racist practices, in Turkey there are still significant non-Turkish and non-Sunni populations, the vast majority of whom are Kurds and Alevis: together they make approximately 25 percent of the population.[17] Members of the alleged "active minority of insurgents" have belonged primarily to these two, at times intersecting, populations, the two largest Indigenous groups in Turkey.

In line with growing left-wing mobilization across the globe, Turkey also witnessed large-scale revolutionary working-class mobilization throughout the 1960s and 1970s. This surge on the Left was met by a concomitant rise in right-wing racist and fascist groups and paramilitary operations, supported by the Turkish security apparatus in collaboration with the NATO's stay-behind forces (Ganser 2005, 225).[18] Although certain segments of the Sunni Turkish working classes took part in the revolutionary working-class mobilization of the 1960s and 1970s, the Turkish ruling elite along with the CIA[19] considered the Alevis and Kurds to be cornerstones of the "communist threat." That large-scale working-class mobilization came to an end with the coup d'état of 1980, which was followed by three years of military rule; the widespread purge of activists via military tribunals, blacklisting, torture, disappearances, shootings, and executions; and the adoption of a new constitution in 1982 that expanded the power and role of the military. The aim of the coup instigators had been to quell left-wing dissent and to create a society based on a so-called Turkish-Islamic synthesis designed to blend Turkish nationalism with political Islam (Kurt 2010). During the years that followed the coup, the Islamists were able to attract ever larger segments of the Sunni Turkish working classes through Islamist charity and benevolence networks and civic associations (White 2011; Tuğal 2009). But as I illustrate in chapter 2, although the coup and the repressive policies that followed were successful in pacifying large segments of the Sunni Turkish working classes, by the late 1980s left-wing dissent began to reemerge in Turkey, with Alevis and Kurds as its main constituents.

One of the primary actors in this leftist revival was the Kurdish liberation movement. By the early 1990s, only a decade after the brutal coup and the 1982 constitution's expansion of military power within the state, the PKK had managed to become popular among Kurdish workers, peasants, and students and had "established hegemony" (Jongerden et al. 2007, 2) in Northern Kurdistan. By the mid-1990s, the PKK had also become active in Kurdish Alevi towns in the countryside (Ertan 2015). In those same years, revolutionary organizations, some of which collaborated with the PKK, regained their former footholds in Istanbul's working-class Alevi neighborhoods. The PKK and the legal pro-Kurdish political parties have since partnered with various leftist organizations. Some revolutionary organizations cooperated with the PKK and some legally registered *socialist* or *social democratic* parties and organizations[20] made alliances with the legally sanctioned pro-Kurdish political parties. Cooperation between the Turkish Left and the Kurdish liberation movement has not been consistent and has never been free of problems, but it continues to this day: the umbrella People's Democracy Party (Halkın Demokrasi Partisi, HDP), currently one of the major opposition parties in parliament, emerged from within the Kurdish liberation movement and have been successful in bringing socialists, anti-capitalists, feminists, and LGBT activists from various ethnoreligious backgrounds together.[21]

In this book, I chart the effectiveness of the Turkish counterinsurgency in achieving one of its primary objectives: driving a wedge between the Turkish Left and the Kurdish liberation movement—as it has played out in Istanbul's predominantly Alevi-populated working-class neighborhoods. I suggest that these urban spaces have been the primary targets of Turkish urban counterinsurgency not only because they are centers of the dissident Left but also, and perhaps more importantly, because they have been significant "spaces of intervention" (Dikeç 2006) for a bottom-up refashioning of leftist dissent in Turkey since the early 1990s. Localized counterinsurgency interventions in these dissident urban spaces have had an impact on much broader segments of society, quickly stirring up ethnosectarian tensions across the country and paving the way for the partitioning of leftist dissent along class, ethnosectarian, and spatial lines. Within this frame, these dissident urban spaces of Istanbul offer important insights into how counterinsurgent policing intervenes in lived spaces so as to inform, transform, and counter dissident activities and subjectivities and fragment otherwise allied dissident forces.

Provocative Counterorganization

Aware of the fact that state violence breeds backlashes, delegitimizes the ruling elite, and increases sympathy for dissident groups, counterinsurgency aims to "destroy the popular insurgency without appearing to be directly waging a war on the populace" (Haysom 1990, 1). Within this framework and congruent with its aim to transform populations and reorganize political forces, much counterinsurgency work involves covert and elusive techniques designed to divorce dissident groups from their constituency, in addition to overt repression where necessary. As archival works on Cold War and decolonial era counterinsurgencies demonstrate, security agents are known to have provoked counterviolence within dissident groups, incited ethnosectarian conflict among and between dissident communities, encouraged rivalries among and within dissident organizations, and mobilized pro-state paramilitary forces and anti-state groups against one another.[22] These interventions have been effective in marginalizing dissident groups by militarizing and transforming them into security threats against society (including their own constituencies), dividing dissident communities from within, exhausting them by inciting them to fight against one another and other nonstate adversary forces, demoralizing and frustrating them, thereby rendering a justified political cause meaningless. These techniques, which are central to counterinsurgency's so-called psychological warfare, are based primarily on Galula's argument that under the conditions of conflict and war the "ideological advantage of the insurgent [hence of the just cause] decreases considerably" (2002, 246). Thus, counterinsurgency's aim is not to end violence but to create the conditions for controllable violence. As clearly stated in NATO's 2011 *Allied Joint Doctrine for Counterinsurgency*: "The strategic goal of the counterinsurgent is to promote legitimate governance by *controlling violence*" (para. 0328; emphasis added).

As I illustrate throughout this book, state security agents in Turkey adopted a similar strategy in their fight against left-wing and anticolonial Kurdish dissent. Galula's classic book on the subject, *Counterinsurgency Warfare: Theory and Practice*, published first in 1964, was translated into Turkish under the title *Hareket Stratejisi* by the publishing house of the Turkish General Staff in 1969 and assigned as required reading in the Turkish Military Academy. At the height of the left-wing mobilization, Cihat Akyol (1971), then commander of the Special Warfare Department (Özel Harp Dairesi; ÖHD)—the Turkish branch of NATO's secret anticommunist stay-behind network, known as "Counter-guerrilla" in Turkey (Söyler 2013, 316)—promoted the idea of creating covert groups and organizing "fake operations" that would perpetrate cruel and violent acts that gave the impression of having been committed by dissident organ-

izations (cited in Mumcu [1990], 1997, 54–57).[23] Likewise, General Sabri
Yirmibesoglu, another leading figure in the ÖHD during the 1970s, argued that
it "encourage[d] incidents which invite retaliation" (Fernandes and Özden
2001, 12). The aim was to stigmatize targeted left-wing groups in the eyes of
their constituency by portraying them as cruelly violent, thereby facilitating
their alienation from their constituency. In the 1990s, Turkish security forces
supported Islamist and other right-wing paramilitary groups against the PKK in
Northern Kurdistan and encouraged fights between Kurds (Jongerden and van
Etten 2007; Aydın and Emrence 2015). I call such state security intervention *provocative counterorganization*: provocation by national security states of conflict,
violence, and ideological, ethnic, and religious divergences and rivalries both
among and within dissident communities, with the aim of countering and reorganizing a population's dissent against the state. As a policing strategy, provocative
counterorganization is not only a Foucauldian project of docility-producing governance but also a Schmittian project of animosity production that actively promotes enmity among diverse populations. Here, I refer to the writings of the fascist
German political theorist Carl Schmitt (2007, 27), for whom the political domain
rests on a friend–enemy distinction. For Schmitt, the enemy is "the other, the
stranger . . . and in a specially intense way, existentially something different and
alien," an integral part of politics. This otherness within the political makes war
"an ever-present possibility" and "the leading presupposition which determines in
a characteristic way human action and thinking and thereby creates a specifically
political behavior" (34). To put this differently, provocative counterorganization is
a primary mechanism of what Achille Mbembe (2016, 23) calls "the society of enmity," noting it is "characterized by forms of exclusion, hostility, hate movements, and, above all, by the struggle against an enemy."

The Space and Psyche

In this book, I show how provocative counterorganization operates on the ground
in Istanbul's predominantly Alevi-populated working-class neighborhoods. I pay
special attention to its spatial and affective dynamics and their effects on dissident identities and practices. If the population is the main target of the counterinsurgency, its two main axes are space and the psyche. Security is a two-way
sociospatial phenomenon that is at once produced and reproduced in and
through sociospatial relations, processes, and practices and that itself produces,
shapes, and transforms space (Glück and Low 2017). As Eyal Weizman (2012)
has demonstrated in his work on the Israeli security state, counterinsurgency,
instead of destroying what security agents perceive as a "hostile space," reorganizes

it in line with its counterorganization aims. At the same time and in relation to this reorganization, it aims to transform political subjectivities and practices within the targeted space.

This book traces the transformation of Devrimova from the late 1970s when it was a sanctuary space built by and for the country's racialized, hence most vulnerable, workers into a low-intensity conflict zone and a sectarian enclave since the mid-1990s. I illustrate how counterinsurgency and its provocative dimensions have become manifest and operate in this space with the aim of countering and reorganizing dissident activities and subjectivities. Police forces' hit-and-run tactics, the targeting of Alevi spaces and bodies, gang and drug dealing activities in the neighborhoods, the selective targeting of the most community-minded revolutionaries by the anti-terror laws and violent interpellations—which I define as calls to a specific subject position and a specific identification made through performative acts of state or state-backed violence—work to incite defensive counterviolence, exaggerate sectarian cleavages, and contain revolutionary activity and violence in the neighborhoods.

Known as a "dirty war", counterinsurgency and its elusive security strategies rely very heavily on shadowy intelligence agents: undercover police, agents provocateurs, spies, and informants. The infiltration of such agents into dissident groups and communities and the coercion of individuals into collusion undoubtedly intervene in, shape, and inform dissident practices and subjectivities.[24] Yet, counterinsurgency's elusive practices and its soi-disant "psychological warfare" also entail various affect-and-emotion-generating strategies employed by state security forces and the mass media. To separate dissident groups from their base of supporters, to drive a wedge between and among dissident communities and isolate them from the so-called passive majority, counterinsurgency relies on what Joseph Masco (2014, 18) calls "affective infrastructures": "historically produced, shared, and officially constituted, sanctioned, and promoted feelings that are deployed as instruments for coordinating citizens as members of a national security state." In his work on the links between the Cold War and the War on Terror in the United States, Masco argues that the official sanctioning and promotion of the effects of fear, anger, and terror by ruling elites are critical to how affective infrastructures produce and maintain a docile public. Indeed, in this book, feelings of fear, terror, rage, and insecurity play an important role. But in this book, rather than the production of docility, I am interested in the ways in which affect-and-emotion-generating *provocative counterorganizational strategies* work to effect a broad range of counterorganizational aims: the strengthening of already existing ethnosectarian and ethnonational cleavages in Turkey, the mobilization of left-wing groups against one another, the creation of intergenerational conflict within working-class Alevi communities, the militarization of revolutionary youth, the continuation of low-intensity conflict in the neighborhoods, and, last but not least, the effective colonization of the political space through policing.

Counterinsurgency as a War on Politics

Laleh Khalili (2012, 5) argues that "counterinsurgency refuses politics, or at least transforms political conflicts and contestations, revolts and insurgencies into technical problems to be solved." For Khalili, this refusal is caused by counterinsurgency's "inability to recognize the politics that defines and structures revolts" (5). Yet counterinsurgency doctrines actually do acknowledge that the source of the insurgency is political. NATO's *Allied Joint Doctrine for Counterinsurgency* stresses that "economic, political or social grievances . . . fuel the insurgency" (2011, para. 0354). It is not so much that the logic of counterinsurgency fails to recognize the political reasons motivating rebellions but that theorists and practitioners of counterinsurgency are reluctant to make the political and structural changes necessary to eradicate their root causes, such as poverty, racism, and colonialism. Counterinsurgency instead aims to maintain social orders that are based on the oppression and exploitation of racialized and dispossessed populations—social orders that by their very nature lead inevitably to rebellions. Thus, it serves to make the inevitable evitable. In this sense, I agree with Harcourt (2018) that counterinsurgency is a "governing paradigm" (8) and a "counterrevolution without revolution" (12). We might even call it a *permanent* counterrevolution, a form of *preventive governance* that remains ever mindful of the possibility of revolt and rebellion against racism, patriarchy, capitalism and colonialism. Counterinsurgency then does not only "refuse politics," as Khalili argues, by transforming already existing revolts and political conflicts into technical issues of security and "terror" but it also actively wages a preventive and permanent war on politics: although fragmentation of populations is a major effect of counterinsurgency, its ultimate aim is depoliticization. As I illustrate throughout this book, generating the conditions for perpetual yet functionally manageable conflict through overt and covert intervention and the use of affect-and-emotion-generating security strategies are key components of counterinsurgency's depoliticization efforts. After all, counterinsurgency builds on the idea that even the most appealing political cause loses its legitimacy under conditions of perpetual conflict.

My understanding of politics here is inspired by Jacques Rancière's juxtaposition of politics as antithetical to the police. For Rancière (1999, 2001), the police are not essentially about repression and discipline; their function "refers to both the activities of the state as well as to the ordering of social relations" (Swyngedouw 2009, 606). The police thus "constitute the assemblage of institutions, actors and practices" (Khalili 2014, 93) and serve as established orders of governance that assign and distribute human bodies, tasks, spaces, roles, voices, and forms of participation in society. The act of distribution is also an act of partition. Rancière employs the term "partition" in the double sense of the word: "on the one hand, that which separates and excludes; on the other, that which allows participation" (Rancière 2001, Thesis VII). Similar to the logic of counterinsurgency, Rancière's police are concerned both with the *partitioning*, the dividing up of people, voices, activities, spaces, and so on, and with defining the forms of participation/part-taking. The "essence" of the police is "the partition of the sensible," a general law that "defines the forms of part-taking by first defining the modes of perception in which they are inscribed" (Rancière 2001, Thesis VII). "The partition of the sensible" is also a "partition between what is visible and what is not, of what can be heard from the inaudible" (2001). In other words, the police are "an order of the visible and the sayable that sees that a particular activity is visible, and another is not, that this speech is understood as discourse and another as noise" (Rancière 1999, 28). In that sense, as Khalili (2015, 93) argues, for Rancière, policing is about "making unrecognizable (and insensible) that which lies beyond the ordinary discourses, practices and institutions in which we are embedded."

Rancière holds that political activity is antithetical to the police. Whereas the police define the forms of participation, politics is an intervention in the forms of partaking and distribution defined, shaped, and made possible by the police. It is an intervention in the roles and definitions assigned to the people and places by the "police order." Therefore, for Rancière "politics *act* on the police" (1999, 33; emphasis in original): "Political activity is whatever shifts a body from the place assigned to it or changes a place's destination. It makes visible what had no business being seen and makes heard a discourse where once there was only place for noise; it makes understood as discourse what was only heard as noise" (30).

Politics works against the grain of the established order and disturbs the policed distribution of things. It intervenes in the police order; it changes or attempts to change places' and bodies' assigned destinations within the existing social order. It opens up new and unexpected possibilities, spaces, and roles.

To put it more concretely using a few examples from this book, whereas the police predestine the racialized working classes and the dispossessed to mere survival, politics opens up the space for them to become active agents of mass social mobilization who dare to challenge established social relations. Whereas the police strive to coerce the working classes of diverse backgrounds into a relationship of enmity, one characterized by ethnoreligious or racialized divergence, and allow their words only to be heard as "ethnic," "racial" or "religious" noise, politics opens up a space for camaraderie that transcends divisive categories while fighting against oppressive structures. Whereas the police locate poor racialized women in domestic space as "ignorant," invisible, and yet reproductive "victims" of patriarchy and capitalism, politics enables them to defy patriarchal public–private divisions and gendered and classed hierarchies to create their own "subaltern counterpublics" (Fraser 1990, 68).[25] Finally, whereas the police push working-class youths of the urban margins into criminal activity, drug dealing, and drug use, politics generates a search for ways to put an end to the criminalization of those youths.

In this sense, this book—by providing an ethnographically grounded analysis of the tension between policing and politics—says as much about policing as it does about politics. On the one hand, this Rancièrian approach can illuminate the ways in which anyone, including those who are targeted by police, can become effective agents and even mediators of counterinsurgency efforts to manipulate, depoliticize, and police dissent. It can shed light on the "broader assemblages of 'policing'" (Garriott 2013a, 10). On the other hand, it can index the many attempts, both successful and abortive, made by these dissident police targets to actively and insistently intervene in the "distribution of the sensible."

Although Rancière approaches police and politics as a binary, ethnographic analysis shows us that excesses and gray zones always lie somewhere between the two. In racialized working-class spaces where multiple and intersecting forms of oppression prevail, political activity designed to resist those oppressive structures does not always fit neatly into clear-cut divisions between the police and politics. As I illustrate throughout the book, although creating a sanctuary for the racialized working classes is a significant political intervention that opens up a safe space for the creation of subaltern counterpublics, it also contributes to these populations' isolation, a primary aim of counterinsurgency.[26] Or, as we shall see in chapter 4, armed revolutionary vigilantism both paves the way for the mimetic reproduction of official sexist and racist policing practices and is a political intervention by making the neighborhoods dangerous places for drug dealers and gangs—thus, policing and politicking at the same time. In an era when a significant percentage of urban poor youth across the globe are destined to become drug consumers and dealers, such antidrug vigilantism disrupts the police distribution of roles by reducing the amount of drug-related activity in the neighborhood. In examining both the Turkish security state's war on left-wing Alevi and Kurdish dissent and the political efforts of the targeted populations to challenge such a war, I present a spatially informed analysis of the tension between policing and politics, as well as of the gray zones between the two.

Martyrs: Spirits of Resistance

Despite their use of overt violence and covert counterinsurgency techniques since the 1970s, the Turkish ruling elite has managed to quench neither revolutionary militancy, Kurdish activism, nor the alignment between them. In my analysis of the tension between policing and politics, I ask how revolutionary activity can carry on in a country that has since its foundation implemented oppressive policies, embedded in its many laws and policies, against its dissident Indigenous populations. My answer takes into account the agentive effects of the dead, specifically the martyred dead. In the left-wing Alevi and Kurdish imaginary, there are two kinds of martyrs: those revolutionaries and rebels who lost their lives while fighting against oppression and those who lost their lives at the hands of the state or state-backed violence. As Robert Hertz (1969, 86) argues, certain deaths cannot be contained by society: the death of those who lost their lives in a "sinister way" "impresses itself most deeply on the memory of the living"; "their souls roam the earth forever."

It is impossible not to notice the inscription of the names and images of Alevi, Kurdish, and revolutionary martyrs into the collective memory, sociality, and space of Devrimova and similar neighborhoods. Were those unfamiliar with Devrimova to walk its streets, they would be immediately struck by the ubiquity of revolutionary slogans spray-painted on walls alongside posters displaying photos of martyrs. The walls of the ramshackle apartment buildings and shanties of Devrimova are sites of public expression on which members and sympathizers of the various revolutionary organizations celebrate the revolutionary struggle ("Long live the revolution and socialism," "Revolution is the only path"), express their rage against the ruling elites ("The murderous state will pay," "People's justice will call [the government] to account,"), and commemorate martyrs ("Revolutionary Martyrs Are Immortal," "Ebru Timtik Is immortal," "Mahir Çayan Is alive"; see figure I.3).[27]

Martyrs do not die. Akin to Avery Gordon's ghost—a "social figure" and an "animated force of the oppressed past" (2008, 8)—they stand at the threshold between life and death: both absent and present, present and past. Inscribed in material space as posters, sculptures, and building names, they are constant reminders of past oppression and of resistance against it, thereby connecting the past to the present. Neighborhood parks, buildings, *cem* houses (Alevi prayer and congregation houses), and neighborhood associations are named after martyrs. Some, such as the Pir Sultan Abdal Cem House in Bir Mayıs Neighborhood, take the name of Ottoman-era Alevi rebels.[28] Others commemorate modern-day revolutionaries like Sibel Yalçın Park in Okmeydanı and the Hasan Ferit Gedik Rehabilitation Center in Gazi. Still others pay tribute to the victims

FIGURE I.3.   The wall of a house on which is written "From Berlin to Istanbul Shoulder to Shoulder against Fascism." The images on the wall are of Mahir Çayan, leader of the People's Liberation Party-Front of Turkey; Subcomandante Marcos, main spokesperson for the Zapatista National Liberation Army; and Dursun Karatas, founder of the Revolutionary People's Liberation Party Front. Image has been modified to protect the identity of the person pictured.

Photo by Sinan Targay.

of state violence, as does Berkin Elvan Park in Güzeltepe.[29] Many neighborhood residents are themselves named after martyred revolutionaries. Hasan Ferit Gedik's grandfather told me that his grandson was named after two revolutionaries, Hasan and Ferit, murdered by state security forces. After the killing of Hasan Ferit by gangs in October 2013, many newborns were named after him.

In her work on memory, space, and the "senses of governance" in Northern Cyprus, Yael Navaro-Yashin (2012) demonstrates that the phantomic can be embodied in material spaces and objects, can linger in a territory, can generate affect, and can even exert a "determinate force over politics" (17). Building on her insight into the potential affective impact of the phantomic on political activity, I show that, by highlighting questions related to ethical self-formation (à la Foucault 1988), martyrs act as invigorating social and political forces that inspire many Devrimovans to take an oppositional stance against the Turkish security state—helping them defy fear, resist counterinsurgent policing, and refuse its divisive strategies. In this sense, martyrs are the spirits of resistance and solidarity who help enable dissident political activity to continue. But the affective power of the martyrs, as I demonstrate, is also affected by structural forces and affective security strategies. At other times, young marginalized men's feelings of rage and the desire for revenge intersecting with patriarchal social formations, can translate the affective power of the martyrs into acts of policing (à la Rancière) that reproduce existing gendered roles.

Research on the Edge of the Sensible

State security officers do not like to share information on their elusive and covert counterinsurgency techniques. Yet state security archives, the published memoirs of remorseful state security officers, and oral histories conducted with former officers are invaluable sources for understanding the logics of Cold War and decolonial era counterinsurgencies and their elusive practices.[30] To illustrate the provocative dimensions of the Turkish counterinsurgency during the Cold War era and in the 1990s, I delved into the writings of high-ranking security officers and pro-military journalists, archival materials from counterinsurgency-related discussions in the Turkish National Assembly, the archives of the Human Rights Foundation of Turkey (Türkiye İnsan Hakları Vakfı), the RAND Corporation's publicly available reports on left-wing dissent in Turkey, and the oral history narratives of Devrimovans who have been targets of counterinsurgent policing for decades. It was more difficult, however, to obtain information on recent, on-the-ground counterinsurgency methods.[31] As Peter K. Manning (2018, 32) emphasizes, when it comes to on-the-ground policing strategies, "the police are secretive in their practices . . . they are devious in their activities." To prevent the development of countertechniques, Turkish security forces are especially secretive about their counterinsurgency techniques.[32] In areas related to state security matters, merely initiating contact with state security officers runs the risk of intervention and poses a threat to independent research.

Therefore, to secure my independence as a scholar in conducting the research required for this book, I decided to refrain from making contact with any and all state security officers. My encounter with a high-ranking police officer during my preliminary research on another, yet related, topic also played a role in that decision. When I began conducting research in the summer of 2010, my focus was on the criminalization of working-class youth. While searching for potential field sites, I went to a small courthouse in a working-class district of Istanbul to consult with a state prosecutor (*savcı*) on crime rates in working-class areas. After explaining my quest for research information to a janitor in the courthouse—because I didn't know which prosecutor I should speak to—he suggested that I knock on prosecutor Metin Bey's office door. "Metin Bey has a

PhD degree; he might be of help," he said. As the janitor predicted, Metin Bey was very helpful. After tea and a brief chat about my education and research interests in his small and gloomy office, dominated by piles of documents, Metin Bey told me that the person I needed to talk to was Ismet Müdür, one of the highest-ranking police officers in Istanbul.[33] He grabbed the phone, dialed Ismet Müdür's number, and within a few minutes arranged a meeting for me with him, without even asking if I wanted one. Astonished by this easy access to such a high-ranking police officer, a week later I went to my appointment in Ismet Müdür's fancy office in downtown Istanbul. He was very welcoming, telling me that the issues of poverty and crime were his special interests and that he would be very happy to help me conduct research on that "extremely important" topic. He enthusiastically added, "We could write that dissertation together!" In that moment, I understood that, were I to conduct my research among the police, it would be extremely difficult for me to write independently on a topic that was of such great interest to Ismet Müdür; my research and writing would be monitored. A week later, I called him to thank him for his offer of support but told him my PhD adviser encouraged me to conduct a neighborhood ethnography instead.

When working on the ground in places where counterinsurgent policing plays out, anthropological methods facilitate the analysis of counterinsurgency techniques through long-term, careful ethnographic attention to the operations and effects of state security practices. In his pivotal book on political violence in Northern Ireland, Allen Feldman (1991, 3) approaches power "from its point of effect and generation" of agency, suggesting that we "look at power where it takes place." In a similar vein, Michel-Rolph Trouillet (2001, 126) claims that "state processes and practices are recognized through their effects." I follow Feldman and Trouillet by focusing on the manifestations, modalities, and agentive effects of state security practices that serve the ends of provocative counterorganization, thereby shedding light on the Turkish security state's present-day elusive counterinsurgent policing techniques. My analysis of current counterinsurgency practices draws primarily on oral history narratives, in-depth interviews, and ethnographic participant observation conducted in Devrimova between 2010 and 2013, as well as during subsequent visits to the neighborhood and similar neighborhoods in 2014, 2015, and 2016. I also analyzed Turkish national newspapers, news reports posted on the websites of various left-wing journals, and video recordings posted on YouTube by the police or by revolutionary groups.

When I began my fieldwork in the fall of 2010, it was a relatively calm period in Turkey. AKP government representatives at the time framed the situation as one of "advanced democracy" (*ileri demokrasi*) in which the government was publicly addressing past state crimes against Kurds, Alevis, and leftists. In a series of investigations known as the Ergenekon Trials, hundreds of security officers, bureaucrats, and others—some of whom were involved in mass murders in the 1990s—were investigated as members of an alleged clandestine organization called Ergenekon. Although they were accused of plotting to overthrow the government, the censorious attention focused on the assassinations, disappearances, and psychological warfare of the past decades gave the impression that the AKP government's promise of "advanced democracy" might not be entirely unfounded.[34] Despite its lack of substantial policy changes supporting Alevi claims for recognition and equal citizenship rights, the AKP-initiated "Alevi opening" (*Alevi açılımı*) of 2007—part of its democratization initiative—raised hopes among some segments of the Alevi community.[35] Finally, the fragile and uneven "solution process" (*çözüm süreci*) initiated in 2009, also known as the "Kurdish opening" (*Kürt açılımı*), further strengthened hopes for realization of the long-awaited peace between the Turkish government and the Kurdish liberation movement.[36] At the time, many of my left-wing, liberal middle-class friends were optimistic about the country's future. I was eager to join in my middle-class friends' optimism, but there was an unbridgeable contradiction between what I was hearing and observing in Devrimova and the AKP's promises of democracy.

Even though in the first phase of my research from the fall of 2010 to the fall of 2012, there were fewer street clashes in Devrimova than there had been in the late 2000s and there were no checkpoints and stop-and-frisks at its entrances, Devrimovans and residents of similar neighborhoods were rather pessimistic in those years. As I illustrated elsewhere (Yonucu 2018a), by 2010, the AKP government's use of "lawfare" against dissent—the "resort to legal instruments, to the violence inherent in the law, to commit acts of political coercion, even erasure" (Comaroff and Comaroff 2006, 30)—which gradually shifted to center to the middle-classes and Turkish Sunni populations, after the alleged coup attempt of 2016, had already begun to be felt in those neighborhoods. After the 2006 expansion of the antiterror law, several hundred revolutionary and pro-Kurdish youths from these neighborhoods were imprisoned without evidence as "terrorists" and were facing decades-long prison sentences or even life sentences.[37] While my middle-class Turkish leftist friends believed in a bright future, for the vast majority of my Devrimovan interlocutors, as well as for my working-class Alevi and Kurdish friends, those years were just the "calm before the storm." And history has proven them right. In the ensuing years, with the increasingly nationalist authoritarianism of the Erdoğan government, even my most privileged and optimistic friends and acquaintances had to leave the country, targeted by the antiterror laws and are facing long prison sentences.

The relatively calm period between 2010 and 2012, however, did enable me to conduct fieldwork in Devrimova on this difficult topic. Yet, from my very first weeks there, the undercover police participated in my research as ghostly figures who threatened to disturb and impede the development of trust between Devrimovans and me. There is no police station in Devrimova, and unless you found yourself in the middle of a police operation, you would never see a police officer in uniform on its streets. In fact, Devrimovan youths like to brag that the police do not dare enter the neighborhood. Yet on any given day, the police are present either as undercover cops or as seen through the darkened windows of their military vehicles on patrol. A senior researcher who had conducted research in Devrimova warned me that any Devrimovan I came into contact with could, in fact, be an undercover police officer or a police informer and, worse, that Devrimovans would suspect me of working with or for the police. Before my work in Devrimova even began, this conspiracy narrative of mutual suspicion and mistrust—the insensibility and illegibility of any given situation that the undercover police presence sought to produce and to which revolutionary fear and defiance of infiltration responded—would be folded into my day-to-day fieldwork in Devrimova.

On January 14, 2011, about three months after I began conducting fieldwork in Devrimova, an undercover policeman made it known to me that I was being followed. When a week later I told three young Devrimovans who were helping me with my research about my experience, none of them were very surprised. Their first response was, "Welcome to Devrimova," implying that undercover surveillance is not the exception for Devrimovan residents. They and a lawyer friend reassured me that because the undercover policeman had made his presence known, the police were not after information. "They just want to intimidate you," they explained. "If they'd wanted to remain unseen, you wouldn't have had the slightest suspicion that you were being followed." That assertion challenged my assumptions about undercover police officers working as clandestine agents who operate on the basis of invisibility.

The solution they advised me to adopt was to become even more visible on the streets of the neighborhood and to spend more time talking to people in public spaces. They suggested that I conduct my interviews in parks and at coffeehouses and cafés where everyone could see what I was doing, thereby making obvious what I was talking about and with whom. They reasoned that doing so would show the police both that I was not afraid of them and that my activities did not involve anything that should be a cause for alarm. They also told me that I should not let the police stop me from doing my research. As I elaborate on in Chapter 5, I later realized that my interlocutors' advice to be visible and unbowed was part of a time-honored tactic gleaned from Devrimova's repertoire of resistance. As Billie Jean Isbell (2009) stresses, being witness to violence burdens one with debt. I suppose that the burden of debt I was left with from what I had witnessed as a high school student in the mid-1990s (see the preface) was more important to me than my own feelings of fear and impulse to flee.

The experience of being followed by the undercover police further reinforced my decision not to be in contact with the police. Fearful that they would ask me information about the community, I neither spoke with the police about my research nor requested consent from them. I nevertheless found that I was compelled to act in compliance with what I assumed was their "distribution of the sensible," which informed where, with whom, and when I could conduct research. In retrospect, an unspoken deal existed between the police and me: I would stay away from certain people—outlawed revolutionary groups, drug dealers, and gangs—and their associated spaces, and the police would not interfere with my research. My research had limitations: I was not free to talk with whomever I pleased or visit just any part of the neighborhood at just any time. My research, too, was being distributed and partitioned by the police.

Despite or perhaps in response to the duplicitous air of the insensible that the undercover police and informant activities introduced into the neighborhood, Devrimovans developed powerful solidarity relations. As Jeff Sluka (1995, 102) has noted, "Ethnographic studies of political life in the ghettos agree that repression and the war have not eroded community solidarity, but in fact, fostered and strengthened it." Solidarity and friendship serve as effective instruments of refusal of and resistance to the force of the police and their allies. My Devrimovan interlocutors and friends, all of whom wanted me to tell the story of their neighborhood, never left me alone during my research process. I never went to parks or cafés on my own or wandered by myself in the neighborhood. "The most important social knowledge" is "knowing what not to know" (Taussig 1999, 2). Conducting research in the company of Devrimovans who steered me clear of possible risky encounters and communications meant that I was monitored, protected, accepted, limited, and tolerated by the community.

As I note in the preface, I was already acquainted with the working-class Alevi neighborhoods when I started my fieldwork. Not only was I cognizant of the history of the oppression and resistance in the neighborhoods and the discrimination that Alevis and Kurds faced in Turkey but also, because of my own working-class background and long-term friendship with working-class Alevis and Kurds, I was familiar with many cultural references in a way that a middle-class Turkish researcher might not be. Although I do not belong to a racialized community in Turkey, I, like many of my interlocutors, grew up in a *gecekondu* (shanty) in an Istanbul working-class neighborhood and am thus well aware of the stigmas attached to working-class spaces and bodies in Turkey.[38] As in Devrimova, the youth in the neighborhood where I grew up also began to engage in petty crime and drug dealing by the early 2000s. When I started my fieldwork in Devrimova, I was thus aware of the processes of working-class criminalization and had conducted and published research on that issue.[39] My musical and other cultural interests were not much different than those of many Devrimovans. Like many Devrimovans, I grew up listening to Turkish and Kurdish folk music and revolutionary bands. When I was a teenager, I read many of the classic socialist fiction that Devrimovan youth still read and discuss—Maxim Gorki's *Mother*, Nikolay Ostrovskiy's *How the Steel Tempered*, and Jack London's *The Iron Heel*, among others. Such common cultural ground helped me feel at home in Devrimova and easily develop a rapport with my interlocutors.

Although I did not live in the neighborhood, I worked for one and a half years as a volunteer teacher at a local Devrimovan education co-op run by neighborhood youth. Being a teacher-researcher at the co-op made it possible for me to be part of the everyday life of the neighborhood and provided me with easy access to my students' families. I conducted more than a hundred interviews with women and men between the ages of eighteen and seventy-eight who had lived in the neighborhood for more than ten years. With the exception of two people, all of the participants allowed me to record the formal part of the interviews; I did not record informal conversations. During the interviews, neither my interlocutors nor I mentioned the real names of persons, places, or revolutionary organizations. During the first phase of my research (2010–2012), my interviews focused on the history and recent past of the neighborhood. Because research and public engagement regarding the 1990s and past state crimes were common in those years, my aim was to give police the impression that my research exclusively focused on the past. Although my interviews did actually focus on the past, the conversations that surrounded the interviews frequently touched on current issues and events. Because I was cognizant of the risk that disclosure of insider information about revolutionary groups might hold for my interlocutors and me, I was not interested in learning more than what the police and public already knew. My research and this narrative were not meant in the spirit of a cloak-and-dagger, behind-the-scenes exposé.

During and after the Gezi uprising of summer 2013, Devrimova and other such neighborhoods once again witnessed increasing gang and police violence and its defensive counterviolence. This made it difficult for me to be present as a researcher and participant-observer, as did the renewed identity checks and interrogations at neighborhood entrances. Given this turn of events, I made only infrequent visits to Devrimova and some of the other predominantly Alevi working-class neighborhoods throughout the second half of 2013 and again in 2014, 2015 and 2016. When I did visit, I checked beforehand to ensure that there were no ongoing clashes or police raids, and conversations with my interlocutors took place unrecorded either in houses or outside the neighborhoods. In that contagious and pervasive atmosphere of fear, I did not have the courage to be publicly visible and present on the streets. Some of my interlocutors later fled to Europe to seek asylum, allowing my interviews and conversations to continue there in 2017 and 2018.

Culture-Centric Warfare and Ethnographic Refusal

Ethnographic insights into racialized and dissident communities can wind up serving the ends of the policing of such communities.[40] As indicated in NATO's 2011 *Allied Joint Doctrine for Counterinsurgency*, counterinsurgency's "culture-centric warfare" (Gregory 2008) requires "intimate knowledge" of those dissident communities being policed and an ethnographic "close reading" (Kilcullen 2007, 8) of their local cultures. In parallel with counterinsurgency's recent "cultural turn," the police in Turkey also began to take a special interest in anthropological studies. A significant number of Turkish police officers have studied anthropology and completed their PhDs in anthropology departments in Turkey or in Europe and the United States within the last decade. Alongside urban ethnography's "historically fraught practice" (Ralph 2015, 442) in reproducing "colonial tropes" (449) and further stigmatizing the racialized urban poor, counterinsurgency's ever-growing interest in anthropology makes ethical questions all the more important for anthropologists who work with and among racialized and dispossessed populations who suffer from overt and covert forms of police violence.[41] Bearing such concerns in mind, in this book, I deliberately refrain from providing detailed ethnographic information and intimate knowledge of the local culture and people that might potentially aid in the policing of the neighborhoods. In other words, I engage in an ethnographic refusal, an ethnographic calculus of "what you need to know and what I refuse to write" (Simpson 2007, 72). My focus is instead on the structural violence, state security practices, and their colonial legacies that lead both to the criminalization of the racialized Alevi and Kurdish urban working classes and to their involvement in violence.

Organization of the Book

The first chapter, "The Possibility of Politics: People's Committees, Sanctuary Spaces, and Dissensus," historicizes the establishment in the 1970s of Devrimova and other such neighborhoods by revolutionaries as sanctuary spaces for socialist workers. Treating Devrimova's short yet oft-recalled experience of local self-governance, this chapter elaborates on the Rancièrian concept of politics as antithetical to policing. It demonstrates how the people's committee experience was an active "world-building practice" (Zerilli 2005) that allowed Devrimovans to come together "in action and speech" (Arendt 2013, 175) to open up political space for transformative disagreements. This experience helped many Devrimovans fashion themselves as political actors capable of challenging their ascribed roles in the policed distribution of the sensible (Rancière 2015), including by mounting challenges to gender and class hierarchies. The chapter also illustrates how the Alevi cultural archive of oppression and resistance, as well as historical Alevi practices of informal lawmaking, helped vernacularize communist politics among working-class Alevi communities in 1970s Turkey. Finally, it shows how Cold War counterinsurgency strategies informed Turkey's war on communism.

The first half of chapter 2, "Gazas of Istanbul": Threatening Alliances and Militarized Spatial Control," examines the leftist revival and reemergence of outlawed revolutionary groups, some of which became allies of the PKK, at the end of the 1980s and the early 1990s. It illustrates how the mutually constitutive relationship between the experience of absolute injustice, the desire for justice, and the urge for revenge was effective in galvanizing sympathy among working-class Alevis and Kurds for revolutionary organizations. The second half of the chapter examines the spatial dimensions of counterinsurgency techniques used by the Turkish state in response to this leftist revival.

By highlighting the parallels between the militarized spatial control in Northern Kurdistan and the dissident in working-class neighborhoods of Istanbul, this chapter also illustrates the colonial "boomerang effect" of Turkish state's spatial counterinsurgency techniques.

Chapter 3, "Provocative Counterorganization: Violent Interpellation, Low-Intensity Conflict, Ethnosectarian Enclaves" opens with the Gazi incidents of 1995 when seventeen people were killed and hundreds wounded as a result of police and military violence in the predominantly Alevi-populated working-class neighborhood of Gazi. Rather than being merely a singular spectacular performance of state violence, the Gazi incidents constituted a "critical event" that gave rise to "new modes of action" (Das 1995) and new forms of political agency, both in and beyond the neighborhoods. Paving the way for the "bottom-up reorganization of political forces" (Haysom 1989), the Gazi incident marked the beginning of a new counterinsurgency strategy in Istanbul that combined overt repressive state violence with urban-centered and affect-and-emotion-generating *provocative counterorganization* techniques in an attempt to quell growing left-wing mobilization and subvert the Turkish and Kurdish left-wing alignment, which was becoming more cohesive at the time. Informed mainly by the British counterinsurgency in Northern Ireland and the French counterinsurgency in Algeria and using various affective security strategies, these new techniques provoked ethnosectarian cleavages, turned dissident Alevi and Kurdish communities against one another, contained counterviolence in the neighborhoods, marginalized revolutionary organizations in the eyes of their constituency, further racialized Alevis and Kurds as "unruly" people, and resulted in the transformation of these urban spaces into low-intensity conflict zones and ethnosectarian enclaves.

Chapter 4, "Good Vigilantism, Bad Vigilantism: Crime, Community Justice, Mimetic Policing, and the Antiterror Law," charts the rise by the early 2000s of petty crime, drug dealing, and gang activities in Devrimova and other neighborhoods, shedding light on the repressive and provocative aspects of the newly expanded antiterror law. The chapter elucidates the ways in which, by selectively targeting the most peaceful and cooperative among the revolutionaries, the expanded antiterror law effectively intervened in local politics and space, reconfiguring political space and activity at the local level and continuing the confinement of violence within the neighborhoods. More specifically, it demonstrates the role of the antiterror law, as well as the conspicuous absences and presences of security forces in generating vigilantism in the neighborhoods and then transforming it from a public, participatory, and unarmed form of informal justice to a clandestine, exclusive, and armed one that mimics official policing practices.

Chapter 5, "Inspirational Hauntings: Undercover Police and the Spirits of Solidarity and Resistance," tackles the affective power of martyrs to inspire a radical refusal of docility and complicity. In Devrimova, the panoptic gaze of the undercover police, the antiterror laws, and police violence do not always manage to compel Devrimovans into a position of compliance. Many Devrimovans—not only revolutionary youth but also others—publicly refuse to collaborate when asked to work as informants. Some openly and defiantly champion outlawed revolutionary groups that have been labeled terrorist organizations. Others—in particular, young men—still engage in public performances of rage. These responses provide ethnographically grounded insight into why, despite its use of extreme forms of state violence, the Turkish ruling elite has since the 1990s managed neither to suppress pro-Kurdish and left-wing dissent nor to eradicate sympathy for revolutionary activism. This chapter demonstrates how what I call *inspirational hauntings*—the hauntings of past resistance and of rebellious and defiant subjects who seep into the present and serve as encouraging, emboldening political, spiritual, and ethical resources—raise questions related to ethical self-formation (à la Foucault 1988) and inspire many Devrimovans to take an oppositional stance against the Turkish security state, thereby freeing them from the immediacy of fear in the present.

The final chapter, "Gezi Uprising: The Long Summer of Solidarity and Resistance and the Great Divide," addresses the much-cherished yet ephemeral coming together in solidarity that occurred during the Gezi uprising of 2013, highlighting the parallels between counterinsurgency practices applied during the Gazi incidents of 1995 and those during the Gezi uprising of 2013. It argues that the violence discharged in predominantly Alevi working-class spaces and on working-class Alevi bodies during the Gezi uprisings exposed the continuing significance of these neighborhoods as "spaces of intervention" (Dikeç 2006) in the ruling elite's attempts to counter existing or emerging forms of alignments within Turkey's left-wing dissident block. This anti-Alevi violence, unleashed at the height of the nationwide uprising, proved to be an effective police intervention in reorganizing and partitioning (Rancière 1999) anti-AKP dissent. Together with the racializing anti-Alevi official and media discourses, this violence triggered historical Alevi fears of massacres, generated an atmosphere of insecurity, and facilitated defensive counterviolence and internal ethnosectarian conflict in the neighborhoods. It was this combination of strategies and impacts that was effective in colonizing political space in the neighborhoods and effectively dividing and fragmenting anti-AKP dissent along ethnosectarian and class lines.

The book's epilogue, "Policing as the Generation of (Dis)Order," concludes that policing is not only about maintaining social order by managing disorder but also about generating disorder. Generating disorder through what I call provocative counterorganization enables ruling elites to intervene in the organization of dissent in a way that counters existing assemblages and alignments among actual or potentially dissident populations and prevents those that are emergent. Police attempts to maintain order by generating and managing disorder is in fact an enduring legacy of the Cold War counterinsurgency doctrine of low-intensity conflict, which is itself informed by the colonial school of warfare. The epilogue suggests that without taking into account the provocative and partitioning dimensions of counterinsurgent policing as a technique not only of governance but also of anti-politics, it is impossible to fully grasp the violence of dissident, non-state actors.

THE POSSIBILITY OF POLITICS

People's Committees, Sanctuary Spaces, and Dissensus

In line with the global rise in left-wing movements, Turkey witnessed large-scale left-wing mobilization throughout the 1960s and 1970s. Living in makeshift squatter shanties (*gecekondu*, a term that translates literally as "settled/perched at night"), the urban working classes of Istanbul from diverse ethnosectarian backgrounds formed a significant part of this mobilization. Although right-wing nationalists and Islamists also found support among certain segments of the Sunni Turkish working classes, the main centers of the revolutionary Marxist movement were to be found in the Alevi-populated working-class neighborhoods. In the 1960s and 1970s, being a leftist became part and parcel of Alevi identity (Markussen 2012). The attraction between Alevis and the revolutionary organizations was mutual. Socialist critiques of capitalism, state domination, and Sunni Islam—the dominant form of Islam in Turkey—gained the support of Alevi workers, who had suffered Islamist and nationalist attacks, discrimination, and capitalist exploitation. Perceiving Alevis as one of the most oppressed groups in Turkey, revolutionaries of all ethnosectarian backgrounds came to see Alevis as their "natural allies" (Van Bruinessen 1996a, 9).[1] For this reason, they invested resources in generating political support and membership among the Alevi population, taking an active role in solving the housing problems of Alevi workers, and building sanctuary spaces for them in the quickly urbanizing cities.[2] As I demonstrate in this chapter, this mutual attraction between Alevis and revolutionary organizations, when combined with what I refer to as the *Alevi cultural archive of oppression and resistance*, was especially effective in vernacularizing revolutionary leftist politics among Alevis.

In the second half of the 1970s Turkey's revolutionaries began to experiment with direct and local self-governance, buoyed by the conviction that a socialist revolution would eventually take place. Inspired by the work of local councils in socialist countries, the first experiments in informal governance were set up in the form of people's committees (*halk komiteleri*) in certain Istanbul *gecekondu* neighborhoods populated predominantly by Alevis. With the establishment in 1979 of people's committees in Fatsa, a town in the Black Sea region, by the elected socialist mayor Fikri Sönmez, and the promise of local direct self-governance by Edip Solmaz, the newly elected socialist Kurdish mayor of the city of Batman in Northern Kurdistan, the idea and practice of people's committees spread from the urban margins of Istanbul to other parts of the country.

Defined as a "crude form of sovereignty" and a major threat to the government's authority by Turkish and US counterinsurgency analysts who argued that such attempts legitimized "terrorist activity" (Sayari and Hoffman 1991, vi), these experiments in self-governance made these areas the primary targets of state and state-backed civilian violence. As a result, these committees in Istanbul's working-class neighborhoods and those in other parts of Turkey did not operate for more than one or two years. Solmaz was killed in an extrajudicial murder only twenty-eight days after his appointment as mayor, his promise of instituting self-rule never fulfilled.[3] Active members of people's committees in Fatsa and the Istanbul neighborhoods became the targets of police violence, and many, including Fatsa's Mayor Sönmez, were eventually incarcerated.[4] But the committee experiences had a significant impact on the communities' political imaginaries and memories. Within leftist circles in Turkey, Fatsa and the Bir Mayıs neighborhood of Istanbul, where the first and most effective committees were established in 1977, these committees are still celebrated as exemplars of socialist self-governance.[5] In Devrimova, people continue to take pride in the neighborhood's committee experience. Considering themselves the successors of past generations who had experimented with self-governance, young revolutionaries often refer to the committee experience to explain their current efforts to protect their neighborhood from police and gang violence and drug-dealing activity.

In this chapter, I elaborate on Devrimova's brief yet oft-recalled experience of local direct governance. Following Jacques Rancière (2001, 2015), I outline my conception of politics as antithetical to policing and expand on the antagonistic relationship between political activity and the *partitioning* act of policing. The people's committees and their attendant people's courts (*halk mahkemesi*) provided an empowering and transformative political experience that enabled many Devrimovans (both men and women) to designate themselves as political actors who were making their own history. Rather than being passive victims of oppressive structures and relations, Devrimovans became people capable of challenging

their ascribed roles and places in the order of things. In the narrative that follows, I illustrate how Devrimovans' ability to come together "in action and speech"
(Arendt 2013, 25) within the space of spontaneity opened up by the people's committees and courts gave rise to productive, liberatory, and transformative debate,
dialogue, and disagreement. This participatory experience helped Devrimovans
negotiate both established patriarchal gender relations and the unequal class relations between middle-class revolutionaries and working-class Devrimovans. It
facilitated the emergence of Devrimovans as political actors on the world-historical
stage who saw themselves as active participants in a global revolutionary struggle.
This chapter also demonstrates the possible links between the centuries-old Alevi
practices of informal justice and the Alevi cultural archive of resistance and oppression that helped vernacularize the communist experiments with direct local
governance of the 1970s.

Alevi Cultural Archive: Oppression and Resistance

Alevi communities in Turkey have long struggled over the meaning of Alevism,
making a clear-cut definition impracticable. Different Alevi communities define
Alevism in various ways. For some Alevis, Alevism is a religion, for others it is a
sect of Islam, and yet for others Alevism is a belief system outside of religion,
a path, a lifestyle, and a philosophy of liberation and resistance (Massicard 2003).
"Whilst some Alevis have no objection to the profession that there is only one
God and that Mohammed is his messenger," Alevis generally do not observe the
other four pillars of Islam (Cetin 2016, 251).[6] All Alevi communities, however,
revere Ali, who was a cousin of the prophet Muhammed. Although Shiites hold
the same reverence for Ali, Alevis do not identify as Shiite. And in contrast to
the two major Shiite and Sunni denominations in Islam, Alevis do not attend
mosque. Rather, they have their own ceremonies, called *cem*. *Cem* ceremonies
take place in *cemevi* (*cem* house).

The original story of oppression and resistance in contemporary Alevi cultural
narratives dates to the assassination of Ali after the prophet's death and the martyrdom of his dissident followers, who are believed to have sacrificed their lives in their
fight against the oppressive rule of Caliph Yazid in Karbala' in 680 AD. Community representatives and activists often link the past and present persecution of Alevis to Karbala' as a way of emphasizing the continuation of Alevi suffering.[7] Alevis
in Turkey commemorate Ali and his Karbala' martyrs during *cem*, mourning the
Karbala' massacre during Muharram, the second-holiest month of the Islamic cal-
endar after Ramadan. For them, the Karbala' massacre is the first in a "long chain

of atrocities" (Çaylı 2014) committed against Ali's disciples. Indexing the struggle against the tyrant Yazid as the original constitutive act of Alevism, many of the Alevi activists and *dedes*[8] I met with argued that the maxim "to not stand against the oppressor is the biggest evil against the oppressed" (*Zalimin zulmüne karşı çıkmamak, mazluma yapılacak en büyük kötülüktür*) lies at the heart of Alevi belief. Inscribed at the entrances of some neighborhood *cemevleri* (plural of *cemevi*) the maxim is attributed to Imam Huseyn, Ali's son who was martyred in Karbala.

"We left our fears back in Karbala' (*Biz korkuyu Kerbela'da bıraktık*)," goes a saying attributed to the renowned Kurdish Alevi revolutionary Hüseyin İnan. Often retold and circulated in Alevi circles after *cem* gatherings and in times of Islamist or state security threat, its use offers a good example of the enduring legacy of Karbala' in the modern-day, intertwining histories of Alevi and revolutionary resistance (see figure 1.1). Although there is no evidence that Hüseyin İnan actually uttered these words, it is widely believed that he spoke them in response to a question posed by another legendary revolutionary figure, Deniz Gezmiş, when they were being led to the scaffold in 1972 to be hung for their revolutionary activities; Gezmiş asked him then, "Aren't you afraid, *dede*?"[9]

FIGURE 1.1.   A scene from the funeral in Gazi Cemevi of two young revolutionaries, Yeliz Erbay and Şirin Öter, who were killed by state security forces on December 22, 2015. Image has been modified to protect the identities of those pictured.

Photo by Sinan Targay.

FIGURE 1.2.   An akrep in front of the Gazi *cemevi*. The photos on the wall from left to right: Ali and the twelve imams, Haci Bektashi Veli, and Pir Sultan Abdal.

Photo by Sinan Targay.

Leftist portrayals of Ottoman-era Alevi rebellions as proto-communist movements also help situate Alevi history within the global history of oppression and resistance, further contributing to the entwinement of Alevi and revolutionary histories (Van Bruinessen 1996a). Although many older and younger revolutionaries of Devrimova born into Alevi culture work actively to distance themselves from their Alevi identity, claiming that revolutionaries are atheists and therefore have "no business with religion," most nevertheless often refer to the Alevi cultural archive of oppression and resistance in explaining their engagement with the revolutionary struggle (*devrimci mücadele*). Sentences that start with "I am not an Alevi" or "I do not consider myself to be an Alevi" often continue with "but the history of resistance and oppression in Alevi society played a crucial role in my decision to become a revolutionary." As we talked together about the roots of their involvement in revolutionary activism, almost all my interlocutors told me that having grown up hearing the heroic tales of Alevi resistance—led by rebels like the fifteenth-century Sheikh Bedreddin, the sixteenth-century poet-rebel Pir Sultan Abdal, and the twentieth-century leader Seyit Riza—along with stories about contemporary revolutionaries, they began to reflect on how oppression and resistance experienced at a very early age and this reflection compelled them to fight against injustice (see figure 1.2). The haunting presence of past Alevi oppression and resistance has been an animating force that, when intersecting with poverty and discrimination, has motivated many Alevi workers to engage in political action against injustice.

Politics, Collective Action, and Dissensus

Drawing on Hannah Arendt's conceptualizations of spontaneous action and political freedom, students of her thought have argued that politics is an active "world-building" practice (Zerilli 2005); that is, the act of voting, solitary and in secret does not meet her understanding of politics and democracy. The goal of politics is to address matters of common concern, and that requires it to be local, direct, and participatory. Arendt believed in the potentiality of human togetherness and the transformative and emancipatory power of the newness that this togetherness of unequal individuals may unleash. For Arendt (2013, 178), the capacity to change the world, begin afresh, and create novel forms of organization in place of what has already been instituted is generated by "being together in the manner of speech and action" in public. Individuals must be able to see, talk to, and meet with one another in public within the spirit of democratic debate, which allows unequals to be "equalized" in certain respects and for specific aspirations (215; d'Entrèves 2002, 17).

Arendt was a persistent advocate of localism against central governance, supporting small networks and gatherings, as well as worker, student, and neighborhood councils. Creation of and participation in the councils provide a venue for "the people," who do not form part of the governing mechanisms of nation-state bureaucracies or party machines, to participate in governance and determine the future of their countries (Arendt 1972, 231). She celebrated Hungarian workers councils, arguing that "the rise of the councils, not the restoration of parties, was the clear sign of a true upsurge of democracy against dictatorship, of freedom against tyranny" (Arendt 1958, 32). As I illustrate later in this chapter, within this Arendtian frame of democratic politics, the people's committee in Devrimova was a unique political space in which unequals—men and women, bourgeois students and impoverished workers—attempted to enter into a relationship of equality, facilitating critical engagement with the existing distribution of sociopolitical roles and positions.[10]

Arendt's conceptualization of workers was, however, contradictory.[11] Although she celebrated the workers' councils as true democratic venues, she held rather conservative views toward the poor and the proletariat, considering them incapable of becoming political actors. As Mustafa Dikeç (2013, 8), with reference to Rancière (1995) underlines, in Arendt's framework, the poor and the proletariat belong to the sphere of needs and reproduction; they are merely concerned with survival.[12] But what made the people's committees a truly political experience in the Rancièrian sense is that they opened up a space for the subaltern—the poorest of the poor—to move beyond demanding their needs and begin engaging in world-building practices.

Although Rancière's understanding of politics resonates with Arendt's emphasis on the transformative potential of people coming together in action and speech within a shared space, his framework goes beyond Arendt's to include intervention in the distribution of roles and positions in the given order. In *Proletarian Nights*, a study of the French working-class movements of the mid-1800s, Rancière (2012) illustrates how workers engaged in nighttime literary and intellectual activities refused to be predetermined as solely, *merely* the proletariat. Rancière considers these nighttime activities as exemplary political acts precisely because they intervened in the established distribution of social roles and places that imprisons proletarians in the sphere of needs and in the space of work.

In contrast to Arendt, Rancière views politics less as a matter of acting in concert with others and more about dissensus. What precisely he means by dissensus matters here. Dissensus is not merely opposition, debate, or quarrel but rather "a dissociation introduced into the correspondence between ways of being and ways of doing, seeing, and speaking" (Rancière 2010, 15). Dissensus is "the making contentious of the givens of a particular situation" (Rancière and Panagia 2000, 124). As I illustrate in the following sections, by opening up a space for simultaneously acting together in concert and engaging in *dissensus*, the people's committees and courts in Devrimova made self-governance a political experience through which subaltern men and women could become active agents in challenging established relations and creating something new.

Devrimova as a Sanctuary Space

Most of the first residents of Devrimova were Alevi Turks and Kurds who had migrated from rural areas to the city in search of jobs in the 1960s and early 1970s and who could not afford to build *gecekondu* houses elsewhere. They were therefore among the poorest of the poor, working as street vendors, construction workers, domestic workers, peddlers, and apprentices to a trade—jobs that many Devrimovans still hold today. Because there were no factories near the neighborhood at the time, the majority of Devrimovans could not benefit from the relatively secure working conditions offered to factory workers. In one way or another, all of the first residents of Devrimova had connections to revolutionary organizations; some were already members or sympathizers, and others had family members in these organizations.

Built on a vacant area, from its inception, Devrimova, like other similar neighborhoods, such as Bir Mayıs, Gazi, Çayan, Okmeydani, and Gülsuyu, was designed as a sanctuary space, not unlike the sanctuaries of Belfast, that was defended against "adverse forces" (Feldman 1991, 38). The most significant of these "adverse forces" was then and still is the state security apparatus, joined by right-wing Turkish nationalists and Islamists from surrounding neighborhoods. With the erection of the first shacks in Devrimova and in other such neighborhoods came frequent clashes with state security forces—police cadres and soldiers—who entered the neighborhoods regularly with military vehicles and bulldozers to demolish the structures; they would be met by stone-throwing residents. The most well-known and bloodiest incidents took place on September 2, 1977, in the Bir Mayıs neighborhood ("May First" neighborhood), named after the May Day celebrations; state security forces killed nine residents and wounded tens of others by shooting directly at the crowd from their military vehicles.[13]

As senior Devrimovans recounted to me, each and every attempt by soldiers and police cadres to demolish the makeshift *gecekondu* houses in the neighborhoods would be met with hundreds of residents who filled the streets so as to block the bulldozers and military vehicles, chanting: "*Gecekondu* is our right! We will take it against all odds!" (*Gecekondu hakkımız söke söke alırız!*).[14] Nedim, a fifty-year-old Devrimovan who was a child in the mid-1970s, painted a vivid picture of the contentious encounters between the security forces and Devrimovans.

> As kids we were used to playing in the empty areas at the periphery of the neighborhood. When we saw the bulldozers coming toward the neighborhood, we would start running and shouting, "The state is coming! The state is coming!" Men were usually at work during the day. But the women who heard our voices would pour into the streets and start collecting stones in their skirts to throw at the bulldozers.

In demystifying the notion of the state as a homogeneous, unified entity that exists over and above individuals, Philip Abrams (1988, 79) has exposed its ideological nature as a mask that obscures the "actual disunity of political power." However, the state's "insubstantiality" (Taussig 1992) does not mean that the idea or fantasy of the state has no real effects. Begoña Aretxaga (2000, 44) warns us that, regardless of "the reality or unreality of the state-subject," we should "take the reality of insubstantial state-being seriously and question how it is imagined by the people who experience it, what its particular manifestations and forms of operation are and what kind of subjectivity it comes to embody." As Nedim's story and the stories of my other interlocutors throughout this book illustrate, since the establishment of the neighborhood, the state has been manifest and experienced as a destructive force in Devrimova. In "the act of producing terror" (49) in the streets of Devrimova, the state has become a subject. This state-subject has not only deprived Devrimovans of their rights to shelter, housing, infrastructure, and other basic needs but has also threatened their lives and their fates.

Contrary to expectations, the state-subject's destructive and threatening presence in the streets did not succeed in debilitating Devrimovans enough to make them leave their sanctuary space. The violent presence of the state served instead to organize Devrimovans around a common cause: the fight for their right to housing. After each demolition, the entire community would gather together, decide on the division of the labor, and start rebuilding the houses that had been destroyed.[15] Men, women, and children would all take part in this effort. As my senior interlocutors proudly recounted, every single house in the neighborhood was built collectively in those years. But Devrimovans' collective space-building practices extended beyond the fight for housing to include collective world-building practices that opened up space for individual and social transformation. The people's committees and the people's courts were prime instruments of this world-building practice, and their effects are still felt today.

People's Committees and the Experience of Self-Governance

Soon after they built their shacks and staked out residential space in the area, Devrimovans established a neighborhood people's committee. For a little longer than a year, the people's court, created to mediate internal conflicts within the community, and the people's committee, were the only governing bodies in the neighborhood. It is important to note here that the establishment of these institutions in these neighborhoods was not merely a result of the encouragement of local self-governance and organizational assistance given by outside revolutionary organizations. Both the urgent infrastructural needs and the historical Alevi experience of informal justice played a part in their creation. On a winter day in 2011, I spoke with Arif Amca, a seventy-two-year-old Devrimovan founder of the people's committee framework and car mechanic for more than thirty years.[16] Conversing in a coffeehouse where elderly male residents play card games, chit-chat, or watch TV while sipping black tea, Arif Amca explained to me why they felt the need to establish the people's committee in the neighborhood:

> When we started to build the neighborhood, there was nothing here. No electricity, no water, no roads, no infrastructural services. . . . It was

mostly an empty land full of mud. Because the state did not recognize Devrimova as a residential area, there was also no police station, no *muhtarlık* [neighborhood administrative unit]. To get water, we had to walk for more than half an hour to reach the wells. When people began to move into the neighborhood, we got together and discussed what could be done. At the time, revolutionary organizations were already discussing the establishment of people's committees. We organized a public meeting, and at that meeting I and some other friends who, like me, were also revolutionaries, suggested the establishment of people's committees. The idea sounded plausible to many. Honestly, we had no other choice. We had to develop our own instruments with which to solve our problems as quickly as possible. It was not just a political choice. It was also a basic necessity [*temel ihtiyaç*].

According to Arif Amca and other elderly residents I interviewed who had participated in this first meeting, there were around fifty to sixty people present, almost all men. Yet once the committee began to work, more and more women took part in its activities. Over time, women became more active than men, posing a challenge to the conventional gendered distribution of roles.

The participants decided at the first meeting to divide the neighborhood into regions. Because members and supporters of the various revolutionary organizations were already concentrated in specific regions, this division enabled the organizations to participate in local governance equally. Each region had its own elected committee representatives who were monitored by an elected head committee (*baş komite*), consisting of all men. Committee meetings took place once a week, and depending on the urgency of the matters, the number of participants varied between twenty to thirty people to as many as four hundred. The meetings held after police house demolitions were invariably the most crowded.

In the meetings, my senior interlocutors explained, residents brought forward their day-to-day problems—issues of security, health, electricity, sanitation, mud in the streets, and domestic violence—for debate and possibly solution. The task of the committee representatives from the regions was to prioritize the problems, determine the best possible solutions from among those proposed, and form volunteer working groups with which to tackle them. There were working groups for electricity, water, public security (*asayiş*), and urban planning—whatever the situation demanded. For example, the electricity group located a power distribution unit not too far away from the neighborhood and managed to bring electricity into the neighborhood illegally. Revolutionary university students regularly visiting Devrimova and similar neighborhoods also took part in these working groups. Medical students established health groups and provided residents with basic health care services and public health education. Urban planning and architecture students helped residents divide and distribute the land justly as they transformed their shacks into houses and planned the neighborhoods' streets and public spaces. The Marxist principle of "to each according to his/her need" was applied in decisions on the just distribution of land, with need calculated according to the number of family members per household.

Among the various working groups, the *asayiş* group for the provision of informal public security was the most urgently needed. Ibrahim Amca, one of the founders of the *asayiş* group and a retired construction worker, told me about the formation of these groups while we were chatting and eating sunflower seeds, a popular working-class snack, in a neighborhood park on a hot August evening:

> Neighborhoods like ours were exemplary back then. We were experimenting with a new socialist way of living. The nationalists and the Islamists living in the surrounding neighborhoods who were supported by the state saw us as their enemies. For them we were anarchists,[17] communists. They were backed by the state, as is still the case today. We were afraid that they would attack the neighborhood. We had to be vigilant and watch the neighborhood boundaries to prevent them from entering. The state could also send agents provocateurs to the neighborhood. So the number one responsibility of the *asayiş* groups was to prevent such events. We also needed to handle relatively minor events, such as burglaries. And then there were the attacks against Devrimovans outside the neighborhood. There was no public transportation service to Devrimova, so *mahalleli* (neighborhood residents) who worked outside the neighborhood had to get off the bus at least half an hour's walking distance away and walk through a Sunni Turkish-populated neighborhood to get back home. On their walk back home, nationalist and Islamist groups from that neighborhood would beat Devrimovans whenever they saw them alone. We needed to protect them as well.

The *asayiş* group was divided into three subgroups—neighborhood patrol, border patrol, and escorts—to meet the community's functional needs for security. Neighborhood patrol groups were responsible for watching the neighborhood at night when Devrimovans were sleeping, keeping the neighborhood free of petty criminals and any suspicious outsiders, who were assumed to be agents provocateurs. Border patrol groups secured the neighborhood's boundaries, informing Devrimovans in advance when they spotted bulldozers, panzers, or mobs approaching the neighborhood. In such cases, they would blow their whistles to call Devrimovans into the streets to stand united against possible attacks. As many older Devrimovans proudly noted to me in our interviews and informal conversations, "One whistle was enough to bring hundreds of people" into the streets. These groups were also responsible for investigating outsiders before allowing them to enter the neighborhood. Afraid that any outsider could be an agent provocateur sent by the police to trigger violence, they would bar entrance to anyone who was unable to demonstrate a connection to neighborhood residents. Escort groups met Devrimovan workers, especially women workers who worked primarily in affluent neighborhoods as cleaning women, at the bus stop and accompanied them back to the neighborhood. These escort activities are still very much appreciated and remembered by senior female Devrimovans. As Nazê Nene, who worked as a cleaning woman for more than thirty years, claimed, it was thanks to these escort groups that she and her friends could work outside the neighborhood; they "always felt the protective and caring eyes of the revolutionaries on them."

Gary Marx (1974) has compellingly argued that any analysis of social movements that does not take into account the presence of informants and agents provocateurs is incomplete. His investigation of the FBI archives unearthed numerous examples of the presence of secret agents working in left-wing groups as informants and agents provocateurs. As their name suggests, agents provocateurs are operatives who carry out the bulk of counterinsurgency's psychological warfare. Their main task is to secretly intervene in dissident organizations and provoke their use of violence. By so doing, they stigmatize dissident groups in the eyes of the public, encourage paranoia and mistrust among group members and their supporters, gain evidence for use in a trial, and racialize their constituency by creating the conditions for their depiction by politicians and the media as violence-prone "savages" or "barbarians." Agents provocateurs are thus essential figures in provocative counterorganization operations.

Turkish security officers have also employed agents provocateurs in their fight against left-wing dissent. Although there is no publicly available archival material that would show exactly how and where such agents provocateurs were used, firsthand accounts that provide evidence for their use have been published. As mentioned in the introduction, in 1971, Cihat Akyol, then commander of the Special Warfare Department (ÖHD)—the official name of the Turkish counter-guerrilla (Söyler 2013, 316)—and known as one of the architects of Turkey's "deep state," published an article calling for the creation of covert groups that would engage in violent acts but give the impression that they had been committed by dissident organizations (cited in Mumcu 1990; reprinted in Mumcu 1997, 54–57).[18] In a special parliamentary commission meeting on coups held during a 2012 meeting of the Turkish National Assembly, retired staff colonel Talat Turhan testified that in the 1960s and 1970s Turkish military officers were sent to the Special Warfare School at Fort Bragg, North Carolina, and later to Fort Benning in Georgia to receive counterinsurgency training that included provocation and propaganda techniques and psychological warfare (Meclis Araştırması Komisyonu 2012).[19] Although we do not as yet know the exact role agents provocateurs and informants played in the organizations that were active in Devrimova, the residents' fear of agents provocateurs—a fear that still continues in the neighborhood today—was not unfounded. As Ibrahim Amca's account attests, this fear was a productive force that played an important role in Devrimova's becoming a sanctuary space—an enclosed community protected from the outside environment. In fact, because Devrimova was planned as a safe haven for the country's most vulnerable workers, neither its first residents nor the outsider revolutionaries who helped them build it allowed strangers to settle in the neighborhood until 1980—that is, when the military coup crushed the revolutionary movement.

As I illustrate in the following chapters, this complex interplay between perceived and real threat has heightened security concerns over the course of the years, thus paving the way for the containment of revolutionary activities and violence in the neighborhood and for the transformation of Devrimova into an enclosed community preoccupied with protecting itself from a threatening outside.

People's Courts and Alevi Historical Practice

The creation of people's courts soon followed the establishment of the people's committees in the late 1970s. Over the course of an afternoon in his apartment, Hasan Amca, a seventy-six-year-old Devrimovan who worked as a street vendor for more than thirty years, explained to me why there was a need to establish courts and how they operated:

> We were living in shacks back then, and not all of the shacks had doors. This allowed burglary. From time to time, there were disputes between people. We needed a mechanism with which to solve these issues. There was no police station or anything like that in the neighborhood. Actually, even if there had been, people would not trust it enough to go to the police. With people like us, when we would go to the police to complain about something, the police would treat us as if we were the guilty ones. Nothing has changed since then. In the eyes of the police, we have always been terrorists.

As Erika Robb Larkins (2015, 60) in her ethnographic study of violence in a Brazilian favela argues, "The police are not meant to protect the rights of *all* citizens; police work in favela settings in particular centered on maintaining entrenched class divisions between the favela and the city and upholding the status quo rather than implementing some idealistic vision of the law or justice for all." Similarly, as Hasan Amca and countless other interlocutors argued, Devrimovans—Istanbul's racialized and dissident poor—did not experience the police as part of a governmental body that protected their rights and delivered justice. The committees therefore decided that disputes and charges of crime within the neighborhood would need to be resolved locally. If, for instance, someone stole something from a neighbor, that neighbor would bring this complaint to the committee members, and the committee members would assemble a people's court to hear it. The committee members would call the accused, the plaintiff, and witnesses and ask them to provide information about the alleged crime. They would ask the people in attendance if there were any witnesses to the theft. If the accused was found to have stolen something, the court would ask why he or she had committed that deed and then would solicit suggestions for punishment from the audience. After deliberation among the committee members, a sentence would be meted out. In most cases, punishments were not harsh but were meant as a deterrent to repeating the offending act.

Although the founders of the committee cited only the Soviet-style council experience as their main inspiration during our interviews, informal justice was not an entirely new phenomenon for Devrimova's Alevi residents. In response to a history of what Umit Cetin (2017) calls a "persecuted exclusion," a significant percent of Alevis had lived in disguise in remote and mountainous areas for centuries and developed their own communal justice practices (Sökefeld 2008). *Cem* rituals functioned not only as commemoration rituals for revered Alevi figures but also "as a site for the adjudication of social disputes among members of the community" (Tambar 2010, 655). Led by a *dede*, a male descendant of Ali, *cem* ceremonies involved open discussion of disputes between community members and debate on the possible forms of punishment or compensation. Although it is clear that the people's courts were modeled after the Soviet-style council experiences and lacked the economy of emotion, ritual, and history present in *cem* rituals, they may have found particularly fertile soil in Devrimova's Alevi community precisely because Alevis were already comfortable with informal justice practices and the solving of community problems without recourse to historically hostile state authorities. This familiarity with informal justice practices—or what we might call a centuries-long Alevi *habitus* of informal justice—may have played an important role in Devrimovans' quick adoption of the people's courts and the effective vernacularization of revolutionary practice among Alevi communities. Importantly, the absence of gender-based spatial segregation among Alevi communities during *cem* ceremonies must have made it easier for Devrimova's Alevi women to participate in the committee meetings and courts. It is no coincidence that all of the women participants of the committees and courts I met were Alevis.

Committees, Courts, and de facto Feminist Politics

The revolutionaries who initiated the establishment of people's committees and courts in Devrimova did not aim to challenge traditional patriarchal relations. Revolutionaries of that time in Turkey were not interested in gender politics, which they considered a secondary issue that should be addressed after the revolution. Many of the senior activists I spoke with, including the middle-class revolutionaries who used to visit the neighborhood frequently, recounted that initially there was not much space available for women in the committees. Yet, over time, committee and court experiences not only paved the way for Turkish-speaking women's active participation in the meetings but also opened up space for a de facto feminist politics.[20] Ayşe Nene, a seventy-five-year-old Devrimovan known in the neighborhood as a "revolutionary grandmother" (*devrimci nene*), explained to me how she and other women began to take part in the meetings:

> At first, I was not interested in going to the meetings. But we had a lot of problems in the neighborhood. For instance, the wells were located away from the neighborhood, and when we went there to get water, there was sometimes a huge line. I thought it would be good to have some sort of order, as in a timetable. This was something we discussed among the women in our region, but we needed to reach the others. My uncle's son was a committee representative. I told him to take this issue to the committee meeting. He said, "Why don't you come and share your ideas with the people there by yourself?" I was at first unwilling. I thought, "No one will listen to an ignorant [*cahil*] woman like me." He somehow convinced me to go to the meeting. My husband did not like the idea. But my uncle's son was a respected revolutionary, so he could not object to it. I went to the meeting with three other female neighbors of mine. At first, I was a bit shy. I remember that when I first started talking, I could not look anyone in the eye. There were a lot of men, a lot of revolutionaries at the meeting. You felt like, "Who will care

about what I say when there are all those revolutionaries here?" But in time, that feeling went away. As I participated in more meetings, I became more confident. Of course, some men did not want to listen to us; they were not happy to see us in the meetings. Eventually other women, too, began to participate in the meetings. We became very active. We actually became more active than the men! [Laughs.] We, too, became revolutionaries. Our activities were not limited to the neighborhood. We would go to demonstrations outside the neighborhood, support strikes. We were fighting for the revolution.

Like Ayşe Nene, all eight women I interviewed who had lived in the neighborhood in the 1970s told me how much they enjoyed participating in the meetings and demonstrations. They valued the feeling of being heard and being useful, of working together with other people both in and outside the neighborhood. Participation in decision-making meetings and in collective action and resisting state security operations in the neighborhood transformed how many female Devrimovans were seen: no longer "ignorant poor women," they were recognized as revolutionaries doing work beyond the gendered domestic boundaries of the sanctuary space of the neighborhood. Crossing these gendered boundaries and transcending their ascribed gendered roles empowered them as present and visible actors in the community. To this day, they participate defiantly in the May Day and other demonstrations inside and outside the neighborhood and are respected by neighborhood youth for their dissident activities.

As more and more women began to take part in the meetings, they began to challenge the patriarchal distinction between public and private domains and brought traditionally private matters into public discussion. The increasing participation of women in the committee and court meetings opened up space for feminist practice. Fatma Teyze, Ayşe Nene's comrade in the 1970s, recounted how the difficult issues of domestic violence, male alcoholism, and the gendered dimensions of household finances were eventually brought to the people's court:

> We were fighting [*mücadele ediyorduk*] all together back then. There was unity among the people. We were also fighting the men, fighting our husbands. [Long laughter.] Some men would beat their wives or did not let them work outside [the home]. Some men would drink alcohol and not give enough money to their wives. We thought, "If we discuss [other] neighborhood problems in the committee, why can't we discuss our problems?" We took them to the courts. At first, the committees did not want to discuss these issues. Men tend to back up other men. But we insisted. We said that the courts had to punish those men. Some

women were afraid, of course. They did not want to take their husbands to the courts. But some did. The punishment for those who drank too much was to hand over their salaries to their wives. Once, the court told a man who had harassed some women in the neighborhood to leave the neighborhood and to never come back again. Like it was in the village *cems*.[21]

In her article documenting the people's committees in Fatsa, Yeseren Elicin (2011) argues that women became the most active participants of the committees. They also brought problems of domestic violence and excessive alcohol consumption to the people's courts for public discussion and used the people's committee meetings as platforms for addressing male domination in the community and pressuring men to change their behaviors. Though short-lived and met with concerted resistance by men, women's participation in the people's committees and courts and in collective acts of resistance were effective in cultivating an Arendtian sense of public-spiritedness and joy among women, one that still brings a smile to the faces of women as they describe those victorious moments against male domination. These moments were also political performances of dissensus that forced revolutionary men to confront their own oppressive practices and privileges.

Against the Grain of the Sensible

The people's courts in Devrimova opened up space not only for negotiating gender hierarchies and relations but also for redressing class hierarchies. In the 1970s, revolutionary university students, many of whom came from middle- or upper-middle-class backgrounds, often visited Devrimova and other working-class neighborhoods. Although Devrimovans still speak highly of these students, their encounters were not tension-free. Rather than trying to forge a relationship of comradely solidarity with Devrimovans, some Turkish middle-class revolutionaries, born into class and ethnosectarian privilege, imagined themselves as the "saviors" of the "victims" of capitalism and state domination or as leaders of the "uneducated" masses. People's courts provided the space for working out these unequal class encounters. Ergin Bey, an upper-middle-class Sunni Turkish architect who frequented Devrimova in the 1970s as a student, recounted to me over lunch one day, while sitting at a café in a posh area of central Istanbul, his own people's committee trial experience in Devrimova. His story exemplifies how Devrimovans used the people's courts to challenge this victim–savior binary marked by racialized and class relations.

I would go to the neighborhood regularly with my theater friends. At the time, I was a student in the architecture department and was helping Devrimovans to design the streets. A couple of Devrimovans learned that some among us were active in the theater. They asked us if we could organize a play for them. We told them that we could and agreed that we would perform a play for them two weeks later. But for some reason, we didn't manage to prepare for the play. We went to the neighborhood anyway, as we had promised, but with no intention of performing. I had a jeep. We parked the jeep a little away from the neighborhood and walked there. We didn't want to be seen with the jeep.

As soon as we entered the neighborhood, people began to gather around us and ask us about the play. It turned out that they had already arranged everything. They had carried chairs from a coffeehouse to an empty area in the neighborhood. They had even made a makeshift stage for us. We were surprised. We were not expecting such preparations. We didn't tell them that we weren't prepared but decided to improvise instead. Back then we were into Brechtian theater.[22] When the time came, we went onstage. We tried to improvise something. But it didn't work. There were tens of people—men, women, and children. They understood that we weren't prepared. Some got angry. The women were especially angry. They said that it was their laundry day or something like that, and that they had to change their schedule to see our play. They said, "We arranged everything for you. We had a lot of things to do today. We postponed them because of your play. But it seems that you don't respect us." We made a promise, but we did not keep it.

The women insisted on taking us to the people's court. In court, they asked us to explain what had prevented us from preparing. I don't remember what we said exactly. But they didn't find our excuse convincing. As a result of the trial, we were banned from entering the neighborhood for two months. They decided that we had been disrespectful.

When I asked senior Devrimovans about this event, I could not find anyone who remembered it. But when I recounted it to Hasibe Teyze and Hasan Amca, whom I quoted earlier, their interpretation of the story of Ergin's trial articulated the class tensions that existed between Devrimovans and the revolutionary university students who frequented the neighborhood. Hasan spoke first:

> I don't want to speak badly of the revolutionary students. We were comrades. Some of them were the children of laborers [emekçi çocukları], like us. But some were different. They were from bourgeois families.

They had a bourgeois upbringing. Even though they were revolutionaries, some still saw the world through a bourgeois lens.

When I asked him to elaborate, the hierarchy came into sharper view: "Well,
you know, the bourgeoisie always looks down on the proletariat. They believe
that the working class is ignorant, uneducated, uncultivated."
    Hasibe immediately chimed in:

> That's true. What Hasan says is very true. Even though they were revo-
> lutionaries, some of them saw themselves as above us. Not all of them,
> of course. There were many great revolutionary youths who were from
> very wealthy families, but they would not make you feel it. I don't re-
> member that particular event. But I do remember that we used to talk
> about some arrogant students and consider taking that issue to the
> courts. The women probably wanted to teach them a lesson [laughing]
> and wanted to say to them, "You see us as ignorant people who can't
> understand and appreciate art. But we do." Because some saw us—
> especially saw the women—as completely ignorant [kara cahil]. Maybe
> we didn't know how to read or write, some of us didn't even know how
> to speak Turkish, but it didn't mean that we were stupid; it did not make
> us less of a revolutionary.

In *Proletarian Nights*, Rancière (2012, 249) addresses this uneasy and unequal
relationship between privileged revolutionary intellectuals—the "prophets of the
new world"—and the proletariat. Pointing up the paradox of the revolutionary
desire to abolish "proletarian existence" and the revolutionary predilection to
see the proletariat as "good soldiers of the great militant army and as prototypes
of the worker of the future" (249), Rancière argues that bourgeois revolutionaries could not and did not want to imagine the proletariat as intellectuals and
artists. Those bourgeois revolutionary visions of the proletariat as worker and
as intellectual-artist were mutually exclusive. For the proletariat, however,
nighttime was when men and women engaged in intellectual and artistic activities and "wrenched themselves out of an identity formed by domination and
asserted themselves as inhabitants with full rights of a common world capable
of all refinement or asceticism that had previously been reserved for those
classes relieved of the daily cares of work and bread" (ix).
    Within this frame, Devrimovan women's anger with Ergin and his artist friends
can be understood as a result of the gulf between the bourgeois revolutionary
imaginary of workers and the workers' imagination of themselves. The women's
insistence on taking privileged revolutionaries to the people's court can be seen as
a political attempt to prove that they are more than just "soldiers of the great mili-

tant army" (Rancière 2012, 249) marching under the command of bourgeois revolutionaries. In this sense, the trial was a vehicle to show that they were "inhabitants with full rights of a common world" (ix) and that art can—or, better yet, should—be known and appreciated by both bourgeois and working-class revolutionaries alike. The trial essentially functioned as an exemplary political performance that could challenge the predetermined position of the poorest of the poor in the policed distribution of the sensible as merely "victims" and to remind those predetermined as "saviors" of their equal place in a common world.[23] In this sense, too, the people's courts provided space for the world-building practice of dissensus meant to carve out a "subaltern counterpublic" (Fraser 1990) wherein social hierarchies and relations of power were contested and redressed.

Although fitting, this characterization does not imply that in a very short period—the committee experience lasted for only a year and a half—Devrimovans were able to create an ideal, utopian experience of socialist and feminist democracy. As some of my senior interlocutors noted, certain court and committee members resisted the challenges posed by women and other groups who dared go against the grain of the established and socially policed distribution of roles and relations. In particular, women's attempts to bring domestic issues to the courts were seen by some—including revolutionary students who frequented the neighborhood—as apolitical activities that diverted revolutionary energy from supposedly "real" problems. Others I interviewed noted that the connections, antagonisms, and power struggles among the various revolutionary groups negatively affected the people's committee meetings. Yet the people's committees and courts were nevertheless politically empowering spaces that transcended a predetermined focus on instrumental concerns by spontaneously paving the way for transformative disagreement. Together, the power of public participation in the Arendtian sense and the spontaneous eruption of practices of dissensus opened up a powerful political space in Devrimova where the wretched of the earth were able to experience being active agents of a world in the making. It is perhaps for this reason that the scenes and excitement that surrounded the people's committees and courts of the late 1970s are still fresh in the memory of those who took part in them and why they continue to haunt the neighborhood youths who still long to launch their own experiments in self-governance in the neighborhood.

In subsequent decades and even as late as very recently, Devrimovans have attempted to revive this experience. Yet, despite efforts by Devrimovans and residents of similar neighborhoods to revive the people's committees, they were rapidly stigmatized. In 1997, a group of residents, some of whom were affiliated with various revolutionary organizations, came together and established people's committees in the neighborhoods of Gazi, Okmeydanı, and Nurtepe. In Gazi, residents elected community representatives to address neighborhood issues, such as frequent electricity cuts and lack of public bus routes, before the Turkish National Assembly. The committees quickly caught the attention of the national media. Associating the initiative with an outlawed revolutionary organization, the Revolutionary People's Liberation Party-Front (Devrimci Halk Kurtuluş Partisi-Cephesi; DHKP-C), the right-wing newspaper *Zaman* announced dramatically in a headline, "The DHKP-C Lays Their Hands on the People's Assembly," claiming that the initiative was led by a "terrorist organization."[24]

Liberated Zones

While courts and committees were empowering experiences for the country's poorest and racialized urban working classes, the growing number of attempts to establish people's committees in other working-class neighborhoods of Istanbul resulted in a series of media campaigns of condemnation. A RAND research report—prepared for the US Under Secretary of Defense for Policy—considered these self-governing experiences to be a "crude form of sovereignty," a form of "terrorism" that challenged the sovereignty of the state and legitimized alleged "terrorist" organizations (Sayari and Hoffman 1991). Taking the law into one's own hands is not always antagonistic to the power of the state; in some instances, it can occur in collusion with the state. Ruling elites may encourage informal justice as "a cheap form of law enforcement" (Pratten and Sen 2007, 3) and incorporate it into state security practices.[25] In other contexts, especially when practiced by dissenting religious or political groups such as People against Gangsterism and Drugs (PAGAD) in South Africa in the late 1990s or the Irish Republican Army in Northern Ireland, informal justice is considered a threat to state sovereignty because the activities of such groups promote an alternative worldview and political imagination.[26] Because the committees and courts were set up by dissenters of the state, in the eyes of Turkish ruling elites, the court and committee experiences in the neighborhoods were challenges to the state's distribution of "proper" roles and forms of participation and had to be policed accordingly.

Defaming dissident communities and groups via the media is a widely used counterinsurgency technique aimed at fragmenting them by criminalizing and stigmatizing them in the eyes of other segments of the population. In line with this strategy, the Turkish mainstream media launched a condemnation campaign against those neighborhoods that were experimenting with people's committees. The first wave began in 1977, shortly after the implementation of the people's committee experiments. The pro-government newspaper *Tercüman*

warned the public that "the enemies of the state and the nation" were establishing "liberated zones" (cited in Aslan 2008, 128). The publication of *Tercüman*'s
commentary on the so-called liberated zones was soon followed by the large-
scale destruction of the Bir Mayıs neighborhood where the committees had been
most active. More than one thousand houses were demolished and nine residents, including two children, were killed by state security forces (150).

Newspaper commentaries on the neighborhoods continued to be followed by
police operations. In March 1978, mainstream newspapers once again carried
"the issue of the liberated zones" into their banner headlines and front pages, con-
demning them as little more than havens for "anarchists." All the communities
that had established people's committees were portrayed as violent, chaotic, and
outside the control of the state. Referring to the people's court in the neighborhood of Bir Mayıs, one newspaper claimed that there were execution squads in
the neighborhood (Aslan 2008, 151). Another maintained that committees had
built prisons in the neighborhoods. In spring 1978, hundreds of Devrimovan
houses were raided, hundreds of residents were taken into custody, and Devrimova's people's committee members were forced to flee the neighborhood and
go underground. Such operations put an end to the people's committee meetings and the court experience in Istanbul. The meetings and courts continued
underground for some time. But by being forced into secrecy, they had lost their
Arendtian and Rancièrian dynamism, which lay in the redistribution of public
political participation.

Because mainstream media attention to the neighborhoods had made Devrimova more vulnerable to attacks by nationalist and Islamist mobs, the provision
of security, which eventually led to self-isolation, became one of the main priori-
ties for Devrimovans. Border patrol groups were in need of increasing numbers of
volunteers to prevent mobs from entering the neighborhood. In the lead-up to
the 1980 coup, 1978 proved to be a particularly bloody year for Alevis. The Gray
Wolves (Bozkurtlar), a Turkist, racist, and fascist paramilitary group formed by
Colonel Alparslan Türkeş, the founder of the Nationalist Action Party (Milliyetçi
Hareket Partisi), in the late 1960s, attacked predominantly Alevi-populated towns.
This paramilitary group killed hundreds of Kurdish and Turkish Alevis and incited ostensibly civilian pogroms in Malatya in April 1978, in Maraş (currently
Kahramanmaraş) in December 1978, and in Çorum in May–July 1980; rioters
chanted slogans like "Death to communists" and "Death to Alevis."[27] These events
reverberated through the Alevi community, making millions of Alevis fearful that
they might be among the next to be targeted. Afraid of remaining in their home-
towns, many survivors of the Malatya, Maraş, and Çorum massacres found shelter in Devrimova and other Istanbul working-class Alevi neighborhoods.

As Allen Feldman (1991, 36) argues in his comprehensive study of life in Northern Ireland during the height of the Troubles, the creation of a community sanctuary space "cannot simply be viewed as a withdrawal from an autonomous outside, from a violence-prone public domain, in order to create a relatively violence-free haven." More than a mere withdrawal or separation from the outside world, a community sanctuary space, he argues, attempts to manage violence by directing it into prescribed channels. Within an atmosphere of heightening insecurities, the protection of Devrimova from actual or potential adverse forces went hand in hand with making the neighborhood a threatening place for outsiders. As the neighborhood began to attract state-sanctioned mob violence, pistols that had been carefully hidden in safes were taken out and used at the peripheries of the neighborhood to frighten strangers away. It is no coincidence that, as in Belfast, Devrimova and other sanctuaries of the dissident left-wing working classes began to be marked by violence, as fights and armed clashes between revolutionaries and right-wing and Islamist paramilitary groups throughout the country reached their peak in the late 1970s. This similarity stems from the parallel techniques used by the Turkish and British security elites in Belfast and Istanbul. Turkish security elites read and were informed about British brigadier Frank Kitson's books *Gangs and Counter-Gangs* (1960) and *Low-Intensity Operations* (1971).[28] Using Kitson's counterinsurgency strategies incubated in Belfast, both security forces collaborated with and supported right-wing paramilitary groups (Protestant groups in Belfast and Turkish Sunni groups in Istanbul) against the left-wing working classes (Catholics in Belfast and Alevis in Istanbul).[29] The targeting of dissident working-class Alevi spaces was effective in the spatialization of the conflict—that is, its concentration in and association with certain areas. As I illustrate in chapter 3, the sectarian nature of the targeting was also effective in the transformation of left-wing, working-class sanctuaries into sectarian enclaves, as was also the case in Belfast.

However, it was not until the mid-1990s that Devrimova would become a place of "contained and permitted violence," a phrase Feldman (1991, 37) uses to describe Belfast. All of my interviewees who lived in the neighborhood in its early years took pains to stress that revolutionary violence was used at the community's borders to prevent violent mobs and provocateurs from entering the neighborhood. For elderly Devrimovans who were eyewitnesses to those events, the introduction of guns into the neighborhood in the mid-1990s was a huge turning point: it marked the point when revolutionary violence began to be contained in the neighborhood. As I illustrate in the following chapters, the containment of revolutionary violence in the neighborhoods in relation to changing modalities of state security intervention played a central role in transforming the figure of the revolutionary—from an inseparable part of the community whose "protective eyes," in Nazê Nene's words, provided assurance into an ambiguous figure who stands on the threshold of inside and outside, security and insecurity. This transformation, enabled by Turkish counterinsurgency, was effective in separating revolutionaries from their constituency.

The 1980 Coup

In February 1980, six months before Turkey's military coup d'état, *Aydınlık*—an ostensibly communist and an overtly nationalist newspaper—published a series of articles about Devrimova and other such neighborhoods.[30] In the series, the newspaper printed maps of the neighborhoods and information on revolutionary organizations' areas of influence.[31] This was followed immediately by a series of search-and-destroy operations in these areas. As a result, most of Devrimova's active revolutionaries were imprisoned, became fugitives, or escaped to Europe in search of asylum.

In September 1980, the National Security Council staged a coup d'état to overthrow the civilian government and declared a national state of emergency that lasted for three years. As a result of the coup and the military rule that followed, more than 1200 people died from various causes (execution, torture, under suspicious circumstances, in prison, during prison hunger strikes, while fleeing, during conflict, or as suicides or natural deaths). Some 650,000 people were detained and 230,000 people tried; 1,683,000 people were officially listed in police files as suspects; 348,000 people were banned from traveling abroad, 30,000 fled abroad as political refugees, and 14,000 had their citizenship revoked; 23,677 associations were shut down; 400 journalists were sentenced to prison, 300 journalists were attacked, and 3 were shot dead; 62,864 teachers, 120 professors, and 47 judges were dismissed, and more than 30,000 people were fired from their jobs (Zeydanlıoğlu 2009). In the midst of this three-year state of emergency, a new constitution was introduced in 1982 that significantly strengthened the role of the military in governing the country (Cizre-Sakallıoğlu 1997); this was accompanied by the militarization of the police force. Soon after the coup, two highly militarized police units were established: in 1982, the Rapid Action Forces (Çevik Kuvvet) and, in 1983, the Special Operations Unit (Özel Harekat Birimi). Recruited from among members of the fascist, racist Nationalist Movement Party, the Rapid Action Forces are notorious for their aggressive attacks against civilians and disproportionate use of force, including the killing of civilians during political demonstrations. Resembling Britain's Special Air Service in Northern Ireland, the Special Operations Unit was formed as a paramilitary unit and trained in guerrilla warfare. Engaging in undercover operations, surveillance, and armed intervention, the unit has been responsible for large-scale human rights abuses, including the disappearance and extrajudicial killings of thousands of activists (Berksoy 2007).

The atmosphere of fear and intimidation created by the military government during these years, which terrorized the entire country, was effective in suppressing activity in Devrimova. Devrimovans whom I interviewed characterized the years following the coup as ones of silence, fear, and apathy. Hasibe, a Devrimovan in her seventies, described the mood of the time with poetic intensity:

> There was dead silence in the neighborhood in those years; not even a leaf stirred [*yaprak kımıldamıyordu*]. Many people were imprisoned or ran away. The neighborhood was partially abandoned. We, those of us who remained, had no energy to continue to fight back. A lot of us were interrogated and tortured by the police—both men and women. We witnessed the killings of comrades and relatives. People lost their loved ones. It was as though nothing was left of the revolutionary struggle. Metris and Sağmalcılar prisons had become our second addresses. Half of the *mahalleli* [Devrimova residents], mostly men, were in prison, and the other half were visiting the prisons regularly to see them. The state appointed a *muhtar* (neighborhood administrator) to the neighborhood. His main duty was to spy on us. But there was actually not much to spy on. Because all of the most dedicated revolutionaries [*en adanmış devrimciler*] were already in prison.

But even though Devrimova became insular and Devrimovan's challenges to the existing police distribution of the sensible were dormant, things would not remain this way. As we see in the next chapter, less than a decade after the coup, revolutionaries began to reorganize in the neighborhoods, the factories, and the universities, and Kurdish cadres who had been active in the 1970s' revolutionary movement began to coalesce into a Kurdish liberation movement, a new political actor in the country.

"GAZAS OF ISTANBUL"

Threatening Alliances and Militarized
Spatial Control

Although the 1980 coup had pacified the revolutionary movement, it did not succeed in preventing the remobilization of left-wing dissent in Turkey. Devrimova
may have become insular and its activities gone dormant after the coup, but
Devrimovans' passion for challenging the accepted distribution of the sensible
had not been permanently debilitated. In the late 1980s and early 1990s, Devrimova and other such neighborhoods once again became the main centers of revolutionary organizations in Turkey. In effect, they soon became state-of-emergency
zones occupied by military vehicles and special operation units that constantly
surveilled and delineated their boundaries. If in the 1970s Devrimova had been a
sanctuary space whose boundaries were drawn, watched over, and protected by
Devrimovans themselves so as to keep threatening outsiders away, then by the
1990s the neighborhood had gradually been turned into what Devrimovans experienced as a semi-open prison, to which they gave the nickname "the Gaza of
Istanbul." To go in or out of the neighborhood, Devrimovans had to first pass
through entry and exit checkpoints manned by armed and masked policemen
standing next to military vehicles. At the checkpoints, they had to show their
identity cards and often endure abuse and humiliation.

This transformation after the 1980 coup of their sanctuary into a semi-open
prison can be understood only within the context of the emerging counterinsurgency techniques that the Turkish state was increasingly using to curb a leftist revival. In their attempts to suppress the reemergence of revolutionary
organizations and their alignment with a burgeoning Kurdish liberation movement, Turkish security forces exported the spatial counterinsurgency techniques

they had applied in the Kurdish provinces to the urban margins of Istanbul. As Stephan Graham (2009) argues, colonial techniques are key to the making of "new military urbanism," which entails "the extension of military ideas of tracking, identification and targeting into the quotidian spaces and circulations of everyday city life" (386). By highlighting the parallels between militarized spatial control in Northern Kurdistan, which can be considered an internal colony of sorts (Beşikçi 2004; Kurt 2019), and in dissident working-class neighborhoods of Istanbul, this chapter illustrates the colonial "boomerang effect" of Turkish state spatial counterinsurgency techniques. As described by Aimé Césaire (2001) Michel Foucault (2013), and Hannah Arendt (2007), colonial violence and techniques of power eventually make their way back to and form the basis for violence and repression in the colonial country.

Leftist Revival after the Coup

The late 1980s and early 1990s witnessed the growth of worker, public employee, student, feminist, Kurdish, and Alevi movements; the reemergence of revolutionary organizations; and the coalescence of the Kurdish liberation movement in Turkey. Beginning in the mid-1980s, large-scale workers' demonstrations and mass strikes were organized throughout the country in response to the importation and imposition of neoliberal economic policies. Between 1986 and 1995, the average annual number of employees involved in strikes was 71,217.[1] That number was more than three times the average annual number of employees, 21,584, who took part in strikes between 1971 and 1980[2] (though the number of employees who went on strike reached its peak in 1980, with 84,832 striking workers[3]). The first large-scale strike after the coup took place in 1986 in an electric materials factory, *Netaş*, with the participation of 3,150 workers and lasted for ninety-three days; it ended with a collective agreement. This strike was followed by several local walkouts and demonstrations that reached their peak in the spring of 1989. Known as the 1989 Spring Actions (*Bahar Eylemleri*), these collective actions included creative workers' protests such as eating bread and onions in front of workplaces, half-naked and barefoot marches on major highways, and collective buzz cuts, as well as traditional tactics like collective slowdowns of production (Çelik 1996). The scale of the demonstrations was massive. The escalation in strike number and participation continued until 1995, when 199,867 workers were involved in strike actions.

From the mid-1980s to the mid-1990s, revolutionary students began to organize under umbrella student organizations, such as Student Coordination (Öğrenci Koordinasyonu) and the University Students' Platform (Üniversite

Öğrenciler Platformu), and staging campus occupations, marches, and demonstrations with thousands participating (Oğuz et al. 2012). In June 1995, after organizing a two-day sit-in of 150,000 public employees, left-wing public employees established the Confederation of Public Employees' Trade Unions (Kamu Emekçileri Sendikaları Konfederasyonu; KESK). Feminists, Alevis, and Kurds, many of whom had been members of revolutionary organizations before the coup, began to focus on the discrimination they faced within the dominant patriarchal, Sunni Turk-majority society in Turkey, writing about the prior suspension of their identity-related problems with revolutionary organizations.[4] In the process, various Alevi, Kurdish and feminist organizations and journals were established both in Turkey and in the diaspora. Issues related to cultural diversity, difference, and coexistence began to be discussed more openly in these venues.[5]

At the same time, spurred by the release of revolutionaries from prison, revolutionary groups began to reorganize. Two main trends resurfaced. Legal socialist parties such the umbrella Freedom and Solidarity Party (Özgürlük ve Dayanışma Partisi; ÖDP), People's Labor Party (Halkın Emek Partisi; HEP), the Labor Party (Emek Partisi; EP), and the Socialist Power Party (Sosyalist İktidar Partisi; SİP) were established.[6] Outlawed revolutionary socialist groups also reappeared, including Marxist, Leninist, and Maoist clandestine organizations such as the Revolutionary Left (Devrimci Sol; Dev-Sol), which in 1994 became the Revolutionary People's Liberation Party Front (Devrimci Halk Kurtuluş Partisi-Cephesi; DHKP-C), the Marxist-Leninist Communist Party (Marksist-Leninist Komünist Partisi; MLKP), and the Workers and Peasant Liberation Army of Turkey (Türkiye İşçi Köylü Kurtuluş Ordusu; TİKKO).[7]

In an atmosphere of left-wing mobilization and growing dissent, the burgeoning Kurdish liberation movement, which included the guerrilla organization PKK, presented a major challenge to the Turkish ruling elites. Established in 1978 and staging its first guerilla action in 1984, the PKK has been waging an active anticolonial guerrilla war against the Turkish state ever since. Despite being outlawed as a designated "terrorist" organization by the Turkish lawmakers, by the early 1990s the PKK had been able to garner widespread popular support among Kurdish workers and peasants (Jongerden et al. 2007). To make things worse for the Turkish ruling elites, the PKK also became active in Alevi Kurdish towns and began to gain support among Alevis at this time (Göner 2005; Ertan 2015). In his book on global counterinsurgencies, the pro-military journalist responsible for military media relations, Mehmet Ali Kışlalı (1996), lamented that Turkish military forces could not succeed in their psychological war against the PKK (160); they had been unable to separate the PKK from its popular base. Yet the Kurdish liberation movement's challenge to Turkish ruling elites and to the policed distribution of the sensible reflected more than the PKK's increasing hegemony in the Kurdish provinces. Both the PKK and the legal segments of the Kurdish liberation movement such as the People's Labor Party (HEP) made alliances with certain segments of the Left. Dev-Sol and TIKKO, for instance, received training in PKK camps in the Bekaa Valley in Lebanon and engaged in joint actions with the PKK (Aydın and Emrence 2015, 64). In 1991, twenty-two pro-Kurdish deputies entered parliament as a result of the alignment between the pro-Kurdish HEP and the Social Democratic Populist Party (Sosyal Demokrat Halkçı Parti; SHP), the junior partner of the then-coalition government; it was led by Erdal Inönü, the son of Ismet Inönü whose Turkish supremacist words I cite in the introduction to this book.[8] At the time, the SHP was popular among Alevis and secularist middle- and working-class Turks.

In addition to these collaborations at the organizational level, leftist support for the Kurdish liberation movement became manifest within the cultural sphere as well. In the 1990s, famous left-wing music bands, able to reach millions and popular among Alevis, students, and working-class Turkish leftists, voiced their support for Kurdish resistance through their songs. In 1991, a popular revolutionary band, Grup Kızılırmak, released an elegy titled "Nevala Kasaba" (Nevala Creek) dedicated to those Kurds murdered by Turkish paramilitary squads, including the legendary PKK commander Mahsun Korkmaz, and thrown into Nevala Creek. In the opening section of the elegy, the renowned Kurdish writer and activist Musa Anter, whom Kurds call Apê Musa (Uncle Musa), reads a poem in Turkish about Kurdish suffering and resistance in Turkey.[9] And in 1995, the most popular revolutionary music band, Grup Yorum, released on their highly successful album İleri (Forward) the unofficial Kurdish national anthem in Turkey, "Herne Pêş" (Go Forward), with lyrics by the prominent Kurdish poet Cigerxwîn and composed by the exiled Kurdish musician Şivan Perwer. Such public manifestations of sympathy for Kurdish suffering and resistance indicated that by the 1990s recognition of the legitimacy of the Kurdish struggle for freedom had spilled over beyond the boundaries of Northern Kurdistan to reach a larger public.

That overflow of sympathy for the Kurdish liberation movement occurred in parallel with the outpouring of the Kurdish population from Northern Kurdistan to Western Turkey. Turkish security forces applied lessons learned from the British counterinsurgency against communist guerrilla forces in Malaya in their fight against the Kurdish liberation movement (Kışlalı 1996, 57).[10] Following the British example, Turkish security forces displaced more than a million Kurdish peasants throughout the 1990s in an effort to isolate the PKK and cut its ties with the Kurdish villagers and force the guerrillas into starvation (Ayata and Yükseker 2005; Jongerden 2010). The unintended consequence of this mass displacement was the migration of Kurdish dissent along with dispossessed

Kurdish peasants into the slums of large cities. In the process, Devrimova and other dissident working-class neighborhoods became places of refuge for displaced Kurds. At a time when many Turkish revolutionary organizations were collaborating with the Kurdish liberation movement, this led to increasing left-wing mobilization in Turkey's big cities, especially Istanbul.[11]

Even though the many new successors to those revolutionary organizations de-activated by the coup were gaining support from workers, students, and middle-class intellectuals from diverse backgrounds all across the country, Devrimova and other Alevi-populated working-class neighborhoods became the main centers of the left-wing revival. While waiting in Devrimova for a concert by a revolutionary band to begin, Mahir and I began to chat; the concert was being held in a neighborhood cultural center named after a local revolutionary martyr. It was a cold winter evening of 2011, but this famous band from the 1990s brought our memories flooding back. Mahir, a construction worker in his early forties, recalled those years melancholically:

> In the 1990s the spirit of the old revolutionary days was back in the neighborhood again. We were very organized. The Kurdish movement was powerful. There was collaboration between the Kurdish movement and the revolutionary movement. There were a lot of strikes and demonstrations back then. We would rent big buses to go to the strikes from the neighborhood. Young people, old people, men and women, Kurds and Alevis—we used to all go together. For the May Day demonstrations, for instance, we used to rent fifty or sixty big intercity buses in which to go to the demonstration area from the neighborhood. Our neighborhood, like the other revolutionary neighborhoods of Okmeydani, Gazi, Gülsuyu, Armutlu, and Bir Mayis, was at the heart of the new mobilization. We were organizing series of mass street demonstrations on political issues ranging from Palestine to economic liberalization policies, from the hunger strikes of political prisoners to the problems in the education system.[12] We were organizing reading and discussion groups at schools and workplaces. There were cultural centers of the revolutionary organizations in Taksim and Kadıköy [two central districts of Istanbul]. We, especially the youth, used to go to these places very often. There were great teachers and artists in those places. For instance, I learned how to play the guitar at BEKSAV.[13] BEKSAV also had a great movie hall where you could see alternative, noncommercial films. I watched all of the Tarkovsky films there.

The picture he drew of Devrimova of the early 1990s was similar to what I witnessed during my visits to such neighborhoods in those years. I told Mahir that I remembered very vividly how my high school friends would go regularly to demonstrations with fellow neighborhood residents, visiting workers, spending their weekends at BEKSAV and other cultural centers run by revolutionary organizations, taking art courses and participating in reading and discussion groups there. As I noted in the preface, in my own predominantly Sunni Turkish working-class neighborhood, only a few were interested in art or politics. A significant percentage of the Sunni Turkish working-class youth were instead developing an appetite for drugs, religion, or the global popular culture of the time—American brands of clothes, breakdancing, American music on MTV, Turkish pop, or sad *arabesk* music. In contrast, by the early to mid-1990s, the residents of predominantly Alevi working-class neighborhoods such as Devrimova had once again become political actors on the world-historical stage. By becoming publicly visible as acting and speaking subjects demanding justice and better living conditions, by daring to engage in artistic activities, and by showing solidarity with oppressed groups around the world, they were intervening in the distribution of the sensible. They were going against the grain of their ascribed roles as poor and passive "victims" of capitalism who belonged solely to the sphere of "needs" and reproduction (Rancière 1995). At the same time, the neighborhoods became centers for the reorganization of outlawed revolutionary groups.

The Appeal of the Revolutionary Left

Outlawed revolutionary groups deemed terrorist by the Turkish state, such as Dev-Sol/DHKP-C, MLKP, and the PKK, were inspired by the 1970s' Turkish revolutionary leader Mahir Çayan's (1992) revolutionary strategies of *politicized military war* and *armed propaganda*, both based on a theoretical approach he called the *artificial balance theory*. According to Çayan, there is an artificial balance between the state, which he views as an apparatus of the ruling class, and the people. The seemingly all-powerful state is, in fact, far less powerful than the people's power to resist. The state, which is not a hegemonic power in the eyes of the oppressed majority, only appears to have power over the people because of its provision of social services and its use of violence. Its powerful appearance is therefore based on an artificial balance of power, and the revolutionary strategy must be to show the people that the state is not as strong as it appears. For Çayan, armed propaganda activities, such as kidnappings, murder, and hostage taking, selectively directed at those who represent the state and its imperialist allies—high-ranking military officers, businesspeople, US consulates—demonstrate that the state in fact does not possess a monopoly on violence and that state apparatuses are vulnerable. These actions will then give the people the courage to side with revolutionaries.

The most popular organization among the postcoup revolutionary Turkish Left to adopt Çayan's strategy was Dev-Sol, still active today as DHKP-C. In line with Çayan's theoretical approach and strategy, the first half of the 1990s witnessed a series of assassinations directed against state and coup regime representatives, as well as their alleged allies—businesspeople and members of rival groups perceived to be "collaborators" of the state.[14] Dev-Sol's assassinations and unsuccessful attempts in 1990 alone give a sense of this strategy. On January 30, Mehmet Kazım Çakmakçı, the policeman who killed eighteen-year-old leftist Mehmet Akif Dalcı during the May Day demonstrations of 1989, was shot to death.[15] On August 26, Dev-Sol militants attempted to assassinate Adnan Özbey, a retired army major who had served at Metris Military Prison and was notorious for torturing political prisoners.[16] On September 22, Hiram Abas, a member of the Turkish National Intelligence Agency (Milli Istihbarat Teşkilatı), who was trained in the United States in covert action operations (Ganser 2005, 232), was assassinated.[17] On October 30, Bayrampaşa Prison judge, Niyazi Aygen, known for his encouragement of torture, was shot to death.[18] On December 18, another member of the National Intelligence Agency, Ferdi Tamer, was shot to death.[19] Over the ensuing two years, Dev-Sol militants killed several others who had taken an active part in the infamous coup regime, including Şakir Koç, the deputy provincial police chief of Istanbul; Ata Burcu, a retired lieutenant colonel; Memduh Ünlütürk, a retired army general; and Kemal Kayacan, a retired admiral.[20]

In the early 1990s, Dev-Sol also carried out assassinations to show solidarity with Kurdish resistance. In response to the indiscriminate killing by Turkish state security forces of more than eighty Kurds while they were celebrating Newroz, the Kurdish spring feast, in Cizre and other Kurdish towns, Dev-Sol opened fire on a military vehicle on March 24, 1992, killing two soldiers. After the incident, the organization declared, "We will break the hands reaching the Kurdish people. We will not let enmity grow between Turkish and Kurdish peoples" (Aydın 2005, 89).

Although these outlawed and armed revolutionary organizations and their violent methods were integral parts of the revolutionary remobilization that took place during the first half of the 1990s, their activities were not limited to political assassinations and joint guerrilla attacks carried out together with the PKK. Members and sympathizers of these groups were also active in trade unions and in the student movement, actively fighting for workers' and students' rights through legal channels. Each militant group had its affiliated legal organization, association, and cultural center. Today, several associations and cultural centers in Devrimova are still run by revolutionary organizations. These venues usually function as gathering places where people get together to have tea, eat, chat, or participate in public events, such as panels, movie screenings, music recitals, and free courses.

The very large attendance at the funeral of eighteen-year-old DHKP-C militant Sibel Yalçın offers a good example of the extent of public sympathy for that organization in those years. In June 1995, Yalçın had taken part in a DHKP-C raid on a local branch of the True Path Party (Doğru Yol Partisi), a right-wing party in the coalition government that worked closely with right-wing paramilitary groups. The raid resulted in the killing of a policeman and the wounding of another. After the raid, Yalçın was shot to death by the police forces in Okmeydanı, a predominantly Alevi-populated working-class neighborhood. Yalçın's funeral took place in Alibeyköy Cemevi, with around four thousand people in attendance.[21] To honor her memory, Okmeydanı residents named a neighborhood park after her. Sibel Yalçın Park still serves as a reminder of her legacy and a meeting point for demonstrations in the neighborhood.

The popularity of these revolutionary organizations reached its peak during the May Day demonstrations of 1996, attended by an estimated 150,000 people. The largest contingent that May Day was from the pro-Kurdish People's Democracy Party (Halkın Demokrasi Partisi), an official party that had sprung up in 1994 to replace the People's Labor Party, banned in 1993. The second largest group was from outlawed revolutionary organizations. In his commentary on the May Day demonstrations of 1996, left-wing liberal intellectual Ömer Laçiner (1996) described his astonishment that more than twenty thousand people were walking behind the banners of outlawed revolutionary organizations. Laçiner noted that the largest group among them was the DHKP-C group and that a significant percentage of these people were urban poor from the *varoş*, a pejorative Turkish word used to refer to working-class neighborhoods. In puzzlement, Laçiner (5) asked, "How is it that even under intense repression by the government, the people had the courage to walk behind the banners of the most stigmatized political groups?"

Injustice, Outrage, and Revenge

With the expansion of military power under the 1982 constitution and the re-emergence of dissenting groups in the aftermath of the coup, the 1990s were years of extensive state repression and violence against revolutionary and pro-Kurdish dissent. To separate revolutionaries and militants from their constituencies, major penalties were imposed on those accused of being sympathetic to or of helping Turkish revolutionary organizations and the PKK (Aydın and Emrence 2015, 79). Like many of my high school friends from those neighborhoods mentioned in the preface, most active revolutionaries of Devrimova were imprisoned, kidnapped, tortured, or became exiles in Europe and elsewhere. Disappearances, extrajudicial political executions, illegal detentions, and kidnappings, as well as the mass displacement of Kurdish rural populations and the institutionalization of the village guard system in Northern Kurdistan, emerged as new patterns of Turkish state counterinsurgency.[22]

Yet, state violence does not always lead to pacification; it sometimes backfires, inspiring backlash and giving rise to outrage and dissent. Zelal, Mahir's cousin who left the country in 1997 to become a political refugee in France, walked behind the DHKP-C cortege in the mass May Day demonstrations of 1996. Hearing that I was to attend a conference in Paris, Mahir put me in touch with Zelal. I spent an afternoon in the kebab shop where Zelal now works, listening to her relive her memories of those years and watching her prepare the kebabs for the evening's customers. Her account of the 1996 May Day and its connections to the postcoup resurgence of leftist dissident dynamism helps us understand why, despite the violent state repression of dissident groups, thousands did not hesitate to show their open support for outlawed revolutionary organizations:

> I was a high school student from 1992 to 1995. Our school was in the neighborhood. We were all sympathetic to or members of each other's revolutionary organizations back then. The neighborhood was under occupation. Our high school garden was used as the parking lot for the military vehicles. Special operation forces would hang out all around the school. Sometimes they would interrupt the classes to take one of us into custody. They were especially hard on the high school students. You know, there's a saying, "You must crush the head of a boil when it's still small (*Çıbanın başını küçükken ezeceksin*)." The state had the same mentality. Students who were taken into custody would come back a few days later with bruises all over their bodies. Under those conditions, the assassinations made in the name of "people's justice" were attractive to many of us. Hearing that a notorious torturer was killed and knowing that that creature had tortured hundreds of people—perhaps even your own brother, sister, son, or daughter—was a relief. People want justice. [Pause.] People want those responsible for all that cruelty to eventually be punished.
>
> I remember Sibel Yalçın's funeral, for instance. For many of us, she was a hero. She and her comrades had targeted the building of the DYP [Doğru

Yol Partisi; True Path Party], the party responsible for the killings of young revolutionaries, of thousands of Kurds. She was very young. But when the police came to her door, she resisted up to the very last moment. She didn't surrender. When the police asked her to surrender, she yelled back at them, "You have to surrender instead!" When you see it in the news, when you hear about it, you feel strong, hopeful. Actually, the very first demonstration I attended outside the neighborhood was her funeral. How old I was back then? [Silence as she calculates her age at the time] Fifteen, sixteen. Yes, sixteen. At first, the state didn't want to give her body to her family. But the people resisted. The people were outraged. People went every day to Yenibosna [a working-class neighborhood of Istanbul], where Sibel Yalçın's family lived. There were police attacks, but they didn't give up. In the end, the state had to back off. Thousands of people participated in her funeral. I remember it very vividly. People rented buses from the neighborhoods to go to her funeral. The people embraced her.

Those years were different. The revolutionaries had an impact on the people. There was oppression but also resistance. We experienced many conflicting feelings all at the same time: anger and hope, fear and courage.

In 1995, fifteen years after the coup d'état, state violence no longer had a deterrent effect in these neighborhoods: oppression went hand in hand with resistance. Echoing Zelal, many of my interviewees who lived in Devrimova and other such neighborhoods during the 1990s also stressed this double condition of the 1990s and the conflicted feelings they had about it. The repressive instruments of beatings, torture, disappearances, extrajudicial killings, kidnappings, and illegal detentions were not effective in pacifying working-class Alevi and Kurdish dissent. Instead, by producing an ever-increasing desire for justice and revenge, these instruments of repression contributed to the growth of dissent.

In her study on the German and Italian radical Left, Donatella Della Porta (2006, 191) argues that state repression and police violence contribute to "the delegitimization of the state in the eyes of the activists, not only by creating injustice frames, but by arousing the sense of an 'absolute injustice.'" For Della Porta, the sense of absolute injustice produced within the context of state violence is key to understanding the emergence or continuation of radical leftist organizations. Counterinsurgency strategists themselves are aware of the backlash effects of state violence. As anthropologists of defense and national security analysis, Montgomery McFate and Andrea Jackson (2006, 4), argue, "'Winning' through overwhelming force is often inapplicable," because it has the "unintended effect of strengthening the insurgency."

Yet, the widespread state violence of the coup and its aftermath did have a repressive effect on certain segments of the population. For those who have privileges—however limited—state violence can be debilitating. The atmosphere of fear that circulated during the coup and its aftermath had a deterrent effect on the Sunni Turkish urban working classes, who for the most part encountered large-scale state violence for the first time, all the while enjoying the many privileges that accrue to being Sunni Turkish in a country hostile to non-Muslims, non-Sunnis, and non-Turks. Once a major element of left-wing dissent, many members of the Sunni Turkish urban working classes gravitated toward conservative and Islamist parties after the repressive coup of 1980 (Tuğal 2009; White 1997, 2004). The aim of the coup instigators had been to mobilize nationalist political Islam in Turkey and create a society based on a so-called Turkish-Islamic Synthesis designed to blend Sunni Turkish nationalism and political Islam (Kurt 2010). In his book on the incorporation of radical Islamist groups into existing power structures through the emerging neoliberal AKP, Cihan Tuğal (2009) demonstrates that Islamist organizations appropriated the 1970s leftist strategy of "dual power" whereby alternatives to state authority structures were created, much as in Devrimova in the 1970s, but via structures of patronage and economic resource redistribution. By engaging in a "vernacular politics" (White 2011, 27)—"a value-centered political process rooted in local culture, interpersonal relations, and community networks"—Islamists were able to attract ever larger segments of the Sunni Turkish working classes via Islamist charity and benevolence networks and civic associations.

To benefit from these networks, Sunni Kurds had to actively and assertively distance themselves from the Kurdish liberation movement, deny their Kurdishness, and prove their loyalty to the Turkish state and its nationalist ideology (Tuğal 2009). Regarded as heretics in the Sunni imaginary, the Alevi working classes were excluded from the benevolence networks that helped the Sunni Turkish urban working classes survive the increasing economic pressures of that period. Provoking historical fears of Islamist violence against them, the postcoup rise of political Islam disquieted Alevis, and Alevis once again became the targets of Islamist violence.

In July 1993, an Islamist mob attacked an Alevi festival organized by a leftwing Alevi organization, the Pir Sultan Abdal Culture Association (Pir Sultan Abdal Kültür Derneği) in Sivas. An angry mob that was chanting Islamist slogans attacked the hotel where Alevi and left-wing intellectuals and artists were staying during the festival and set the building on fire; thirty-seven people, mostly Alevis, lost their lives. Two years later, in March 1995, an unknown gunman fired on three coffeehouses frequented by Alevis in the Gazi neighborhood of Istanbul. An Alevi *dede*, a revered religious figure in Alevi culture, was killed, and many Alevis were wounded. When the people took over the streets of Gazi and of the Bir Mayıs neighborhood to protest that night and over the following days, police and their gunmen fired into the crowd, killing twenty-two people and wounding hundreds more. For Turkey's non-Sunni, non-Turkish socialists, the repressive coup and the repressive policies that followed it only added "to the long chain of atrocities" (Çaylı 2014, 20). For working-class Alevis born into a culture in which narratives of oppression always went hand in hand with narratives of resistance, these atrocities further strengthened their conviction of "absolute injustice" (Della Porta 2006) and provoked feelings of outrage and demands for recompense.

Those who consider themselves victims of state violence and who believe that their collective suffering is unrecognized may engage in vengeful activities as redress (Fletcher and Weinstein 2002; Wilson et al. 2000). As Zelal's story illustrates, the political assassinations that permeated the political atmosphere of the early 1990s met many people's desire for justice and revenge. The following slogans of outlawed revolutionary organizations in the 1990s were often chanted at May Day demonstrations, strikes, campus occupations, and marches, reflecting these desires: "People's justice will bring [the state] to account" (*Halkın adaleti hesap soracak*); "Long live the people's justice" (*Yaşasın halkın adaleti*); "We will drown fascism in the very blood it has shed" (*Faşizmi döktüğü kanda boğacağız*); "The murderous state will pay the price" (*Katil devlet hesap verecek*); and "Mothers' anger will strangle the murderers" (*Anaların öfkesi katilleri boğacak*). The popularity of the outlawed revolutionary left among the Alevi urban poor in the 1990s, therefore, needs to be understood within the context of the long history of state and state-backed Islamist violence against Turkey's Alevi populations, the series of economic liberalization policies that led to further impoverishment of an already poor working-class, the postcoup ruling elite's promotion of the new ideology of the Turkish-Islamic Synthesis, and the Alevi cultural archive of oppression and resistance, which inspires working-class Alevis to take action against injustice.

Despite increasing state repression, in 2021, the struggle against oppression continues in Devrimova and other similar neighborhoods. As I elaborate in chapter 5, the "spirits" of those martyrs who lost their lives fighting oppression or died as the result of state violence disseminate an affective energy that inspires working-class Alevis to keep resisting despite the potentially grave consequences. Those who were killed by state security forces in Sivas in 1993, or in Gazi in 1995, or, as Zelal suggests, militants like Sibel Yalçın have had a potent, energizing effect on the political activities of the working-class Alevis of the urban margins. As the number of people targeted for death by state violence increased in the 1990s and the 2010s, so did the invigorating and dissident effects of the dead over the living.

"Gazas of Istanbul"

As Eyal Weizman (2012) argues in his work on the Israeli security apparatus, by the 1990s counterinsurgencies had primarily become a spatial phenomenon aimed both at transforming and reorganizing—rather than destroying—lived spaces. In 1991, Turkish security forces had also started to invest in the reorganization of space as a "medium" of their counterinsurgency war against the PKK, especially in the rural areas of Northern Kurdistan (Jongerden 2010). It was at this time that, in their efforts to weaken growing left-wing mobilization and the Left's collaboration with the Kurdish liberation movement, Turkey's ruling elites began to apply new spatial counterinsurgency measures in the dissident working-class neighborhoods of Istanbul. In my interlocutors' words, these new techniques led to the transformation of these areas into "Gazas of Istanbul." In his analysis of the Gaza Strip under Israeli occupation, Achille Mbembé (2003, 26), argues that space is the "raw material of sovereignty." One of the key dynamics of Israeli security's attempts to construct and display their sovereignty in Gaza is the strategy of territorial fragmentation, which creates a collection of isolated zones and population enclaves physically disconnected from one another. The isolation of Gaza, the all-encompassing surveillance of its space and the populations in it, and its designation as a "hostile entity" (Weizman 2011) by the Israeli political authorities combine to contain it, legitimize the occupation, and to "capture resistance itself" (Puar 2015, 5).

The spatial counterinsurgency techniques applied in the neighborhoods were directly exported from Northern Kurdistan. The separation of the predominantly Kurdish territories of Turkey's southeast region from the rest of the country has been a key strategy in the Turkish state's counterinsurgency war against the Kurdish liberation movement. This territorial separation and isolation of Kurdish populations of the Kurdish provinces were enabled by the introduction of a state of emergency (*olağanüstü hal*) in Northern Kurdistan in 1987 that created the OHAL emergency region. Lifted in 2002 and replaced by the declaration of parts of the region as security zones (*güvenlik bölgesi*), the fifteen-year emergency rule was a kind of *endocolonization* (Feldman 1991, 85). The state of emergency suspended the most basic rights and civil liberties in the Kurdish provinces, allowing the governor to summarily relocate populations and exile individuals from the region, detain suspects without charge, ban publications and political activities, and implement a paramilitary village guard system designed to surveil residents at the local level and divide the population from within through the co-optation and armament of local collaborators (Bozarslan 2001). This state of exception was inscribed in Kurdish space in the form of military, paramilitary, and police forces; checkpoints, barracks, and circulating military vehicles

(Gambetti and Jongerden 2015). As Ramazan Aras (2013, 93) argues, under the OHAL regime's invasive police surveillance and "state-sponsored spying systems," many Kurdish towns and cities became "open prisons." Northern Kurdistan was isolated from the surrounding areas, and it became extremely difficult for outsiders, including journalists and human rights activists, to travel there.

Another tool of isolation was strict censorship of the media. Circulation of information about what had been going on in Northern Kurdistan was scrupulously regulated, and the Kurdish press was harshly repressed.[23] Police, counterguerrilla, and state-backed right-wing paramilitary violence against human rights activists was carried out with the aim of silencing witnesses who might communicate to the wider public the scope of the violence taking place in the region. As a result, until very recently, what happened in Northern Kurdistan under OHAL rule remained largely unknown to those who lived outside these areas. A Kurdish human rights activist who had been an active member of the Diyarbakır branch of the Human Rights Association (Insan Hakları Derneği; IHD) in the 1990s told me that he was always devastated to see during his visits to the western parts of Turkey that even the Kurds who lived there weren't aware of the scope of state violence in Northern Kurdistan.[24] This is likely one of the reasons why Devrimovans used the metaphor of Gaza—a place well known for its history of oppression and resistance—to define their neighborhoods in those years.

In an attempt to repress the growing Kurdish and Turkish leftist remobilization and engagement in armed acts of revenge against representatives of the state, similar spatial techniques were adopted in dissident working-class neighborhoods in the urban Turkish heartland. Although the scope and intensity of the violence taking place in Istanbul's neighborhoods and Northern Kurdistan were (and still are) incommensurable, by the early 1990s, Devrimova and other predominantly working-class Alevi neighborhoods had become de facto state of emergency zones through a process of spatial control pioneered by those who had been centrally involved in counterinsurgency operations in Northern Kurdistan.

In 1991, Hayri Kozakçıoğlu, who had served as OHAL's first state-of-emergency governor in Northern Kurdistan, was appointed governor of Istanbul.[25] In 1992, Hanefi Avcı, a police chief centrally involved in implementing counterterrorism measures in the Kurdish OHAL region, was transferred to the post of chief of Istanbul's intelligence branch.[26] Soon after his appointment, Kozakçıoğlu declared that Istanbul, too, had become a city of emergency (olağanüstü şehir) in need of additional police units with which to fight off "left terror."[27] But for the new governor, increasing the number of police cadres would not be enough to solve the problem. In his second year in that post, Kozakçıoğlu announced that his team was conducting scientific research so as to end what he called "left terror" in Istanbul and that the police department would create pilot areas in which to test new scientific techniques.[28] He also stated that both these new techniques and the pilot areas would remain confidential to prevent the development of counterstrategies.[29] Shortly after governor Kozakçıoğlu's appointment, Devrimova and other Alevi working-class neighborhoods began to be segregated from surrounding areas using militarized spatial control techniques. Checkpoints, house raids, cruising white Renault cars notoriously used for kidnapping dissidents, and roving armored vehicles became a part of ordinary life in Devrimova and other neighborhoods.

I had the opportunity to interview Halime and Zehra, two female Devrimovans in their mid-forties, in Halime's small *gecekondu* house. An assistant nurse in a small health clinic, Halime told me in detail about life in the Devrimova of the early 1990s:

> They turned this neighborhood into Gaza in the 1990s. In 1993, in 1994, in 1995, the special operation units would walk regularly on the rooftops. We had to go through checkpoints to leave or enter the neighborhood. Sometimes there were even checkpoints at street entrances inside the neighborhood. Some of the street entrances were yellow-taped, like in crime movies. The checkpoints were ostensibly for protest days, but according to the state there were protests every day. If you ask me, they were here merely to punish us. The state saw us as enemies. If you were from Devrimova, that was then and still is now enough to be considered a terrorist by the state. With the checkpoints, they wanted to tell others, "Hey, do you see? These people are terrorists. They are very dangerous people. Keep away from them!"

Jumping into the conversation, Zehra, who works as a cleaner in a hotel, made the point even stronger:

> And it was effective. The buses would avoid the neighborhood in those years for security reasons. [Laughs sarcastically.] That's how they used to put it: "for security reasons." Why? Because according to the state, we were very dangerous people. We had to get off the bus at Örentepe [pseudonym for a nearby neighborhood where Devrimovans were subjected to the attacks of the Islamists and nationalists in the 1970s]. There was one stop at the Örentepe–Devrimova border. We used to get off at that stop. Örentepe residents didn't use that stop much. I think it was because they didn't want to be confused with us, the terrorists. I remember that when I would push the button to get off the bus, the

people on the bus would move away from me. They would look at me as though I belonged to a different species, as if I had a contagious disease like AIDS or something like that.

Halime piggybacked on this theme:

> That's true. They would look at us as though we were some weird creature. And when you got off the bus, you were confronted with the police. They would ask you questions. Sometimes they would keep you there at the checkpoint for hours, just for fun. We were forced to respond to their stupid questions, face their humiliation and harassment. They enjoyed threatening us, thinking that we would get scared. If you were lucky, you would get home by passing through one checkpoint. But sometimes there were several checkpoints. It was torturous. You came back to the neighborhood after working for eight or nine hours, and then you had to endure police harassment. Because of the checkpoints, people didn't want to leave the neighborhood back then. And it was the aim of the state, too, to keep us in the neighborhoods. It was the same in Okmeydanı, Armutlu, Gülsuyu, Gazi.

Checkpoints and armored vehicles were instruments of confinement, a practice of inscription of the state's sovereign power into a place occupied by dissident populations. They were also sites of interpellation and subjugation. Embodied in the armored vehicles that patrolled the streets and in the members of the masked special operation units, rifles in hand, standing beside the parked armored vehicles and checking identities of passersby, the state's strategy was to interpellate Devrimovans as terrorist subjects, as the enemies of the state and the public, and Devrimova as a "terrain of anticipated violence" (Jeganathan 2004, 72).[30] The metaphoric use of Gaza—a "hostile territory" (Allen 2012, 266) that was "regarded as exceptional and exceptionally problematic" (262)— is suggestive of the hostility Devrimovans had to endure during their encounters with representatives of the state in their own space. Such hostility was effective in confining residents to the neighborhoods, limiting their use of city space, and encumbering their encounters with other groups. Under these circumstances, going out of the neighborhood despite police harassment and humiliation at the checkpoints became an act of refusal—a refusal to be contained in the space allocated to them under constant state security threat.

It was not then and is not now easy to avoid violent encounters. An everyday part of Devrimovan street life for several decades, armored vehicles have been used in many instances of violence, not least in killings and kidnappings of revolutionaries and Kurdish activists and residents. One of the most well-known and earliest examples of the potential violence embodied in these vehicles occurred when Sevcan, a seven-year-old girl, was run over by an armored vehicle while playing in her school playground in Armutlu in 1992 (İşeri 2010). The lyrics of the song "Sevcan" by the leftist band Grup Özgürlük Türküsü, provide insight into the militarized spatial control of the neighborhoods.

> The schools of Armutlu were a police station (*karakol*),
> a panzer standing in the school yard.
> The children grew up beneath the shadow of the panzer.
> When the panzer stole the child's ball,
> the child ran after it.
> The panzer walked,
> and the child remained seven.[31]

Granted sovereign impunity, the policeman who ran over Sevcan was not brought to trial (İşeri 2010).

The constitution of such revolutionary neighborhoods in the 1990s as hostile entities under occupation and segregation was further strengthened by their avoidance by public buses and cabs and their portrayal in the media as dangerous places. Recycled after the Gezi uprisings of 2013, such practices were once again effective in keeping nonresidents out of the neighborhoods by rendering them as no-go areas. I still remember the fear I had when I would go to visit my high school friends in their neighborhoods in those years. As a way of proving my "innocence," I used to carry my schoolbooks in my hands to show that I was in the area for no other reason than to study with my classmates. What you carried with you mattered a great deal in those neighborhoods. Those with revolutionary books or journals in their hands or backpacks were easy targets for the security forces. As I learned from the archives of the Human Rights Foundation of Turkey, in those years countless young revolutionaries were kidnapped and tortured simply because the police found revolutionary journals or books in their backpacks.

During my fieldwork, I learned that I was very lucky not to have been punished for visiting those neighborhoods in the 1990s. Some outsiders had faced police violence. Ihsan, a thirty-six-year-old man who lived in a neighborhood close to Devrimova, explained to me why he stopped going to Devrimova in the 1990s:

> I used to go to Devrimova for guitar lessons when I was a high school student. Once, at the checkpoint, policemen stopped me and asked me to show them my ID. One of them examined my ID and asked me where I lived. I told them where I lived and then, pointing at my guitar, I told them that I came to Devrimova to take guitar lessons. Glaring angrily

at me, the policeman put me in the military vehicle. I was so scared. I waited there for a while; then a car came and took me to the police station. I was only sixteen then. And it was the 1990s, you know. The police could do anything. A policeman at the police station shouted at me, saying things like, "Are you a terrorist? What are you doing in Devrimova? Don't you know that that place is a den of terror? What are you up to?" Then he told me that if I ever dared go to Devrimova again, they would kill me. I never went to the neighborhood again. I later heard that the same thing happened to others who wanted to visit the neighborhood. Later, for example, a friend of mine was severely beaten at the same police station just for wanting to go to Devrimova.

The simple act of going to Devrimova had become a criminal act, one that would render you suspect in the eyes of the police. Writing of the social appraisal of women's respectability, Sara Ahmed (2013) argues that women are expected to move through public space in such a way as to demonstrate their desire to stay safe: "movement becomes a form of subject constitution: *where* 'one' goes or does not go determines *what* one 'is,' or *where* one is seen to be, determines *what* one is seen to be" (33; emphasis in the original). By telling nonresidents to *not be seen* in Devrimova, the police were defining the bounds of both respectability and suspectability and tying them to the *where* of Devrimova. The checkpoints and military vehicles were telling people that, to remain citizens while retaining citizens' rights—those who cannot be detained, interrogated, or tortured with impunity—they had to *not to be seen* in these neighborhoods. Being seen in those places made them into a deserving target of violence. In this way, police waiting at the checkpoints could actively separate those who were to be seen in Devrimova from those who were not, a distribution of the *respectable* from the *suspectable*.

This strategy of separation was so effective that—even though during the first phase of my research between 2010 and 2012 there were no longer checkpoints at the entrances to mark the neighborhoods as dangerous—the neighborhoods were still known as no-go areas that even taxi drivers would not enter. Many of my interviewees talked about the reactions of acquaintances from their workplaces or schools on learning that they lived in Devrimova. These acquaintances would invariably ask questions conveying disbelief: "How can you live in such a dangerous place? There are a lot of terrorists in that neighborhood! How do you stay safe there? How can you live among terrorists?"

These techniques of spatial control prevented the redevelopment of alternative self-governance bodies like the people's committees and courts of the 1970s. Yet, with the continued support of left-wing organizations, Alevi and Kurdish workers of the urban margins continued to plan and conduct strikes, demonstrations, and May Day marches. The suppressive techniques of the checkpoints, roving armored vehicles, and raids, which turned the neighborhoods into occupied zones, were not entirely effective in frightening their targeted populations away from the streets. Just as state violence in the Kurdish cities of the OHAL region engendered strong counterreaction and resistance and facilitated the growth of the PKK (Aras 2013, 92), so too did the ongoing police presence, surveillance, and violence in the neighborhood serve to delegitimize the state and encourage residents to side with the dissident Left.

Postcoup leftist dissent in the neighborhoods peaked in the mid-1990s and dwindled in the decade's second half. The next chapter suggests that this decrease in resistance as well as the collaboration between the revolutionary left and the Kurdish liberation movement was caused by a shift in the modes of counterinsurgency techniques used in the neighborhoods toward those based on the low-intensity conflict doctrine. By the mid-1990s, less overt but more brazenly manipulative affect-and-emotion-generating *provocative counterorganization* strategies joined the counterterrorism repertoire. Ümit Özdağ, one of the Turkish nationalist ruling elites, highlighted the effectiveness of the psychological warfare of low-intensity conflict in his 2005 book, *Low-Intensity Conflict in Turkey and the PKK* (Türkiye'de Düşük Yoğunluklu Çatışma ve PKK). Özdağ argues that in 1994 Turkish security forces specifically invested in the psychological warfare with the PKK (82). Although he does not specify which psychological warfare techniques were applied against the Kurdish movement, he does acknowledge that overtly repressive military techniques were not effective in suppressing the PKK's political success and advises that military operations should go hand in hand with psychological warfare techniques informed by the low-intensity conflict doctrine.

The year 1995 was an important turning point for the predominantly Alevi-populated working-class neighborhoods of Istanbul and also because of the use of *provocative counterorganization*'s affect-and-emotion-generating techniques. As we see in chapter 3, by 1995 these technique were effective in driving a wedge between certain segments of the Alevi leftists and the Kurdish liberation movement and between revolutionaries and their constituency. This fragmentation paved the way for the containment of revolutionary violence within neighborhoods while stirring up ethnosectarian tensions throughout the country. These new techniques were effective in distributing spaces and roles along prescribed ethnosectarian, class, and spatial lines and in limiting the room for politics that would go against their grain.

PROVOCATIVE COUNTERORGANIZATION

Violent Interpellation, Low-Intensity Conflict, Ethnosectarian Enclaves

On March 12, 1995, unknown gunmen fired on three coffeehouses in the Gazi neighborhood of Istanbul at around 8:45 p.m. An Alevi *dede*, a revered male figure within the Alevi community, was killed in the shootings, and many others were wounded. According to eyewitnesses, the police did not take immediate action; instead of pursuing the perpetrators, they left the scene in another direction. In effect, the eyewitnesses reached the conclusion that the police were helping the assailants. Word spread quickly, and large numbers of Gazi residents went onto the streets that night, marching toward the police station chanting, "Where are the police? Stand together against fascism! Down with oligarchy!"

The next day, thousands of people from other parts of the city marched to Gazi to join its residents in their protest. As the demonstrations continued into a third day, large numbers of police and military troops poured into the neighborhood. As though it were a war zone, the police and soldiers fenced off the perimeter of Gazi with barbed wire. Shooting directly into the crowd, the police shouted such things as "Death to Alevis!" and "Hey leftists and Alevis, we will kill you all!"[1] Eighteen people lost their lives, hundreds were wounded, and countless numbers were severely beaten, all while the TV cameras were rolling. Millions watched in their homes this spectacular performance of state violence. Because access to Gazi had been cut off, marches were organized in other dissident, predominantly Alevi-populated working-class neighborhoods such as Alibeyköy, Bir Mayıs, Okmeydanı, and Gülsuyu to show solidarity on March 15. In response, large numbers of police and soldiers poured into those neighborhoods with the aim of suppressing those demonstrations. In Bir Mayıs, the police again shot directly into the crowd, killing five residents and wounding several others (Tüleylioğlu 2011).[2]

In this chapter, I demonstrate that together the Gazi incidents constituted a "critical event" that gave rise to "new modes of action" (Das 1995, 5) and new forms of political agency both in and beyond the neighborhoods. Paving the way for the "bottom-up reorganization of political forces" (Haysom 1989), the Gazi incidents marked the beginning of a new counterinsurgency strategy in Istanbul that combined overt repressive state violence with urban-centered and affect- and emotion-generating *provocative counterorganization* techniques to quell the growing left-wing mobilization and weaken the Turkish and Kurdish left-wing alignment, which was gaining in strength at the time. That new strategy was informed by the principles of the low-intensity conflict doctrine—a doctrine that came to prominence in South America, the Philippines, Northern Ireland, South Africa, and the United States under the Reagan administration in the early 1980s and was imported into Northern Kurdistan in 1993 (Kışlalı 1996, 26). This new phase of the war on the Left and on Kurdish dissent succeeded in transforming Gazi, Devrimova, and similar racialized and dissident urban spaces into permanent conflict zones and ethnosectarian enclaves.

The RAND Corporation played a significant role in crafting "new warfare paradigms" for counterinsurgencies in the United States and beyond (Harcourt 2018). The RAND report, *Urbanization and Insurgency: The Turkish Case, 1976–1980*, sponsored by the US Under Secretary of Defense for Policy as part of the research project "Low-Intensity Warfare in the Year 2000," and coauthored by US and Turkish counterinsurgency analysts, was published in 1991. The report characterized revolutionary socialist working-class mobilization in Turkey between 1976 and 1980 as "urban terrorism" and claimed that Istanbul's and Ankara's dissident working-class neighborhoods were its main centers (Sayari and Hoffman 1991, 1994). Arguing that "urban terror" in Turkey resembled "urban terror" in Latin America—a major target of the low-intensity conflict doctrine—and that Turkey's working-class neighborhoods are similar to the slums of Latin American cities such as Lima, Bogota, San Salvador, and Mexico City, the report recommended that the fight against terrorism in Turkey take its urban dimension into account when developing counterinsurgency strategies. It warned Turkey's ruling elites that its cities would remain an important source of terrorism and violence for the foreseeable future.

That the report was commissioned as part of the military research project, "Low-Intensity Warfare in the Year 2000," suggests that Turkey's future urban-centered counterinsurgency practices would employ low-intensity warfare tactics. Indeed, according to then-chief of the general staff Doğan Güreş, high-ranking Turkish military and security officers received counterinsurgency and low-intensity conflict training in the early 1990s (Kışlalı 1996, 216–17). In 1993, Güreş officially announced the use of low-intensity conflict strategies in Northern Kurdistan (26), some of which were inspired by the British counterinsurgency in Northern Ireland, another location the authors of the RAND report felt resembled Turkey in its "sectarian violence." As I show in this chapter, these strategies traveled to Devrimova and similar neighborhoods in Istanbul, where overt repressive techniques began to be accompanied with increasing frequency by urban-centered and affect-and-emotion-generating provocative counterorganization—techniques by national security states that are designed to provoke individual and communal fear, counterviolence, intergenerational conflict, and ethnosectarian discord to refashion a population's dissent against the state.

As in earlier chapters, the material here draws both on oral history narratives and archival sources. Had I not witnessed firsthand the events that later took place in these neighborhoods during the Gezi uprising of 2013 (see chapter 6), it would have been difficult for me to reach the conclusions I present here. Witnessing the police's simultaneous presence and absence in the neighborhoods during and after the Gezi uprising of the summer of 2013 and watching minute by minute the scapegoating of Alevis as putative organizers of the uprising as it unfolded in the mainstream media helped me understand why my interlocutors insisted on dividing the decade of the 1990s into two parts: the first half characterized by rebellion and repression and the second by radical fragmentation and a weakened resistance.

Framing as Counterinsurgency

Media matter a great deal in counterinsurgencies. Whenever counterinsurgency operations take place, counterinsurgents need a narrator "who explains to the audience what has happened, its significance and where events might lead" (Smith 2008, 401). As indicated in NATO's *Allied Joint Doctrine for Counterinsurgency*, the media help counterinsurgents "to manage how the general public understands specific events" (2011, para. 0230). Narration performed in this frame renders visible those things that serve the logics of counterinsurgency and other things invisible; it makes certain voices audible and others inaudible. Accordingly, a focus on the Turkish ruling elite's (including government members and the security officers) and mainstream media's approach to and representations of the Gazi incidents of 1995 will help us understand these events within the framework of policing. The craft of framing and generating affect and emotions effectively distributes roles and types of participation and shapes modes of perception. Such an analysis of representations as frames also gives us insight into the provocative counterorganization effects of the Gazi incidents.

Aliza Marcus (1996) argues that Gazi residents' reactions to the shootings in their neighborhood and their subsequent march to the police station were shaped by their long-standing conflicts and tensions with the police. In the 1990s, Turkish and Kurdish Alevi, as well as Kurdish Sunni, residents of Gazi were, like Devrimovans, organizers of and active participants in antigovernment demonstrations and strikes (Kazmaz 2016). Many were either affiliated with or sympathetic to revolutionary parties and groups, whether officially authorized or outlawed, and to pro-Kurdish organizations; many were also members of left-wing trade unions. Like Devrimova, Gazi was known as a hotbed of revolutionary organizations and had been under militarized spatial control since the early 1990s. Gazi was also a refuge for large numbers of Kurds who had been forcibly displaced from Northern Kurdistan by state security forces in the early 1990s. Subjected to routine police violence and harassment, Gazi residents experienced armored police vehicle patrols, house raids, and kidnappings by the police as part of everyday life. In the early 1990s, dozens of young revolutionaries and pro-Kurdish activists from Gazi were kidnapped, tortured, and found days later lying severely wounded alongside nearby highways. The killing of a thirty-five-year-old Gazi resident and *simit* (bread rings) seller, Bayram Duran, on October 16, 1994, while being held in custody at the Gazi police station had an enormous impact on the community (Tüleylioğlu 2011). Although Gazi residents were enraged by the police's murder of Duran, as well as the years of police violence in the neighborhood before the coffeehouse shootings, the governing elites and media focused their presentations of the coffeehouse incident on alleged Alevi discontent not with police violence in their neighborhoods, but with government policies in general.

Right-wing prime minister Tansu Çiller, Istanbul chief of police Hasan Kocadağ, and Istanbul governor Hayri Kozakçıoğlu all argued that the Gazi shootings and demonstrations had been staged to provoke Alevis to rise up against both the state and its majority Sunni population. Government officials either implied or stated directly that the PKK and radical Islamists were behind the coffee house shootings. Kozakçıoğlu alleged without evidence that all of the shops looted during the events belonged to Sunnis and argued that the "provocateurs" had succeeded in inciting and mobilizing Alevis against Sunnis (Tüleylioğlu 2011, 176).

The lone high-ranking officer arguing against such sectarianism-based explanations was Hanefi Avcı, then head of the intelligence division of the Istanbul police. Avcı, who would later become a marginalized and persecuted figure within the police department, argued that the intelligence division did not view

Gazi as an Alevi neighborhood but as a hotbed of the radical Left.[3] Consider Avcı's testimony to the Turkish National Assembly's Gazi Investigation Committee: "For us, Küçük Armutlu, Gazi, Alibeyköy, and Sarıgazi are analogous neighborhoods. When we attack [saldırı yaptığımızda] or move into these neighborhoods, we are never thinking that we will come face-to-face with members of the Alevi community or that we will provoke Alevis. Instead, we're thinking of the leftists" (Tüleylioğlu 2011, 191). Avcı also claimed in his testimony that the first café targeted by the gunmen was known by the police as a place frequented by "radical leftists and those who are affiliated with terrorist groups," by which he meant the PKK and other outlawed revolutionary organizations (83). For Avcı, the assailants very well may have been targeting leftists, but their aim would not have been to provoke Alevi–Sunni polarization. The Gazi Investigation Committee ignored the implications of Avcı's testimony and chose instead to focus on sectarian causes.

In their coverage of the protests of the coffeehouse shootings, the mainstream secularist and center-left media followed by Alevis also drew attention to the sectarian makeup of Gazi's residents. Headlines in newspapers such as *Cumhuriyet*, *Yeni Yüzyıl*, *Milliyet*, and *Akşam* stated unequivocally that they were designed to exacerbate Alevi–Sunni polarization. The secularist daily *Cumhuriyet*'s headline read "Attack against Alevis,"[4] *Yeni Yüzyıl*'s headline read "Alevi Groups Clash with Police,"[5] and the center-right *Milliyet*'s headline was simply "Provocation."[6] Popular columnists also characterized the events as being steeped in sectarian sentiment. In line with official government discourses on Alevis, the prominent columnists of the time echoed racialized colonial binaries of "the natives" by portraying Alevis either as childlike dupes or as a rebellious and violence-prone people who could easily be manipulated to rise up against state security forces and Sunnis. For those sympathetic to the Alevi community, the Alevis were both targets and victims of a provocation carried out by "terrorist" forces—if indeed the Alevi community had been "duped," it was surmised, the entire country would be caught up in the scam.[7] Right-wing columnists, unsympathetic to the Alevis, portrayed Alevis as violence prone, claiming that the incidents had been successful in mobilizing the Alevi community against the state and Sunni citizens.[8] Some columnists posited that the unrest in Gazi was caused by radical left-wing organizations who "hide behind Alevis" so that they can carry on with their extremist activities.[9] Others argued that the events represented the eruption of long pent-up "Alevi anger." [10] As I show in chapter 6, similar racializing discourses circulated in the mainstream media in 2013 during the country-wide Gezi uprising when state violence was directed against working-class Alevi spaces and bodies.

These two very different approaches to Alevis—one sympathetic and depicting the Alevis as victims, the other unsympathetic and portraying them as prone to violence—had two points in common: both considered Alevis to be open to manipulation, and both saw them as a homogeneous community. By focusing on sectarian identity, the two sides rendered invisible both the collective struggle and demands of Gazi's left-wing Alevi and Kurdish workers and the ongoing state violence in Gazi. The result was that the political voices of Gazi residents, who together had transcended in solidarity the ethnosectarian divisions between them to demand better working and living conditions, equality, peace, and justice, were translated into unintelligible noise (Rancière 1999). Or perhaps it is more accurate to say that their voices were reduced in the social imaginary into a singular sectarian voice, one allegedly provoked by "radical" and "terrorist" organizations. Discriminated against because of their Alevi identity, the Alevi residents of Gazi, Bir Mayıs, Devrimova, and similar predominantly Alevi-populated neighborhoods were subjected to the racializing effects of the representations that circulated around these instances of large-scale state violence. My argument aims to make visible the precise ways in which these affect-and-emotion-generating representations contributed to the transformation of these places into sectarian enclaves, thereby disrupting relations of solidarity between Sunni Kurds and Alevis, two major dissenting population groups in Turkey, and exacerbating already existing ethnosectarian cleavages between the two groups. In this respect, both the Gazi events and their representations by government officials and the media worked as *violent interpellations*—which I define as calls to a specific subject position and a specific identification made through performative acts of state or state-backed violence—that hailed their targeted citizens as sectarian subjects and their targeted locations as sectarian spaces.

Violent Interpellations

In a discussion of the relationship between the state and subjectivation, Louis Althusser (1976) offers an example of a police officer who calls out to a passerby, "Hey, you there!" The person becomes a subject by realizing she has been hailed and by turning around and responding. As Judith Butler (2013, 25) puts it, "the act of recognition becomes an act of constitution: the address animates the subject into existence." In other words, this "'Hey you' has the effect of binding the law [represented by the police] to the one who is hailed" (Butler 1997, 381). This "unilateral act" harnesses the "power and force of the law to compel fear at the same time that it offers recognition at an expense" (82). Although this Althusserian schema may appear insufficient in explaining the complex and dynamic processes of subjectivation in many situations, the force of interpellation in the context of policing, as Phillip Chong Ho Shon (2000, 169) notes, stems from the fact that "it is oblivious to the subjects' protests." Regardless of her identification with the subject position she is called to occupy, the subject cannot easily escape from or dismiss the interpellation. Deriving its power from the historically embedded structural violence of racism, sexism, and classism, interpellation exerts a powerful force on the subject. By producing affects and emotions that force the interpellated to engage with the interpellation, it is able to intervene in interpellated individuals' imaginaries of themselves and of the world.

Hannah Arendt provides insights into the concept of violent interpellation that I propose here. Raised by a nonreligious mother, Arendt recounts in a 1964 interview with Günter Gaus that she became aware of her ascribed ethnoreligious identity as a Jew only by hearing racist, antisemitic insults from children outside her home. In this context, Arendt articulates the power of violent interpellation without naming it as such: "If one is attacked as a Jew, one must defend oneself *as a Jew*. Not as a German, or a world citizen, or an upholder of human rights" (video, minute 34:53). The simultaneity of attacking and hailing implicit in violent interpellation elicits defense within the frame of the interpellation. Seen in this way, the action of the police in Gazi who shot at the crowd while chanting "Death to Alevis!" was a *violent interpellation* in that it worked in two modes. The chant informed the protesters that, despite their multiple and layered identities as Alevis, Kurds, Turks, workers, revolutionaries, leftists, atheists, feminists, and women, they were all Alevis in the eyes of the police, who were the embodiment of state sovereignty. The accompanying bullets reminded the now-Alevi protesters and bystanders that, as Alevis, they were all killable subjects.

Violent interpellation is a *negative interpellation*, as Ghassan Hage (2010) points out in the context of the increasingly racializing language used against Muslims in and of Europe. Being attacked as a Muslim in Europe effectively racializes the hailed subject, making him "fall from being a universal to being a particular" and fixing that particularity with "negative attributes" via hailing (122). Representations of Alevis in the media and in political speeches as rebellious, as easily provoked or manipulated, as anti-Sunni, and as anti-state are negative interpellations that served to associate Alevis with racialized particulars rather than with human universals.

As Didier Fassin (2013, 8) informs us, interpellation does not simply tell the hailed-after subject "that is what you are" (for example, a racialized subject). It also *orders* her to "become what you are." Violent interpellation is thus also an *imperious interpellation*. The Istanbul police not only told the hailed-after residents of this dissident neighborhood that their assigned roles were only to be Alevi. In hailing them, the police ordered them to become Alevi, to disassociate themselves from all their other identities—revolutionaries on the world-historical stage, workers fighting for better living conditions, Kurds (for Alevi Kurds[11]) demanding recognition and respect, advocates for human rights and democracy—and to defend themselves as Alevi. Reflecting on the Gazi incidents, Yüksel, a Gazi resident in his early thirties, illustrated the relationship between violent and negative interpellation and sectarian identification:

> I was sixteen when the Gazi uprising took place. Our house was close to one of the coffeehouses that got shot up. When we first heard the gunshots, we thought there must have been a clash between the revolutionaries and the police. In those days, the state was always targeting revolutionaries. Usually such clashes occurred around the revolutionaries' safe houses, in bourgeois neighborhoods where the militants were in hiding. The neighborhood wasn't safe for revolutionary militants. Special operation forces were here every day. Because of that, we were a bit confused. We later heard that one person had been killed in the shooting. Everyone was angry. The police were brutal with revolutionaries and pro-Kurdish activists in those days. Kidnappings were common. Torture was common. Gazi residents [*mahalleli*] were sick and tired of the police. People went out onto the streets to protest. It lasted for days. There were thousands in the streets.
>
> In the beginning, everything was normal. But then the police started to shoot into the crowd. Some people were throwing stones at the police and at the shop windows. I don't know who they were. They may have been revolutionaries or maybe provocateurs. Some of the revolutionaries were trying to prevent those people from throwing stones at the shop windows. They were shouting, "There are provocateurs! We have to stay calm!" It went on like that for days.... There were provocateurs pretending that they were one of us and shouting, "Let's throw stones at the mosque." Hasan Ocak,[12] for instance, was one of the people who prevented people from directing their anger toward the mosque. He led the people toward the police station, instead of the mosque. Yet soon after the events he was killed by the state. No wonder. He was trying to prevent people from getting too agitated. I remember him very vividly. He was trying to calm the people down and make them act reasonably. But things got very hectic. There were the police, the soldiers, the agents provocateurs, the *mahalleli*. It was total chaos. It was like a war zone.

I heard the police cursing at the Alevis as they were shooting. They were shouting, "All Alevis are sons of bitches." They were also shouting, "We are going to kill you all!" To tell you the truth, I was surprised to hear that. The majority of Gazi's residents may be Alevi, but it has always been known as a revolutionary neighborhood. One would expect them to curse at the revolutionaries, but that was not the case. They were against Alevis. As the shootings continued, I thought they were going to kill us. I thought about what had happened in Sivas. I thought there was going to be another Sivas or Maraş or Çorum.[13] I think others felt the same way. People started shouting on the streets, "Gazi is not going to be another Sivas!" I remember thinking, "If they killed thirty-seven people in Sivas, I mean if they killed thirty-seven intellectuals (aydın) and artists, among them famous Turkish intellectuals, they will surely kill us here. We are poor laborers. Who cares about us? They could kill us there and prevent others from coming to protect us." I think that's why people didn't want to go back to their homes. The police even put barbed-wire fences across the entrances of the neighborhood and locked us in.

As was the case with many of my Alevi friends and interviewees from these neighborhoods and others, Yüksel told me that it was only after the Sivas and Gazi incidents of the mid-1990s that he began to realize his own identity as an Alevi:

My most important sense of identity back then was being a revolutionary, and it still is. If you're a revolutionary, you're an atheist; you're an internationalist. You have no religion. You believe in the unity of the workers of all nations. But Gazi and the Bir Mayıs uprising made me realize that I am also an Alevi. The Sivas massacre also had an impact on me. But Gazi and Bir Mayıs were different. It was in the neighborhoods. The state came to our neighborhoods to attack us. As an atheist, I'm not very interested in Alevism as a religion. But I am interested in Alevi history, the history of Alevi resistance. Alevis have been oppressed for centuries. But there is also resistance within the history of Alevis. There's Pir Sultan Abdal, there's Hallacı Mansur, there's Şeyh Bedreddin. They all rebelled against oppressive regimes and sided with the oppressed. After Gazi and Sivas, I realized that what made me a revolutionary was related to my being an Alevi.

Yüksel's reflections illustrate how the fear created during the Sivas, Gazi, and Bir Mayıs incidents drove those who had previously not internalized their ascribed sectarian identities to situate their personal history within the history of the Alevi community and to identify as Alevi.[14] Most of these were socialist Alevi youth who had never before witnessed violence unleashed against Alevis and who regarded ethnosectarian identifications as divisive. More interesting still, the interpellative effects of the incidents were not limited to those residents who had been directly confronted with state violence in their neighborhoods but extended beyond the borders of the neighborhoods and of Turkey. As Sökefeld (2008, 69) observes, following these two incidents, Alevi youths in the diaspora also began to identify and "declare themselves openly as Alevis." Given the concomitant increases in the memberships of diasporic Alevi associations, Sökefeld concluded that "without the events of Sivas and Gazi, the Alevi movement would have acquired much less strength" (67). To put it in Arendtian terms, being attacked as Alevis made many people feel a need to defend themselves as Alevis.

The spatial dimension of the violence—that it was directed against working-class spaces inhabited by dissenting Alevi and Kurdish populations—was also an effective "place-making practice" (Dikeç 2011, 5) that transformed the neighborhoods in the social imaginary from places occupied by dissident political subjects into places occupied by "unruly" Alevi subjects. This process of place-making is not unlike what Mustafa Dikeç (2006, 2011) detects in French policymakers' approach to the Paris's banlieues in the late twentieth century. Beginning in the early 1990s, French ruling elites emphasized "the 'ethnic' nature of the problem of social housing estates in banlieues, seen to be threatening the integrity of the republic and its values" (72). As a result, "when the youth in the banlieues revolt, they always 'revolt as' (as blacks, as Arabs, as Muslims, as the children of immigrants)" (177). Likewise, official government and media representations of the Gazi incidents marked Gazi and the other neighborhoods as ethnosectarian enclaves, rendering the dissent in the neighborhoods visible only as *sectarian or ethnic dissent* and disappearing all political struggle that transcended ethnosectarian divisions and matters.

Yet, what served the ends of policing and provocative counterorganization here was not the growing Alevi identification of those who had not previously strongly identified as Alevi. To avoid being the targets of racist physical and verbal aggression and discrimination, many Alevis in Turkey have chosen to keep their identities hidden. One indication of the acute stigmatization of Alevi identity is that Alevis are commonly accused in racist stereotypes of breaking the taboo against incest, a "universal" law of humanity. Time and again, my interlocutors who were born and raised in big cities, not in small Alevi-majority towns or villages, told me that from the time they learned of their Alevi identity they also learned not to proclaim it openly outside the neighborhoods. Many hear that they are Alevi only as a warning that must be kept secret from the non-Alevi public. In as much as it intervenes in the police distribution of the sensible, the mere act of affirming proudly or addressing openly one's Alevi identity becomes an important political act. Such affirmative identification can be seen as an excess of the violent interpellation of Alevis and the police call for sectarian identification. As detailed in the previous chapter, by the early and mid-1990s Alevis were already organizing into various Alevi organizations, many of which provided a venue for debate about the discrimination Alevis faced in a Sunni-dominated society. Rather than serving the ends of provocative organization, these platforms thus became important *political* venues for fighting anti-Alevi discrimination and polices.

What made violent interpellation an effective tool of provocative counterorganization and hence of the police was that the fear it provoked became a divisive force: it intensified ethnosectarian and ethnonationalist divisions and weakened the existing but perhaps already fragile political alignments between Alevis and Kurds. As part of such counterorganization attempts, the government provided resources to help establish Turkish nationalist Alevi organizations. Despite the fact that not all Alevis consider Alevism to be part of Islam or even to be a religion at all, these nationalist Turkish Alevi organizations are, interestingly for our discussion here, strictly anti-Kurdish, promoting the idea that Alevism is the original Turkish form of Islam (Coşan-Eke 2019).

Sectarian Imaginary 1.0: Fear of the Violent Past

The alarmingly violent events in Gazi and the ways in which the media and ruling elite framed them served to trigger Alevi fears of past massacres and strengthen what Nosheen Ali (2010, 739) calls the *sectarian imaginary,* "a normalized mode of seeing and interacting with the sectarian other through feelings of suspicion and resentment." The sectarian imaginary invites the subject to attribute meaning to sectarian difference. It dominates interactions with the sectarianized other and heightens "the potential for conflict" (747) along sectarian lines. In effect, it was not only Alevis who became conscious (or more conscious) of their sectarian identity after the incidents but also the neighborhood Sunnis, a significant percent of whom are Kurds, who lived alongside the Alevis.

Having lived in the neighborhood since the late 1970s, some of my Sunni Turkish and Sunni Kurdish Devrimovan interlocutors nevertheless recounted how they, too, had experienced the Gazi incidents as a rite of passage after which they became mindful of their Sunni background. In a neighborhood café in the winter of 2011, Osman, a sixty-year-old Devrimovan who had been born into a Sunni Kurdish family, recounted to me how this process worked in the aftermath of Gazi:

I came to this neighborhood when I was a child. My father was a revolutionary. I was also a member of a revolutionary organization for a long time. I always considered myself to be a revolutionary and thus an atheist. It was not until the Gazi incidents that I learned that I was also a Sunni.

A few months after the Gazi incidents, there were elections for the neighborhood head [*muhtar*]. I was a candidate. Some revolutionary friends were helping me organize the election campaign. We would go to coffeehouses and people's homes to talk about the elections, sometimes together and sometimes separately. A revolutionary friend approached me one day and said, "Brother, I have to tell you something. I heard that some people are saying, 'We won't vote for the Yazid [the caliph responsible for the death of the son of Ali, the most revered figure in Alevism].'" I am so ignorant of religion. I naively asked. "What is a Yazid?" We are revolutionaries, we don't have a religion. When did this happen? How did this happen? All of a sudden, I became a Sunni, a Yazid.[15] After Gazi, people began to talk about who is Alevi and who is Sunni. Maybe it was already there, but it became all the more explicit after that.

Ismail, a middle-aged Devrimovan who had been born into a Sunni Turkish family, shared a similar story:

After Gazi, I had the feeling that my friends, whom I had known for decades, with whom I had been active in the same revolutionary organization before 1980 [the coup], and with whom I had even shared the same prison cell, began to be suspicious of me. For instance, when I would go to the coffeehouse [*kahvehane*, coffeehouses for men] and approach them, they would all fall silent or change the topic. Why? Because I was not Alevi. One day I asked one of my friends about it. I said, "You are like my brother, my comrade. But I feel that sometimes when I sit down with you [and your friends] at the coffeehouse, you stop talking about what you were talking about before, and you change the topic. Or am I getting paranoid? Is that what is actually happening?" He said, "Brother, you're right. Don't get me wrong, but people are afraid. Alevis are afraid. They are also afraid to offend you." I said, "Why would I be offended? I do not believe in religion. I have no religion." He said, "I know. I understand that. But some people do not."

What to say? Whom to blame? They were really afraid. It was as though they began to suspect that all Sunnis might one day become Islamists. There were people like that, of course. Revolutionaries who became Islamists after the coup. But still . . . I could not have cared less about religion. People began to be afraid of one another. This was what

the state wanted: to divide and rule. I took part in the Kurdish liberation movement in the nineties. After the Gazi incidents, it became much
harder to co-organize demonstrations and events with revolutionary
friends in the neighborhood.

The DHKP-C-affiliated periodical *Kurtuluş* in the 1990s devoted a section to
anecdotes about everyday experiences in the neighborhoods, at universities, in
factories, and so on, submitted by its members and sympathizers. There, too,
after the Gazi incidents, people brought up the issue of sectarian tension among
the revolutionaries in the neighborhood. An anonymous man from Gazi, for instance, wrote in an alarming tone that one of his revolutionary friends had
asked him, "Can Sunnis possibly be revolutionaries? Can we trust them?"[16]

Negative interpellation was effective not only in racializing Alevis by associating them with violence, threat, and danger in the eyes of the non-Alevi public; by raising the specter of past anti-Alevi violence it also associated Sunnis with
persecutors in the eyes of Alevis. Because the majority of Sunnis in the neighborhoods—as well as in the trade unions and left-wing organizations in which
many working-class Alevis were members—were Kurds, it was most often the
Sunni Kurd who was transformed into a potential persecutor in the perceptions
of working-class Alevis. A Kurd who was once a comrade could easily become
a "Yazid," a potential perpetrator, or a prospective Islamist, regardless of that
person's self-identification. At the same time, several of the major revolutionary
organizations that had previously cooperated with the PKK began to distance
themselves from or stopped working together with the Kurdish liberation movement. Adopting a Turkish nationalist discourse disguised in anti-imperialist
terminology, they accused the Kurdish liberation movement of seeking to divide the class movement by putting the interests of the Kurdish people before
those of the working classes.[17] According to my interlocutors from Gazi and
Devrimova, the rancor at times reached the level of physical fighting between
pro-Kurdish activists and members of certain revolutionary groups. Because
Kurds were new to these neighborhoods and fewer in number than the Alevis,
the neighborhoods no longer functioned as safe shelters for them.

After the Gazi incidents, many people began to seek shelter in the comfort
and familiarity of family and kinship networks. While describing the fear that
pervaded the community after 1995, my interlocutors pointed out that almost
every village and *hemşehri* (hometown) association—there were more than a
dozen in Devrimova alone—had been established after the Gazi incidents.[18]
These *hemşehri* associations took the place of the neighborhood *kahvehanes*, the
coffeehouses that used to be significant spaces of encounter for male residents
from diverse backgrounds. For the senior residents of Devrimova, it was fear that

prompted many to retreat to their kin group and give up the ideal of becoming part of a larger community and collectivity that transcended ethnosectarian divisions. Alevi, Sunni, village, and *hemşehri* communities of sameness promised shelter from the risks that could come with associating with others. Fear of the state was thereby projected onto others.

Provocateurs and Politics

The British counterinsurgency in Northern Ireland, too, had a sectarian dynamic. Loyalist paramilitary groups closely associated with Kitson's strategy of "counter-gangs" (see chapter 1 and the later discussion in this chapter) collaborated with the British security apparatus in targeting Catholics, the constituency of the anticolonial, anti-sectarian Irish Republican Army in Belfast.[19] Fear of sectarian violence was effective in transforming the nature of politics and space in Belfast, leading to ever-increasing sectarianism and segregation. Emphasizing the productive force of fear in shaping Belfast into an ethnosectarian landscape, Peter Shirlow (2003, 76) argues that "the construction of ethnosectarian landscapes is influential but does not convert everyone who lives in such places towards accepting homogeneous senses of belonging and affiliation." In other words, violent interpellation and its partitioning effects (à la Rancière) can be refused, ruptured, or rearticulated.

The story of Hasan Ocak, whose heroism in leading the Gazi protestors toward the police station instead of the Sunni mosque was recounted by Yüksel earlier in the chapter, demonstrates how the police's fragmentation of the neighborhoods into ethnosectarian camps through violent interpellation was refused, ruptured, or rearticulated via the realm of politics. Then a schoolteacher, Hasan Ocak is now seen as a legendary revolutionary martyr, killed by state security forces after being taken into custody a week after the 1995 Gazi incidents. He is celebrated today for his intervention in police attempts to provoke Alevis into directing their anger against Sunnis. As we see in chapter 6, this intervention is remembered and taken as a model by young revolutionaries at times of increasing sectarian conflict in the country. Maside Ocak, Hasan's sister, was with him during the Gazi incidents and, in an interview with Doğu Eroğlu, explained her brother's role in preventing an attempt to provoke sectarian discord:

> We were in a cortege of approximately thirty thousand people, marching from Alibeyköy [another predominantly Alevi-populated working-class neighborhood] to Gazi. While walking with Hasan, we heard someone behind us was shouting, "There is Nizam-ı Alem Ocakları [an

Islamist, nationalist organization] behind us! Let's attack there. Let's throw stones at the mosque over there." Süleyman Yeter was with us at that moment. Süleyman and Hasan linked arms with the guy and took him out of the cortege. They asked him who he was. He responded, "I am the people [*halkım*]. I am being killed. I am being burned. I am being shot at." They were not convinced by his answers. They body-searched him and found a card in his wallet that showed that he was actually a member of the Nizam-ı Alem Ocakları. Then they fretted over what to do with him. If they let him go, he'd leave, then enter a different part of the cortege, perhaps ten meters ahead of us, and do the same thing. You couldn't know how people would respond to his provocation. It is impossible to keep thirty thousand people under control. If they did something there, then it might cause a lynching. They went back and forth about it over and over, and then they thought, "The best is to keep him with us until we reach Gazi." People created a people's committee [*halk komitesi*] in Gazi then. "We will give him to the people's commit-tee, and they will decide what is to be done." We kept that provocateur with us until Gazi. There was a colonel there. He gave a speech, saying, "We thank those friends who brought the provocateur all the way here for their prudence." One week after this incident, Hasan disappeared in police custody. This does not seem like a coincidence to me. I do not know how else to name it. Four years later, in 1999, Süleyman Yeter was killed under police torture. Perhaps it was a game staged by the state.[20]

All those involved in the Gazi incidents—the ruling elites, the mainstream media, the residents of Gazi, and their allies—acknowledge the presence of provocateurs—but they identify them differently. For the ruling elites and the media, the provocateurs were the radical Islamist organizations, revolutionary organizations, or the PKK. In contrast, for many of my interlocutors, the pro-vocateur was the "state," an entity already waging a war against Gazi's dissident residents. In Gazi, Devrimova, and similar neighborhoods, Hasan Ocak is still remembered as one of the first to understand that the ruling elites meant to frame the protests as an Alevi insurgency against Sunnis and so stir up sectarian ten-sions. Many of my interlocutors believe that Hasan Ocak was able to prevent a major provocation.[21] He and his comrades were successful in denying "the state" the material evidence with which to prove that the Gazi incidents had been an Alevi uprising against the Sunni state and its privileged Sunni citizens. But de-spite their lack of material evidence, the Turkish ruling elite, who have the power to frame events via the media, still spun the incidents as an Alevi insurgency. This shows the contingent location of acts of intervention, rupture, and rearticulation that function from positions relative to violent interpellation and the institutional violence from whence it derives its strength.

Then again, such relative positioning of acts of political intervention in the realm of policing does not necessarily mean that the violent interpellation of ethnosectarian division was completely successful. As I argued in the introduction and elaborate on in chapter 5, the "spirits" of those torn from this life by unjust instances of oppression continue to wander the earth and serve as empowering and emboldening political and ethical resources. Although Hasan Ocak was killed in custody soon after his intervention in a major counterinsurgency operation, his action and the recounting of it still surface in the neighborhoods, inspiring many to take up their part in interventions to counteract sectarian cleavage (see chapter 6). Every year in the month of March, Hasan Ocak's face reappears on the neighborhood walls along with images of the twenty-two people who lost their lives in the Gazi and Bir Mayis neighborhoods (see figure 3.1). Despite ongoing provocation of ethnosectarian and ethnonationalist enmities

FIGURE 3.1.   A scene from the funerals of Yeliz Erbay and Şirin Öter at the Gazi neighborhood cemetery. You see the gravestone of Hasan Ocak, who was disappeared and murdered after being taken into custody on March 21, 1995. Next to his grave are the graves of the people who lost their lives in the Gazi Massacre of 1995. Image has been modified to protect the identities of those pictured.

Photo by Sinan Targay.

by the ruling elites and their allies, his memory haunts the neighborhoods as a reminder of the perils of such hostilities, inspiring many people to collaborate with other oppressed populations.

Fear and Defensive Counterviolence

The fear triggered in the context of such violent interpellation not only strengthens sectarian cleavages but also spurs the targeted people to engage in what David Altheide (2003, 9) calls "defensive action": "it is not the fear of danger that is the most crucial, but that into which this fear can be transformed, what it can become." When the "fear of annihilation" is provoked by state-initiated or state-backed violence against historically persecuted communities, it paves the way for "countering fear by the right of self-defense" (Yassin 2010, 7). The Gazi incidents, which led local Gazi residents and residents of similar neighborhoods to believe that they, too, could be massacred in their own neighborhoods, also prompted a felt need for self-defense. That need played a crucial role in the retreat into and containment of revolutionary violence within the neighborhoods.

Immediately following the incidents, youths from various revolutionary organizations set up makeshift barricades at the entrances and exits of the neighborhoods to prevent the police from entering, manning them for several days as a line of defense.[22] At the same time, revolutionary vigilante groups serving as security patrols and defense units were formed; some called on their militants and supporters to clear the neighborhoods of the police and "fascists" through "revolutionary violence."[23] Only a few months after the Gazi incidents, revolutionary urban armed units conducted what they called "neighborhood raids" in which large numbers of militants participated. Their actions included damaging local shops and cars belonging to the police and their alleged allies (purported informers), bombing suspected undercover police cars, and bombing local bank offices and right-wing party offices located in or near the neighborhoods.[24] In December 1995, the DHKP-C-affiliated journal *Dev-Sol* called the working-class neighborhoods sites of "civil war" and devoted nine pages to a discussion about the significance of the ongoing fighting there.[25] Arguing that everyone from sixteen-year-old teens to sixty-year-old grandmothers should learn how to make bombs, the journal provided detailed information about how to create explosive substances at home.[26]

The DHKP-C's arguments about the concentration of "revolutionary violence" in the neighborhoods were taken up by other outlawed revolutionary organizations, who engaged in similar types of violent activities in those years. The neighborhoods became dangerous places for the police and their allies, and for strangers as well. With the exception of armored military vehicles, police cars avoided the neighborhoods. Years later, when I met him in Paris, Eylem, who like Zelal had left the country when he was still a high school student after being kidnapped and tortured by the police, explained to me his rationale for engaging in violence after the Gazi events:

> I was fifteen when the Gazi events took place. Gazi was a turning point in my life. I was a leftist, but not a member of any revolutionary organization. After Gazi, I realized the urgency of things. I thought that if we didn't protect our neighborhoods, the state and the Islamists might commit another massacre. The strange thing was that after the Gazi uprising the police disappeared from the neighborhood. Yes, there were still *akreps* (military vehicles). But the checkpoints were gone. Police cars avoided the neighborhoods. We were proud at the time, believing that we had scared the police off. But in retrospect, I now realize that they were in reality allowing us to engage in violence in the neighborhood. That is not to say that the police abandoned the neighborhoods altogether. Just like with guerilla tactics, the police would come to stir things up and would then withdraw.

Eylem's words illustrate both the role that provoking the fear of massacres played in motivating youth to engage in violence and the use of other provocative counterorganization methods, which Eylem likens to guerrilla hit-and-run tactics, in the containment of revolutionary counterviolence in the neighborhoods. Not unlike Belfast's Catholic working-class neighborhoods, the working-class neighborhoods in Istanbul became places of "contained and permitted" violence (Feldman 1991). For a while, the attempts of revolutionary youth to protect their neighborhoods from the police and their alleged allies gained the sympathy of many residents and made them respected guardians of the neighborhoods. The large-scale participation in the May Day 1996 demonstrations under the banners of outlawed socialist organizations can be seen as an indicator of that sympathy.[27] However, such a sympathetic outlook was short-lived, and soon enough the revolutionary youth began to be marginalized.

Parting Ways

Many of my interlocutors who lived in the neighborhoods in the 1990s spoke critically of the revolutionary violence that had taken place and accused the revolutionary youth of "inviting the police" into the areas where they lived. When reflecting on the second half of the 1990s, many complained about the revolutionary youths' "obsession with barricades," "throwing Molotov cocktails all over the place for no reason," burning buses, and so on. In other words, as the violent acts aimed at pushing the police and their allies from the neighborhoods became routinized, the revolutionary youth began to be perceived by residents as the culprits who were disrupting order.[28] Such perceptions led to an intergenerational conflict within the community as adults began accusing the youth of acting irresponsibly. Contrasting the tactics of the youth in the late 1990s from those in the 1970s, Halime, a socialist Devrimovan in her mid-forties, was clear in her denunciation:

> While we are criticizing the state, we should look at ourselves, too. Our revolutionaries, our revolutionary youth, are not innocent either. They go out and throw Molotov cocktails at ATM machines or at the markets. Devrimova residents [mahalleli] use those places. When you break the ATM machine in the neighborhood, people have to go to another neighborhood. They have to take the bus. And, back then, in the 1990s, some days no buses would come to the neighborhood. If they did come, they would come only once an hour. So, people either had to walk to ·another neighborhood or wait for a long time to catch the bus. What happens then? People say, "It's because of them that I have to wait and pay for the bus." Or, "It's because of the revolutionaries that I have to walk all the way to another neighborhood." The state likes us to suffer and what those revolutionary youth achieved [was] nothing more than to serve the purpose of the state. But if you ask them, they will say that they were protecting the neighborhoods from the police and the fascists. They invite the police into the neighborhood. In the 1970s, the revolutionaries would keep the violence away from the neighborhood. Their main duty was to keep the neighborhood safe. These guys did the opposite.

Halime's recollection is a common one. By the second half of the 1990s, the respected revolutionary gradually devolved into a marginalized figure accused of bringing violence into the neighborhoods. Two developments were important in this transformation. As many of my interlocutors argued, and as I witnessed later in a similar process during my fieldwork, the revolutionaries who were most respected because they sought cooperation with others—those who could bring the community and various organizations together at the local level—were either subjected to extrajudicial killings, as in the case of Hasan Ocak; imprisoned; or forced into exile to escape a long prison sentence.[29] This was also the case in Northern Kurdistan.[30] With the more experienced and collaborative revolutionaries gone, young male teenagers engaged in performative counterviolence to defend the neighborhoods and expressed their rage against the system to establish themselves as fearless political actors. As I illustrate in chapter 5, such performative demonstrations of fearlessness were encouraged by the masculinist discourses of certain revolutionary groups.

The containment of counterviolence in the neighborhoods was also made possible by the relative withdrawal of the police from the neighborhoods and by their provocative hit-and-run tactics. By the second half of the 1990s, the military checkpoints and special operation forces had vanished from the neighborhoods. The arbitrary raids by special operation units occurred less frequently, and many interviewees noted that the number of military vehicles in the neighborhoods had decreased. To this day, neighborhood youths still proudly claim that the police do not dare to enter the neighborhoods. Yet today, too, the police's sudden use of hit-and-run tactics can turn the streets into low-intensity conflict zones where revolutionary youths set garbage cans alight to use them as barricades and respond to police forces with Molotov cocktails, fireworks, and stones. As Ilana Feldman (2015, 9), in her analysis of colonial policing argues, "If police exercised self-control, it was easier for authorities to cast criminality as a 'native problem.'" As state violence became less visible in the neighborhoods, revolutionary youth began to be considered as the source of violence.

In 2000, four years after the May Day marches of 1996 when more than twenty thousand people walked behind the banners of long-outlawed revolutionary organizations, the DHKP-C leadership addressed their own marginalization with the following words: "The main question we need to ask [ourselves] is this: How did the rift between the people's feelings, excitement, and reactions and those of leftists appear and then begin to widen over the years?"[31] I suggest here that the development of a radical schism within the dissident bloc must be understood within the context of Turkish ruling elites' adaptation of counterinsurgency techniques informed by the low-intensity conflict doctrine. The Gazi incidents were a rite of passage in the history of counterinsurgency techniques applied in Istanbul, marking a transition to the use of a more hybrid counterinsurgency strategy. Overtly repressive techniques designed to contain inhabitants and violence in the neighborhoods began to be accompanied by more covert and provocative counterorganization techniques designed to incite intercommunal conflict and counterviolence.

Low-Intensity Conflict

British military officer Frank Kitson's notorious low-intensity operations in Northern Ireland are informative here. Recognizing that state violence and overt repression—such as occurred in house raids, mass arrests, shoot-to-kill policies—increased the public's support for the IRA, Kitson chose to implement a counterinsurgency strategy involving a particularly provocative form of "collusion": "the involvement of state agents, directly or indirectly, through commission, collaboration or connivance, in non-state political violence" (McGovern 2011, 2016). In line with this strategy, Kitson created "counter-gangs" consisting of British Army officers in plain clothes, their local collaborators from Irish Protestant paramilitary groups as well as informants turned from the IRA. By targeting Catholics—the main constituency of the left-wing and anti-sectarian IRA—these "counter-gangs" were able to keep a decades-long low-intensity conflict in play in the Catholic working-class areas of Northern Ireland. This strategy was so effective that it succeeded in changing the nature of political struggles in Northern Ireland, increasing sectarian cleavages and militarizing the fabric of everyday life (Sluka 2010). The scope of the conflict and its duration transformed the working-class areas of Northern Ireland, especially the densely populated Catholic working-class neighborhoods of Belfast, into "killing fields"—"they represent the major sites of violence, the battlegrounds where domination and resistance in general and the war in particular are concentrated, contained, and isolated" (Sluka 2015, 284). Such continual "troubles" frustrated and intimidated the residents and "undermine[d] their will to resist" (McGovern 2015, 8).

This indirect activity in turn allowed the British Army to be less visible in Northern Ireland, while still controlling and interfering in local political activity by means of collusion. At the time of the Gazi incidents, the Turkish authorities were aware of the effect of Kitson's strategies. While praising Kitson's low-intensity operations in Belfast, Kışlalı (1996), a Turkish journalist who worked closely with the military and conducted research on global counterinsurgencies, argues that the relative retreat of the state security forces from Belfast—a retreat allowed by collusion and indirect intervention—created the impression that the IRA was merely fighting for the sake of fighting, which frustrated residents and made the IRA's political cause appear pointless in the eyes of its own constituency (99).

After all, as counterinsurgency theorist David Galula (2002, 70) has argued, "the best cause loses its power under war conditions." The aim of counterinsurgents is thus not to end violence but to control it. Kışlalı (1996, 160), agrees, noting that the aim of counterinsurgency is to reach an "acceptable level" of violence. Likewise, NATO's *Allied Joint Doctrine for Counterinsurgency* declares that "the strategic goal of the counterinsurgent is to promote legitimate governance by *controlling* violence" (2011, para. 0328; emphasis added). Controlling (not aiming to end) crime and disorder is also a key aspect of neoliberal policing (Fassin 2013; Comaroff and Comaroff 2016).

As we saw in the previous chapter, by the early 1990s, the Turkish ruling elite had acknowledged that their psychological war against the PKK had been unsuccessful: it was unable to separate the PKK from its popular base (Kışlalı 1996, 160). At the same time, Doğan Güreş, then-chief of general staff, officially announced that Turkish security forces had adopted a strategy of low-intensity conflict in Northern Kurdistan (25). To develop their skills in conducting low-intensity conflict operations, Turkish military officers received counterinsurgency training in the United Kingdom, and high-ranking officers made paid consultancy visits there (Gordon 1987). Then-chief of the general staff Doğan Güreş personally conducted research in Belfast (interview with Güreş in Kışlalı 1996, 233). In line with Kitson's low-intensity operational strategy, the Turkish security apparatus created clandestine counterguerrilla groups and armed and collaborated with local right-wing paramilitary groups (Işık 2019; Jongerden 2007). It also supported Islamist Hezbollah against the PKK so to divide Kurdish society from within (Aydın and Emrence 2015; Kurt 2017). As Aysegul Aydın and Cem Emrence (2015) argue that the promotion of rivalries among and within local communities was a pacification strategy that Turkish ruling elites also learned from their Ottoman predecessors. Aimed at turning Kurdish populations against one another and transforming the Kurdish space into a low-intensity conflict zone, these strategies were effective not only in inciting intercommunal violence among Kurds but also in promoting an Islamist ideology as a counter to the PKK's Marxist, anticolonial, left-wing, and secular political stance.[32]

Although no archival evidence on collusion in Devrimova and the neighborhoods has yet come to light, while analyzing the rift that occurred between revolutionary groups and their support base, the concentration and containment of revolutionary violence in the neighborhoods, and the increase in sectarian divisions between Kurds and Alevis after the Gazi incident, it is important to keep in mind that at the time the Turkish security state adopted a strategy of low-intensity conflict.[33] As we also see in chapter 6, this strategy involves various provocative and affect-and-emotion-generating counterorganizational strategies: the affective strategies of fueling sectarian fears and feelings of insecurity gave rise to defensive counterviolence, effectively marginalized the revolutionaries and distanced dissident Alevi and Kurdish populations from one another. The counterviolence that ensued transformed these dissident working-class spaces into places of "contained and permitted violence" (Feldman 1991).

It is important to note here that not all revolutionary violence is initiated, provoked, or permitted by state security agents. Many other contingencies may lead dissidents to engage in violent acts. As we have seen in the previous chapter, the desire to express rage and take revenge or, as we see in the following chapters, attempts to repair injured working-class masculinity and manifest power are powerful motivators for dissident group engagement in violence. Then again, violent dissident acts are not all of a kind, nor do they always separate dissidents from their base of support. As we saw in the previous chapter, because they meet the desire for revenge and justice, the killings of high-ranking security officers and other oppressive ruling elites are often effective in gaining the sympathy of oppressed populations. Yet it is only those acts of dissident violence that do not garner legitimacy in the eyes of their constituency—acts that manage to transform dissident groups into the perceived causes of insecurity—that are encouraged, provoked, and permitted by the ruling elites. To recall Halime's earlier words about the revolutionary youth, "Their main duty was to keep the neighborhood safe. These guys did the opposite."

In fact, as I pointed out in the introduction, the Turkish ruling elite were aware of the delegitimizing effect of certain forms of dissident violence even before the 1990s. At the height of the left-wing mobilization, then commander of the Special Warfare Department, ÖHD, Cihat Akyol (1971) wrote a high-profile article that was meant to circulate exclusively within the military but was years later leaked to the public.[34] It promoted the military's creation of covert groups and its organizing "fake operations" that would involve "cruel and unjust acts" while giving the impression that they had been committed by dissident organizations (Akyol 1971, 1990; cited in Mumcu [1990], 1997, 54–57). Such techniques that involved provocative collusion and infiltration are commonly applied counterinsurgency techniques. Because they effectively serve one of the main purposes of the so-called psychological operations: to destroy "the legitimacy and credibility of the enemy" (Gill 2004, 129). In the United States, Gary Marx (1974) showed how FBI agents infiltrating the Black Panthers to delegitimize the group incited their use of counterviolence. This disguised intervention contributed to the militarization of the group and its effective separation from their constituency and from otherwise sympathetic white liberals. In South Africa, Nicholas Haysom (1989, 1990) has demonstrated how white ruling elites, also adopting the low-intensity conflict strategy, encouraged black vigilante violence in black townships as a way to fragment the growing anti-apartheid struggle. Haysom notes that South African security officers who were present as observers during the Algerian War imported French general André Beaufre's (1965) "extended battlefield" techniques—also adopted and modified by the US Army (Haysom 1989)—for inciting violence among dissident groups into their security policies. In 1969, the Turkish translation of Beaufre's book, *Introduction to Strategy*, was published by the publishing house of the Turkish General Staff as *Harekat Stratejisi*. It was assigned alongside the Turkish translation, *Ayaklanma Bastırma*

Hareketleri: Teori ve Tatbikatı (1965) of David Galula's book, *Counterinsurgency Warfare* (1964), as required reading in the Turkish Military Academy.

Without taking the provocative and partitioning dimensions of counterinsurgency into account, it is impossible to fully grasp the violence of the nonstate actors or the fragmentation of the Left along ethno-sectarian, racial, class, and spatial lines. In Istanbul, the strategies of provocative counterorganization were particularly productive, because they were not only effective in divorcing revolutionaries from their constituency but also were able to contribute to the racialization of Alevis and Kurds in the eyes of the wider public and to divide the Left along ethnosectarian, class, and spatial lines. Drawing on a case study of the confinement of violence and counterviolence in the Gaza Strip, Lori Allen (2012) illustrates that at the same time that "the scale of the violence that was unleashed on Gaza-as-target" transformed Gaza "into a scary place that holds scary people" (269) in the eyes of the Israelis, it also stigmatized Gazans in the eyes of other Palestinians as "uneducated, unsophisticated, easily persuaded" (270) people who are "duped by Hamas." Allen argues that this sense of separation created an impression that "we are not even part of the same game" (271) even among some segments of Palestinian society. Similarly, the confinement of counterviolence to the neighborhoods served to marginalize their residents in the eyes of the wider public as "violence prone" and in the eyes of middle-class leftists as people duped by "radical, extremist" organizations. Turnout over the last two decades of May Day demonstrations in Istanbul is evidence enough of how fragmented the Turkish Left has become. The corteges of outlawed revolutionary organizations were made up almost exclusively of the working classes (mainly Alevis and Kurds), whereas the corteges of legal socialist parties generally contained middle- and upper-class professionals, intellectuals, and college students.

Although the practice of confining dissident counterviolence and conflict to the neighborhoods generated much discontent among residents, revolutionary organizations have managed since the mid-1990s to maintain an ambivalent relationship with local residents. As I illustrate in the chapters that follow, this is because, the state security apparatus still posed a significant security threat in the neighborhoods, deploying overtly repressive techniques when they found it necessary. Just as state and state-sponsored paramilitary violence in Northern Ireland facilitated support for the IRA and INLA (Sluka 2010) and in Northern Kurdistan for the PKK (Aras 2013), in light of the ongoing security threats to residents posed by the state, and with the introduction of novel security threats in the form of drug gangs, that revolutionary activity still held value and sway among Devrimovans.

GOOD VIGILANTISM, BAD VIGILANTISM

Crime, Community Justice, Mimetic Policing,
and the Antiterror Laws

On October 8, 2007, at around 11:00 p.m., two thousand heavily armed police officers poured into Devrimova.[1] Accompanied by military tanks, the police officers, who were from antiterrorism units, stood on the neighborhood's main street until 1.30 a.m., at which point helicopters began to fly overhead and the operation began. The police raided the houses of ten young men, all of whom were living with their parents, and took them into custody. All ten were accused of being members of a "terrorist" organization. While I was conducting my fieldwork in 2011 and 2012, five were granted pretrial release after spending four and a half years in a high-security cell, and their insights form a part of this analysis; the others spent six years in the same type of cell as pretrial detainees. In the fall of 2013, all ten were sentenced to twenty-six years in prison.

All of these young people were engaged in an unarmed and participatory form of extralegal justice/vigilantism in their neighborhood as active members of the Neighborhood Association (NA: discussed later in the section, "Vigilantism 1:0").[2] They were also members of a socialist organization. Had they considered themselves guilty and subject to arrest, these ten young men would have had enough time to leave the neighborhood before the launch of the operation and the raids. However, as the ones granted pretrial release in 2012 told me then, because the police who had streamed into the neighborhood were from antiterrorism units and the young men did not believe they had committed any terror-related crimes, they did not think that they were the targets of the operation. Even after spending four and a half years in prison, they believed that the terrorism charges against them would be dropped.

Over the following years, Devrimova residents witnessed similar operations against other local youths, all of whom also self-identified as revolutionaries and engaged in a similar type of vigilantism in the neighborhood. Similar operations took place in other working-class neighborhoods with a high Alevi population, such as Gazi, Okmeydanı, Gülsuyu, Armutlu, and Bir Mayıs. Hundreds of youths from these neighborhoods who were engaged in vigilantism were imprisoned as terrorists. These operations, however, did not end vigilante activity in the neighborhoods. On the contrary, over the years, armed vigilantism has gained popularity among the youth, and this form of vigilantism still continues in these neighborhoods.

As detailed in the previous chapter, by the late 1990s, outlawed revolutionary organizations had been marginalized both inside and outside the neighborhoods, yet they never entirely lost their local base of support. By the 2000s, new actors and forces entered the scene. Throughout the first two decades of the twenty-first century, drug dealers, small-scale drug gangs, and the amended antiterror law all conspired to preserve the new status quo whereby violence was confined within the neighborhoods. At a time when they were needed to provide security to respond to increasing drug dealing and petty crime in the neighborhoods, state security forces were ruinously absent. Yet they were overwhelmingly present in the form of mass antiterror operations targeting the neighborhood's most respected revolutionaries and pro-Kurdish activists, the very ones who were successfully mobilizing the community against drug dealing and petty crime. Focusing on the rise of petty crime and drug-dealing activities in the neighborhood, this chapter sheds light on the repressive and provocative aspects of the antiterror law by showing how the great expansion of its parameters in 2006 enabled its successful intervention in local political space.[3] As we see, one of the most powerful effects of the antiterror law was to transform the vigilantism in predominantly Alevi-populated working-class neighborhoods of Istanbul from a public, participatory, and unarmed form of informal justice to a clandestine, exclusive, and armed one. In this chapter I demonstrate how the strategic use of antiterror laws served the aims of provocative counterorganization by confining the most collaborative and community-minded revolutionaries behind bars and paving the way for armed vigilantism, hence for the militarization of local revolutionary activity, and continuation of low-intensity conflict in the neighborhoods.

Crime and Criminalization

The global neoliberal turn in the late twentieth century had fostered a new kind of poverty. Although Turkey's neoliberalization process began immediately after the 1980 coup, its working-class neighborhoods remained largely free of crime, gang violence, and drug-related activities up to the end of the 1990s. That is mainly because, during the 1980s and 1990s, family and charity networks had prevented the working class from falling into absolute poverty and thus from engaging in petty crime.[4] Yet, as growing numbers of working-class people were rendered redundant and excluded from wage and labor processes, social solidarity and charity networks that had previously worked to bridge the gap left by the lack of state welfare provision were weakened, and working-class neighborhoods were gradually transformed into places of absolute poverty (Adaman and Ardıç 2008; Buğra and Keyder 2003). Moreover, until the early 2000s, Turkey had not functioned as a final market in the global drug trade, and drugs were therefore not available in working-class areas. When it finally became a marketplace for drugs, cannabis, cocaine, and ecstasy became widely available in the working-class neighborhoods of Istanbul. Many working-class youths first began to buy drugs as consumers, but their inability to afford their growing drug habits, which turned into addictions, meant that they were later recruited as dealers to work with the drug gangs.

While neoliberal policies and relations have worked to exclude certain segments of the working class from wage and labor processes, such policies have also produced in them a desire to be respected members of society as consumers. Engaging in crime, gang violence, and drug dealing emerged as alternative income-generating activities and means by which stigmatized and impoverished populations might seek to acquire respect (Bourgois 2003; Wacquant 2009; Comaroff and Comaroff 2016). In Turkey, too, with increasing poverty and the growing availability of drugs in working-class areas, working-class youth in particular began to commit car thefts, shop robberies, pickpocketing, sex work, and drug dealing.[5] Thus, the early 2000s marked the beginning of a new era in Devrimova and, indeed, in all working-class neighborhoods of Istanbul.

As I have shown elsewhere (Yonucu 2008), one of the primary dynamics that led to the engagement of Istanbulite working-class youth in petty crime and drug dealing is the dialectical tension between these two structurally produced affective poles: their rage against a system that impoverishes and stigmatizes them and their desire to be respected as members of society by becoming successful consumers. What I found in my work on criminalization in the Zeytinburnu district of Istanbul also held true for Devrimova and the other neighborhoods studied here: by the early 2000s, certain segments of Devrimovan youth began to use and sell drugs and to engage in petty crime. Although the main drug suppliers came from elsewhere, the small-time dealers were from the neighborhoods.

It is in this context that discussions of crime—the way that crime is represented and made sense of—become important. As Richard Sparks, Evi Girling, and Ian Loader (2001, 889), with reference to Mary Douglas (1992) argue, crime "is something for which we seek explanation and accountability—and how we explain it and whom we blame may be highly symptomatic of who we are and how we organize our relations with others." In Devrimova and other similar neighborhoods, some residents blamed the parents, arguing that to "protect their children from politics" (by which they meant revolutionary activism and its inevitable consequence, state violence), they would encourage their children's consumerist desires, thereby driving them into drugs and drug gangs. With the move of forcibly displaced Kurds into Devrimova and the other neighborhoods in the late 1990s, some Devrimovans, particularly those who held anti-Kurdish sentiments and were invested in their Turkish (nationalist) identity, began to blame the Kurds for having brought drugs into the neighborhood. For others, drug use and dealing were effects of capitalism. But above all, the majority of Devrimovans I spoke with blamed the state security apparatus.

Studies have shown that the urban poor who live in crime-dominated areas often complain about the failure of the police to provide security and about police corruption—their collaboration with criminals in pursuit of individual gain. In relation to drug dealing and petty crime, the urban poor experience the police either as an absent force or as a force that collaborates with drug gangs and criminals. William Garriott (2013b, 57), in his ethnographic research on the impact of methamphetamine and narcopolitics on a small, rural community in the United States, finds that "frustration with police inaction led to speculation that local police, lawyers, and politicians might themselves be behind the rising drug problem in the community. When someone that 'every-body knows is selling drugs' failed to be arrested or convicted, it seemed to be the only possible explanation." In a similar vein, Donna Goldstein (2013) points out that Rio de Janeiro's favela dwellers use the term "police-bandits" to underline the intertwinement of the police and criminals. When I conducted fieldwork in predominantly Turkish- and Sunni-populated Istanbul neighborhoods in 2003 and 2010, many of the residents complained either of police absence or their partnership with drug dealers as a moneymaking arrangement. Even small-scale dealers complained that police officers saw them as easy sources of money.

But the flourishing of drug dealing in poor neighborhoods is more than a simple matter of police corruption, be it individual or systemic. According to the majority of my Devrimovan interlocutors the arrival of the drug dealers in the neighborhoods was deliberate and under the control of the police. Many saw it as part of a new counterinsurgency project developed with the aim of depoliticizing the community. The novelty, as one of my senior interlocutors put it, was that "in the 1990s, they [state security forces] used to terrorize; now they *also* criminalize" (emphasis added).

In communities where the state security apparatus is considered either a major cause of crime or as allies of criminal gangs, security is sought by other means. In the United States, South Africa, and Brazil, for example, unless they overflow their margins and threaten white middle- and upper-class citizens and their properties, urban poor populations are often left in large measure to their own devices to police themselves, meaning that vigilantes police the neighborhoods.[6] Facing similar processes, during the first two decades of the twentieth century, residents of Devrimova and other dissident working-class neighborhoods of Istanbul increasingly engaged in informal justice vigilantism to fight rising crime. In what follows, I elaborate on three phases of vigilante activism in the neighborhoods—roughly separated into the early 2000s, the mid-2000s, and post-2007—and their transformation in relation to the state security presence and absence.

Vigilantism 1.0: The Legacy of the People's Committees

Vigilante activities in Devrimova were initiated in the early 2000s by a group of predominantly male residents in their fifties and sixties who had been active in the people's committees (*halk komiteleri*) of the 1970s. Their aim was to protect the youth from drug consumption. Pointing to police absence and the state's failure to provide security in the neighborhood, in 2003 a group of residents established the Neighborhood Association (*mahalle derneği*; NA; mentioned on p. 1) with the aim of heightening public awareness of the increasing threat of drug consumption and dealing. Similar vigilante group initiatives originating from within the same demographic occurred around the same time in other predominantly Alevi-populated working-class neighborhoods. I came to understand the dynamics of this early phase of Devrimovan vigilantism in the summer of 2011 while sipping tea with three of the founding members of the NA, Ihsan, Naim, and Mahmut. Ihsan, the owner of the coffeehouse (*kahvehane*)[7] in which the interview took place, was the first to explain how and why he and his friends had ultimately decided to do something about the rise in local crime:

> I came to this neighborhood when I was eighteen. We built this neighborhood together back then, and we of course want to protect what we built collectively. . . . Then all of a sudden, at the beginning of the 2000s several new coffeehouses and gambling dens opened. These new coffeehouses were not just your ordinary coffeehouses. Gambling and other sorts of shady things were going on in these places. Some guys from

outside the neighborhood began selling drugs here. We realized that our youth were hanging out with them, using and even selling drugs. My friends and I got together to talk about the situation and came to the conclusion that if we did nothing to stop it, things would get worse. The neighborhood would become unlivable and our youth would end up either in prison or in the hospital. We wanted to protect our neighborhood and our youth.

At the time, Ihsan and his friends assumed that developing a crime awareness and prevention campaign within a legally established association would be considered legal and legitimate activities both by neighborhood residents and by the police. Established in the fall of 2003 with around fifty members, the NA initially worked to identify the hard-core drug addicts and marijuana users in the neighborhood, eventually pinpointing 127 young habitual users. NA members would then visit the users' homes, talking with their parents and family members and leveraging social pressure to convince them to stop using. These efforts were coordinated with psychologists from the neighborhood community center who offered free rehabilitation services to drug addicts. The NA members compiled a list of coffeehouses, gambling houses, and bars in the neighborhood and gave talks on the dangers of gambling and drug use and the need to protect their community. They located dealers' homes and went to talk to them, warning them to stop. At times they went out with batons to chase glue sniffers or to threaten or beat up known criminals. Their aim was to show the drug dealers and casino owners that they were not wanted in the neighborhood.

Based on their experiences of establishing the neighborhood in the early 1970s, forming people's committees in the face of state opposition, and ousting the police from the neighborhood in the second half of the 1990s, the NA members believed that if residents were united around the issue of crime, the casino owners and dealers would feel uncomfortable in the neighborhood and would eventually leave. In those days in the early 2000s, they were optimistic. Naim, another NA founder, described the reasoning underlying their initial "naiveté":

> There has always been police suppression in this neighborhood. But the people of Devrimova have known how to come together to defend their neighborhood and resist the police. At least that was what we thought back then. We thought the neighborhood would eventually come together and push the drug dealers and the gangsters [çeteci] out of the neighborhood. Because even in the early 1990s, when the police turned this neighborhood into a police station [karakol], the people here knew how to stand together. With just one call to action they would take over the streets. We didn't realize that things had changed.

To raise public awareness and encourage solidarity against the gangs, the NA organized a concert in September 2004 in one of the wedding halls. During the concert, gunmen entered the coffeehouse owned by Ihsan, then head of the NA, and fired at random. A week after the shooting, a group of masked men raided the coffeehouse at night, looting the empty establishment. A few days later Ihsan's wife was shot in the leg while walking down the street. Despite the constant surveillance of undercover police and security cameras in Devrimova, my interviewees described the police as having been unhelpful in finding the attacker.

The police's unwillingness to investigate these incidents reinforced community perceptions that they were siding with the gangs or that the gangs were working for the police. I even heard rumors from several residents that the bullets found in the coffeehouse belonged to the police. These violent developments frightened active NA members from engaging in vigilante activities. They concluded that they were not simply fighting a handful of drug dealers and gangsters but were instead fighting the state. Mahmut, another founder of the NA, commented on the surprising systematicity of the attacks:

> The people we were fighting against were not disorganized. They were not just gangs, not just drug users. They were as organized as the people gathered at Silivri Prison [high-ranking military officers, who at the time had been tried by the AKP government].[8] They work as systematically and with as much organization as those at Silivri. You have to take them seriously. There is a huge force behind them; the force of the state is behind them.

Hasan chimed in on an even more pessimistic note:

> He's right. It became impossible to do any good in this neighborhood. Whenever you want to do something, the state is right there working against you! I got tired of it. . . . Look at people our age in this neighborhood. They've all become alcoholics now. They're all depressed. Even I drink. How can I *not* drink, dear sister? How can anyone stand it without drinking?

Hearing Hasan's words, I remembered how often I had witnessed young revolutionaries in the neighborhood criticizing middle-aged male residents for their excessive alcohol consumption and for being "cowards" and "conformists." The seriousness of neighborhood problems and the overwhelming demands of the fight against drug dealing eventually led to schisms in the community. Those who continued to engage in vigilantism despite the danger to residents it entailed began to blame those who had stopped of cowardice. This moralistic pressure on those critical of armed vigilantism continues today.

Vigilantism 2.0: Addressing the Sociopolitical Roots of Crime

Wary of the violent gang attacks and convinced of police collusion in them, the NA's founding members stepped back from the association, and a younger group of activists in their early and late twenties began to take over in 2005. The new members belonged to a legal socialist party, and like their predecessors they believed that the fight against crime could only be successful if the community stood united. But they also viewed the problem of youth engagement in gang violence, petty crime, drug use, and drug dealing through the critical lens of academic works on the depoliticizing effects of working-class criminalization (Karandinos et al. 2014; Parenti 2000). Having witnessed the quarrels that had erupted among Devrimova residents, the new NA members sought to build common ground around solutions to the problem of youth criminalization and gang violence.

Echoing an argument put forward by Karandinos and colleagues (2014, 18) that criminalization of poor urban areas "profoundly depoliticizes the poor, turning violence inward—neighbor on neighbor," the NA's new young members, including the five young people I mentioned above, who were on pretrial release during the first years of my research, later told me that they "believed that if they could not manage to bring the community together around a common cause, the community's anger would turn inward and residents would focus on crime-related problems rather than on wider social issues that gave rise to crime." In an interview conducted when he was on pretrial release, Ulaş, one of the most active members of the NA, told me how the group approached the issue of crime and why he took part in the fight against crime in the neighborhood:

> Young people engage in crime for several reasons. First of all, they can't find work and they're depressed about it. They feel discriminated against. Also, you see, a lot of new shopping malls have opened up around the neighborhood. Young people want to be able to consume. The TV shows they watch—they all promote consumerist culture and a bourgeois lifestyle. They think they can make easy money if they sell drugs and all that. They also believe that being a member of a gang will bring them power. But on top of this, the state supports the gangs and drug dealing here. This neighborhood is still a political neighborhood. The state would rather have gangs here than revolutionaries. Go to Gazi, it's the same. In Okmeydanı, the same . . . [9] All the revolutionary and political neighborhoods suffer from the same problem. They want young people to use drugs and not question the state. So we decided to prevent it. We had to stop it. But you can't just stop it by force.

Having witnessed firsthand the dialectical tension in Devrimova between recent economic impoverishment of and cultural discrimination against the poor
and the concomitant rise in the poor's desire to gain respect and express their
rage against the system, Ulaş and other NA members saw the engagement of
working-class youth in petty crime as its outcome. They therefore concluded that
even though criminal gangs were being supported by the state, young people engaged in crime for a variety of reasons: doing so was a means of livelihood and
indulgence in consumerism, an expression of defiance against mainstream culture, and a respect-generating activity. Viewed through this lens, they believed
that crime could not be stopped by force alone and that what was needed was a
sense of community and a common understanding of the problem. Ali, a former NA member, explained the logic of these new members' approach:

> You can't simply tell young people, "Stay away from gangs and drugs!"
> There's a reason they are attracted to gangs: to make money, to gain re-
> spect, to acquire power, etcetera. You have to show them *why* what
> they are doing is wrong. You have to show them that it is a *class issue*
> and that capitalism and the state don't care about them. And that gangs
> and drugs are no solution. You have to tell them that for the workers,
> for the laborers, there is no individual salvation. You also have to offer
> them something beautiful. We would organize movie screenings in the
> neighborhood. We would organize discussions on capitalism, on the
> history of the socialist struggle in Turkey. We would read novels that
> helped to develop class consciousness, such as *How the Steel Was Tem-
> pered, And Quiet Flows the Don*. We would organize masculinity work-
> shops to develop a critical perspective on our internalized masculine
> values and behaviors. We would organize picnics and football games
> to increase solidarity in the neighborhood. Solidarity is the key.

NA members approached crime as a social and political problem that could
not be solved solely through performances of security. Accordingly, they planned
social, educational, and recreational activities aimed at encouraging a culture
of solidarity and public discussion in the neighborhood. They were also successful in bringing other local socialist and pro-Kurdish groups together in an attempt to raise public awareness about crime. Together with older residents in
the neighborhood they paid visits to a police station in the district to which
Devrimova was administratively attached and talked to the police chief, but with
no positive response. As Ulaş emphasized, they believed that if a wider public
became aware of the problem, "the police would eventually have to throw the
gangs out of the neighborhood." And so, they contacted human rights organizations to apprise them of the new developments. They organized public meetings

to discuss the dynamics of rising crime in the neighborhood and published the video recordings on the internet.[10] They contacted journalists to raise awareness of the new developments in Devrimova and other neighborhoods, and one national newspaper printed a one-page interview with members of the NA in November 2005.[11]

Although the people's committees were short-lived and were prevented by the Turkish security apparatus from being reconstituted, that experience continues to inspire Devrimovan political activities: not only those of the NA's founders but also of the younger socialist members who were not even alive when the people's committees and courts were flourishing. Yet the spatial control of the neighborhood by state security forces, the increasing surveillance by undercover police, and the unremitting criminalization of any attempt to rebuild the people's committees did not allow for many public gatherings or spontaneous actions.

Thus, despite NA members' attempts to build common ground for discussion and action, the NA functioned differently than had the people's committees. Whereas the committees had enabled a space for public discussion, the NA had to function primarily behind closed doors, providing a community center to which residents could go to seek help regarding problems of domestic violence, sexual harassment, mistreatment by their bosses, and the like. In such cases, members would discuss possible solutions among themselves and with those who submitted a complaint.

Yet, as I expand on in the following chapter, despite the increase in undercover police presence and surveillance cameras (locally known as *mobese* cameras) in the neighborhood, Devrimova's young revolutionaries refused to retreat from the streets. Instead, being visible and vocal in the street became an important political act. The NA organized public demonstrations essentially to expose certain criminal or undesirable actors and entities. They organized protests of hundreds of residents in front of casinos and bars to send the message that they were not wanted in the neighborhood. In the summer of 2005, the NA and other groups organized a march down Devrimova's main street to protest a business owner known for sexually harassing his female employees. As with the people's committees and courts of the 1970s, the NA's female members and women from the neighborhood played an important part in the struggle and were most influential in organizing such civic demonstrations. At the behest of the NA's female members, the NA organized critical masculinity workshops and gender discussions designed to hold up the community's patriarchal relations to public scrutiny.

A number of female members of the NA described to me their feelings of empowerment in having succeeded in raising the issues of gender relations and male domination in group discussions. Ekin, who was an active member of the

NA in the mid-2000s, told me about the women's approach to vigilantism while we were on our way to the above mentioned ten NA member's court hearing to begin in an Istanbul courthouse in the winter of 2012:

> Men and women act differently. Men sometimes are more inclined to solve problems with force. For instance, there was a man who harassed several women in the neighborhood. He was a small shop owner and he used to sexually harass his female employees. Some women from the neighborhood came to the NA to complain about him. Some young male friends from the NA got agitated; they were like, "We should find him and beat him up." But we women told them that this would not be a solution. We had to find other ways, alternative ways, ways that were more deterrent. We organized a meeting on the issue at the NA. We invited those who had been harassed by that man. Five women showed up. We concluded that the guy had been doing this for a long time. Then we got in touch with some other organizations in the neighborhood and decided to organize a public demonstration to shame him. At the time [2005], we were organizing masculinity workshops at the NA. Thanks to those workshops, the men began to question and reflect on their own patriarchal attitudes. That also helped them to work with women, listen to them, learn from them. That, of course, empowered us. Such workshops were especially important in the neighborhoods whenever we had to deal with drug dealers, crime, and such. Later, our organization took part in the "We Are Not Men Initiative" (Biz Erkek Değiliz Inisiyatifi).[12]

In an environment that has forced young men either into gang activity (drug dealing, petty crime) or vigilantism, both of which promote performative demonstrations of masculine power, these attempts by female members of NA were important political acts aimed at challenging the hegemonic gendered distribution of roles and places. But the ongoing urgency of security demands and the overwhelming presence of the violent gangs and drug dealers made the young men the main actors in the fight against crime, rendering feminist-inspired interventions less influential.

As the activities organized by the association gained public sympathy in Devrimova, young, active male members of the NA became respected figures in the neighborhood. Like their predecessors in the NA, they worked in collaboration with the neighborhood community center and succeeded in enabling people to give up using and selling drugs. In 2011, I met several former drug users and dealers who had since become members both of the NA and of the socialist party to which the NA's active members belonged. While I was conducting my fieldwork, many people from various organizations told me about the NA's contribution to the decline in drug use, the decrease in the number of drug gangs, and the closing of gambling houses and casinos. Residents praised the NA's activities, arguing that this second phase of vigilantism was the most effective effort in the fight against crime in the neighborhood. Many stated that, by working in close collaboration with other socialist and Kurdish groups, NA members in those years were able to transcend ethnosectarian tensions in the neighborhood by bringing residents and those socialist and pro-Kurdish organizations together in a culture of solidarity, precisely what they had been aiming to do.

As the NA gained popular support, however, it also became the focus of gang and police attention, a consequence that its members well understood. The most active members received death threats and were stabbed and hospitalized by gang members several times. Such violent attacks demanded retaliation in the form of physical force, pushing female members further into the background and narrowing the space for political struggle. But as I argued in the previous chapter, violence against dissident groups is not a force capable of suppressing all the actions of its targets. In defiance of the gangs and in the belief that their popularity in the neighborhood would protect them, NA members insisted on continuing their activities until October 2007. After an NA member named Haydar had a fight with an undercover policeman, a massive "antiterror" operation, which I described in the opening vignette of this chapter and in chapter 5, was conducted in the neighborhood in which two thousand security personnel participated in armored vehicles, tanks, and helicopters. Ten key NA members were taken into police custody, accused of membership in a terrorist organization.

Because the activists were members of an officially registered socialist organization and because all of their activities had been conducted in public, they did not expect to be detained for long. Except for the testimony of undercover police and a secret witness for the state prosecution, no material evidence placing them with Haydar at the time of the beating or connecting them with a terrorist organization was ever presented.[13] Nevertheless, as mentioned, five members spent four and half years and six spent six years in pretrial detention, and in 2013, all ten were sentenced to twenty-six years' imprisonment. Throughout this period and in subsequent years, similar operations were launched against Kurdish activists and youth groups who engaged in NA-style vigilantism in Devrimova and other neighborhoods. As a result, hundreds of other local socialist and pro-Kurdish youths who had gained the sympathy and trust of Devrimovan residents and who were working collaboratively with other groups and community members were accused as terrorists and put behind bars. During the first phase of my fieldwork in Devrimova, I often heard people lament the fact that the most cooperative and well-liked revolutionary community organizers and pro-Kurdish activists were now behind bars while the more contentious organizers and those openly engaging in violent acts remained free.[14]

Expansion of the Antiterror Law

In line with global trends in terror legislation, Turkey's antiterror law no. 3713, originally passed in 1991, has a very vague and broad definition of terror.[15] Amendment no. 5532, passed in 2006, retains the imprecision while increasing the number and scope of crimes that could be considered as terrorist offenses.[16] It also makes it easier to apply the law, increases the length of punishments for alleged terrorist acts, legalizes the breach of fair trial rights, and allows for the categorization of political crimes as terror crimes (Demirsu 2017).

With this amendment, the number of prisoners convicted on terrorism charges increased dramatically in Turkey: in 2005, there were 273 terror convicts in Turkey's prisons, and that number reached 12,897 by 2011 (Insel 2012). A significant percentage of these convictions were of Kurdish activists and politicians accused of being members of the Kurdistan Communities Union (Koma Civakên Kurdistan; KCK), an umbrella pro-Kurdish liberation movement organization that included the outlawed PKK. The KCK trials began in 2009 following the mass arrest of Kurdish opposition members and the eventual imprisonment of thousands of Kurdish activists, including trade unionists, elected mayors, active members of the pro-Kurdish Peace and Democracy Party (Barış ve Demokrasi Partisi, BDP), journalists, lawyers, and university students, all on the basis of their alleged connections to the PKK. Noting that the KCK trials began immediately after the electoral victory of the Peace and Democracy Party in Northern Kurdistan, Derya Bayır (2014, 34) argues that the trials constituted a judicial policy of "politicide" against the Kurdish opposition.

Since 2006, antiterror laws have become the preferred tool in the war against politics, à la Rancière. The expanded use of antiterror legislation not only put ever-increasing numbers of community-minded dissidents behind bars but they also became a major tool to "police" dissident communities in the Rancièrian sense (1999, 2001); that is, to intervene in the forms of dissident activity and hence to define the forms of participation. Although the massive security operations launched in October 2007 against NA members under the auspices of the expanded antiterror law give the impression that it was solely repressive in nature, there is another side to the legislation: I suggest that its use should be understood as a legal front in provocative counterorganization and its war on politics. That operation and similar stings targeting pro-Kurdish and socialist youth in the neighborhoods were harbingers of the country's "lawfare"—"the resort to legal instruments, to the violence inherent in the law" (Comaroff and Comaroff 2016a, 36)—against dissent. As seen in the KCK trials and the selective targeting of those engaging in relatively peaceful vigilantism and civil politics had the effect of narrowing the space in which to engage in politics. As I show in the next section, this narrowing effectively moved actors into the only remaining space available to them—armed and violent forms of vigilantism—a highly desirable outcome within the logic of provocative counterorganization.

Vigilantism 3.0: Masked and Armed

Although the operations against NA members did not succeed in ending vigilantism in the neighborhoods, they did transform it. In the years following the mass operation of October 2007, a number of socialist organizations, including the one NA activists belonged to, gradually withdrew from vigilantism. They reasoned that since it was the revolutionaries who had been put behind bars, fighting crime would require finding a way out of the cycle that criminalizes revolutionaries. As with the former generation of NA members, they drew the conclusion that the entity they were dealing with was too powerful to fight. And like the former NA members, they, too, were accused of cowardice by other groups.

Other revolutionary groups argued that the only way to fight back against this "dirty alliance" (*kirli ittifak*) between the state and the gangs was to adopt armed struggle, and so they began to engage in armed vigilantism. Because the antiterror operations had targeted activists who engaged in NA-style vigilantism—that is, transparent, public actions under the rubric of a registered association—these groups became convinced that if they wanted to continue to fight crime in the neighborhood, they would have to cover their faces and conceal their identities from the police. Toward the end of the 2000s, vigilantism by armed and masked youths—mostly men under the age of twenty—began to be the major form of extralegal activity in Devrimova and other neighborhoods and remains the case today. Instead of organizing public and participatory meetings and demonstrations as NA members did, these young men donned masks, took up arms, and undertook extralegal security practices that mimetically reproduced the official practices of the police.

In their work on violence, anthropologists have explored the mimetic nature of the relationship between representatives of the state and their rivals (Aretxaga 1995; Taussig 1993; Zilberg 2007). Following René Girard (1988), Elena Zilberg (2007, 65) notes that the mimetic relation is not a mere imitation of the performances of the rival other but entails "an assimilation into one another, a circulation between selves and anti-selves feeding off each other's correspondence." Can

Açıksöz (2019, 25) claims that Turkish military officers, as part of their counter-insurgency campaign against Kurdish guerrilla forces, trained soldiers fighting against PKK guerrillas in Northern Kurdistan to "mimetically reproduce the military tactics and embodied practices of guerrillas." In the case I analyze here, the various spatial and affect-and-emotion generating provocative counterorganization strategies serve to transform the revolutionary into a mimetic copy of the police. And not just any police—as I illustrate below and in chapter 6—but counterinsurgent police quelling Kurdish dissent.

Although their activism stemmed first and foremost from the ideal aim of bringing about a more just society, these revolutionary youth became increasingly concerned with protecting the neighborhood against drug dealers by establishing their own armed security force. Deliberation on alternative ways of providing justice gave way to the urgency of the violence committed by drug dealers and the police that were overtaking the neighborhood. The youth would go out regularly on the streets with red masks and long-barreled guns and use mimetic policing practices on anyone they deemed suspicious: stop-and-frisks, identity checks, body searches, criminal investigation, and extralegal detention. Unlike the NA activists who were now either imprisoned or had withdrawn from vigilantism, this armed group viewed the causes of crime through a conventional legal and moral lens that did not go against the grain of the policed distribution of the sensible. Everyone from marijuana users and sex workers to drug dealers and thieves were considered criminals who deserved to be punished. These revolutionary armed vigilantes' methods of punishment included beating up and torturing drug dealers, pimps, and thieves and shaving sex workers' hair to shame them in public. They were also highly critical of masculinity workshops that took place in the neighborhood. In their journals, they criticized such activities as anti-revolutionary and petty bourgeois acts.[17] Mimicking the police treatment of neighborhood revolutionaries in the 1990s, they placed the beaten or tortured bodies of their victims on display around the neighborhood; they even posted video recordings of the punishments on YouTube and Facebook.[18] As many of my interlocutors noted, conflicts between the gangs and these revolutionary vigilante groups sometimes escalated to the point of violent armed clashes that resulted in deaths.

Accusing Kurds of dividing the class struggle and embracing hegemonic racist attitudes toward Kurds, some segments of these armed groups also posed a security threat to Kurdish residents. Some of my Kurdish interlocutors told me that they were threatened and beaten by these groups. Azad, a twenty-year-old Kurdish construction worker, told me about his encounter with such vigilantes in a neighborhood park on a hot summer day in 2011:

For us, for the Kurds in the neighborhood, there are two police forces. There are the official police and then there are these anti-Kurdish, Turkish nationalist so-called revolutionaries. They have the same mentality as the state. In the past, it was the police who would stop us, search our bodies, and beat us. Now, these so-called revolutionaries do the same thing. They once threatened me with a gun because I didn't agree with them on a political issue [*siyasi bir mesele*]. After that, I could not leave my home for two months. You never know who these people really are. Their faces are covered, they act like the police. . . . How can you distinguish a revolutionary from the police if they act the same way? Have you ever seen a young Kurdish guy walking alone in the streets of the neighborhood? No, right? You will never see a Kurdish youth walking alone in the streets of Devrimova. Do you know why? Because if we walk alone, either the police in their military vehicles will kidnap us or those so-called revolutionaries will attack us.

This confusion between revolutionaries, gang members, and the police is symptomatic of the armed and masked vigilante practices' mimetic resemblance to police and gang practices. In the end, this rivalrous mimetic assimilation of "selves and anti-selves" (Zilberg 2007, 65) frightened many residents away from the streets and created an atmosphere of insecurity in the neighborhood. Even though some residents felt that they were being shielded from gang violence by the armed and masked groups, the vigilantes also posed a threat in that it was impossible to know who was actually behind the mask. "You never knew," many of my interlocutors complained. "The person behind the mask might be a revolutionary, a gang member, or a policeman." Those who criticized the use of the mask often gave the example of the "Broken-Head Mehmet" (*Kırık Kafa Mehmet*). Mehmet was a member of a revolutionary organization that engaged in armed vigilantism. One day, in 2009, while he was playing card games at a neighborhood coffeehouse, a group of armed and masked vigilantes entered it, asking for everyone's identity card. Instead of taking his card out of his pocket, Mehmet proudly told them the name of the revolutionary organization he belonged to. His organization was the only one engaging in armed vigilantism in those days; he therefore assumed that the vigilantes were his comrades. But in place of a gesture of camaraderie, one of the vigilantes hit him on the head with his gun. To this day, Mehmet has a scar on his forehead. No one has yet discovered who the vigilantes were.

The armed groups were not very visible in the neighborhoods during the first phase of my fieldwork in 2010 and 2012. Every now and then I did hear talk of their ongoing activities, and in 2013 and 2014 they began to dominate the streets again. How they were able to continue and even increase their masked and armed vigilantism under strict police surveillance and the threat of the expanded antiterror law is a question that can only be answered by analyzing the counterinsurgency technique of provocative counterorganization.

Good Vigilantism, Bad Vigilantism

Vigilantism does not always remain outside the purview of the state; it can be unofficially incorporated into state security practices and can occur in collusion with the state as a way of "outsourcing justice" (Comaroff and Comaroff 2016). When vigilantism mimetically reproduces state security practices, it contributes to the reduction of crime to a security issue and thereby helps "secure insecurity," which Mark Neocleous (2011, 192), drawing on Karl Marx ([1844] 1975), argues "gives rise to a politics of security, turning security into the fundamental concept of bourgeois society." For this reason, vigilantism exists in some settings with the approval of the state: it is encouraged by ruling elites as "a cheap form of law enforcement" (Pratten and Sen 2007, 3; Abrahams 1998; see also Auyero 2006). Within this frame, in the eyes of the ruling elites, NA-style vigilantism was bad vigilantism. Instead of mimetically reproducing state security practices, it was an intervention that aspired to challenge the existing police order in its Rancièrian sense. The armed and masked vigilante activities, however, contributed to the police "distribution of the sensible."

NA-style vigilantism aimed to mobilize the community around the social and political roots of crime: its actions can be seen as forms of an Arendtian "world-building" practice that "brings individuals together around a common world" in "an inter-related (in public through action and speech)" way (Dikeç 2013, 82–83). Such political audacity was considered to be an act of terrorism by Turkish law enforcement precisely because it interfered with the distribution of political participation as circumscribed by the Turkish state and its police force. In other words, the NA's active members were "great criminals" (Benjamin 1996, 239)—outlaws who had gained the sympathy of the public and whose violence had the potential to build new law and, hence, a new order (Derrida 1992, 33). Their attempts to desecuritize the problem of rising crime, decriminalize segments of society deemed criminal, and destigmatize their communities ran contrary to the role that had been ascribed to Istanbul's stigmatized Alevi working-class neighborhoods—as places of violence, crime, and conflict. The NA members' success in alleviating ethnosectarian cleavages in the neighborhood by bringing Alevis and Kurds together was an intervention in both the police order and logics of provocative counterorganization, which benefited from partitioning racialized and impoverished populations. NA members had attempted to challenge what had become "sensible"—visible, sayable, knowable, assumed—for racialized urban poor communities in the contemporary capitalist system. They had dared to fight crime without reducing it to an issue of security. Although they did not manage to create alternative peace and justice practices that fully secured their neighborhood, they were successful in mobilizing the community, building a common platform for discussion of the sociopolitical issues around crime, encouraging solidarity relations within the community, and publicizing to a wider audience the sociopolitical issues underlying the crime taking place in their neighborhood. The expansion of the antiterror law brought this to an end, paving the way for a two-pronged police order: a massive state security force intervention designed to enact politicide on locally respected figures and extralegal policing in the form of revolutionary neighborhood youth.

That masked and armed vigilantism has survived in the neighborhoods for almost a decade despite constant police surveillance suggests that it may have been tolerated or even encouraged by the police. As examined in the introduction and in the previous chapter, encouragement of the use of armed violence among dissident groups is an effective counterinsurgency technique employed with the aim of destroying the legitimacy and creditability of dissident groups and effectively separating them from their popular base, securitizing issues that are in reality political, and racializing and stigmatizing dissident groups' constituencies. An enduring legacy of the Cold War and colonial policing, the counterinsurgency technique of "manageable conflict" or sustainable, low-intensity conflict ensures the depoliticization of political problems and their expression as revolutionary violence or counterviolence concentrated and contained in the places of actually or potentially rebellious populations, who are kept busy with ongoing problems of (in)security.

In the initial years of the AKP government, which came to power in 2002, the ruling elites invested effort in creating the impression that they would contribute to the democratization of the country. The symbolically styled Kurdish and Alevi "openings" (Kürt ve Alevi açılımı) promised democratic solutions to the problems that Turkey's Alevis and Kurds had been facing for many decades. But given their experience of being among the first targets of the amended antiterror laws, along with impoverished Kurdish youths in Northern Kurdistan, the residents of Devrimova and similar neighborhoods were well aware of the insubstantial nature of the AKP's promises of democracy. Still, when compared with the counterinsurgency tactics of the previous decade, the early years of the AKP government stood in some contrast: there were no checkpoints at the entrances of the neighborhoods; the kidnappings and disappearances of revolutionaries ended; and the police force's hit-and-run attacks diminished. While these changes may give the impression that the government had reduced its use of provocative counterinsurgency techniques, I suggest, in contrast, that the provocative dimensions of counterinsurgency instead became more disguised. By the mid-2000s, working-class youth had become increasingly drawn into drug dealing, drug use, and petty crime while the state security apparatuses conspicuously failed to take action against them. Instead, the security forces selectively targeted with mass antiterror sting operations those who were successfully and in relative peace mobilizing the community against drug dealing and petty crime; in other words, the neighborhood's most respected revolutionaries and pro-Kurdish activists. This in turn provoked the need for and continuation of revolutionary violence against the drug gangs and enabled a security logic of containment of violence within the neighborhoods.

Turkey has a long history of such arrangements between state security apparatuses and extralegal right-wing vigilante in which they work together to target the country's racialized non-Sunni and non-Turkish populations and left-wing dissidents (Bora 2019; Dölek 2015; Saglam 2021). But by the second half of the 2000s, certain segments of the revolutionary working-class youth, too, became unwitting yet effective agents of government efforts to police dissent. Armed and masked vigilantism in Devrimova and other neighborhoods became an effective means of controlling revolutionary and pro-Kurdish activity, effectively turning the voices of dissidence into slogans of security and channeling the energy of the revolutionary youth into local security practices. As the antiterror laws narrowed down the space in which to launch a public, participatory, political fight against crime and the political void widened, the revolutionary youth stepped in. Transformed into ambiguous figures with police-like powers, these new armed and masked revolutionary youth stood at the threshold of inside and outside, security provider and security threat. Rather than intervening in the policed distribution of what had become sensibly known about these neighborhoods, armed and masked vigilante groups in the neighborhoods reproduced it. In so doing, they achieved one of the prime aims of the low-intensity conflict doctrine—the manufacturing of "violent stability" (Haysom 1989)—in the neighborhoods.

But the creation of a manageable and fully controllable "violent stability" is never cut and dry. Nor do policing and politics always operate as binaries. Although armed vigilantism did play a role in the war on politics, it also contributed to politics à la Rancière in the sense that the presence of these groups made the neighborhoods dangerous places for drug gangs, thereby preventing the advancement of drug-related, security-demanding activities in the neighborhood. They also posed a threat to the covert policing practices, which themselves posed a major security threat for residents. As I discuss in the following chapter, the undercover police became a spectral presence in the neighborhood by the second half of the 2000s, triggering widespread feelings of insecurity and threatening to disrupt trust and solidarity relations within the community. In their efforts to free the neighborhood of the police and the criminal gangs, whom they suspected of collaboration, the armed vigilante groups caught many undercover policemen, forcing them to leave the neighborhood. Yet by the end of the 2000s, armed vigilante groups themselves began to be targeted by the antiterror laws. This is likely why they were not as present in the streets during the first phase of my research in 2010 as they had been in the mid-2000s. But as I demonstrate in chapter 6, they would reappear in the summer of 2013 just as the Gezi uprising shook the political scene throughout the country and reverberated across the world.

INSPIRATIONAL HAUNTINGS

Undercover Police and the Spirits of Solidarity and Resistance

On October 8, 2007 at approximately 5:00 p.m., some six hours before the launching of the antiterror operation against NA members recounted in the previous chapter, Haydar, an active member of the NA, began to quarrel with an undercover policeman on Devrimova's busiest street.[1] Haydar was then unaware of this man's official identity, but he had noticed that this stranger had appeared in every place he had been throughout the day. By the late afternoon, Haydar decided to confront this man. He turned around and started yelling at the stranger, asking him who he was and why he was following him. Soon the two men began brawling, and a crowd gathered around them. Another man from the crowd, who turned out to be another undercover policeman, leaped in to help his colleague. This led others to join in the fray, either to protect Haydar or to separate the two parties. At one point, one of the undercover policemen fell to the ground, and his walkie-talkie slipped out of his pocket. Realizing that the man he was fighting with was an undercover policeman, Haydar shouted to warn his friends, "He's a cop!" whereupon the fight ended abruptly. As witnesses later testified at the trial, the confrontation lasted approximately ten minutes.

Despite corroboration of Haydar's claim that he did not know that the man he was hitting was an undercover policeman, Haydar and his nine friends, whom I mentioned in the previous chapter, all of whom were active members of the NA, were accused of assaulting a policeman and seizing a policeman's gun on the alleged orders of an outlawed revolutionary organization considered to be "terrorist" by Turkish law enforcement.[2]

By the second half of the 2000s, in addition to the drug gangs and the amended antiterror laws, the visible presence of undercover police was yet another force that was brought to bear on the local political scene. In the months and years that followed the operation against NA members, hundreds of revolutionary and pro-Kurdish youths from Devrimova and similar neighborhoods would be detained under the antiterror law and found guilty based on undercover police testimony. Because the judiciary views the testimony of undercover police officers as a key source of evidence, covert policing holds a privileged position in the enforcement of Turkey's antiterror law. Thus, the undercover police are not mere spooks or spies who tail dissident revolutionaries and pro-Kurdish activists. They also have the power to shape the direction of their futures and hence their fates.

As I recounted in the introduction, shortly after I began my fieldwork in Devrimova, I realized that I was being followed by an undercover policeman. The conspicuous presence of the police shadowing me allowed me to understand that undercover police officers do not always hide their identities, nor are their undercover policing activities limited to passive observation and information gathering. At times, the undercover police reveal themselves to targeted individuals and groups so as to induce fear and trigger insecurity. During my interviews and informal chats with people in Devrimova, I was often told that it was quite possible that an undercover police officer was nearby, watching us and listening in on our conversations. As had happened to both Haydar and me, other Devrimovans had become aware that they were being followed by the police only by realizing that the same person was showing up wherever they went. In other cases, police officers openly informed people that they were being followed. One middle-aged shopkeeper I interviewed discovered that he was being tailed by the undercover police when he ran into an officer outside the neighborhood and the policeman told him about his daily routine. A common experience for Devrimovan youths is to be told that they had been followed when they are taken into custody. Such revelations are frequently accompanied by attempts to force them into colluding and working as informants.

As part of efforts to standardize and professionalize the field of police work, the Turkish National Police introduced a system of community-oriented policing in 2006, the same year as amendments to the antiterror law were made.[3] In Devrimova, other dissident neighborhoods, and Northern Kurdistan, where locals view and experience the police as a major security threat, community-oriented policing was a negative development: it translated into forcing increasing numbers of community members to spy on their neighbors. Like undercover police surveillance, collusion is about more than passive information gathering. As a productive tool of counterinsurgency's psychological warfare, it works actively to dispirit activists.

NATO's *Allied Joint Doctrine for Counterinsurgency* states, "Nothing is more demoralizing for insurgents than to realize that people inside their movement or trusted supporters are deserting insurgency or providing information to government authorities" (2011, para. 0324). In the last decade, residents—including children—have been regularly stopped by undercover officers while walking alone in or outside the neighborhood and asked to provide information about the community, even about family members. If they refuse to provide that information, the police issue various types of threats, including putting them behind bars as "terrorists," getting them fired from their jobs, informing their family members of their political activities, and detaining their loved ones. Over the years, many of my interlocutors ended up in prison, lost their jobs, or been beaten up by police officers after refusing collusion.

In *Discipline and Punish*, Michel Foucault (1998) argues that panoptic surveillance derives its power from "soul training." The potentially all-seeing gaze of the undercover police "gains in efficiency in the ability to penetrate into men's [*sic*] behavior," thereby obliging people to police themselves and become the "principal of [their] own subjection" (203). Building on Foucault's approach, studies on undercover police surveillance have emphasized its debilitating effects. In her study of the military regime in Burma, Monique Skidmore (2012, 51) maintains that people's "fear of surveillance, 'of being crushed' . . . culminates in inaction and in alienation for the Burmese." Through an analysis of undercover police surveillance in Syria, John Borneman (2009) demonstrates how the fear it triggers can be used as an effective strategy for suppressing and controlling dissident voices and practices. More recently, Arshas Imitaz Ali (2016, 91) claims in his article about police surveillance of Muslim student activists in New York City that it has driven student activists away from activism and "limited their political subjectivities," thereby limiting "their political identities . . . to simply affirming their humanity and presence in the United States."

Undercover policing's powerful effects also derive from influencing and transforming existing social relations within the community that is under surveillance (Feldman 2015; Verdery 2014). As has been documented in contemporary Palestine (Kelly 2010; Shalhoub-Kevorkian 2015), Cold War–era Guatemala (Green 1999) and Romania (Verdery 2014; 2018), undercover policing and informant activities create an environment of suspicion and uncertainty, triggering feelings of mistrust between and among community members. It is not surprising then that informant activities are described under the subheading "Internal Divisions" in NATO's *Allied Joint Doctrine for Counterinsurgency* (2011, para. 0317). Suspicion of infiltration divides dissident groups from within, leading to stringent in-group vigilance and punitive mechanisms (Marx 1989). Rumors that certain individuals or even revolutionary groups are collaborating with the police are not uncommon in Devrimova. Some I spoke with also believed that some revolutionary groups imposed extremely harsh punitive polices against informant activities. The researcher who introduced me to the neighborhood warned me that some of the Devrimovans I contacted could be undercover police officers or informers, adding that the locals might also harbor suspicions that I was working for the police.

But despite the formidable consequences to life, limb, and freedom that pertain in Devrimova, the panoptic gaze of the undercover police does not always manage to compel residents into a position of compliance and self-policing. Nor has it put an end to relations of solidarity in the neighborhood. Many Devrimovans—and not only the revolutionary youth—publicly refuse to collaborate when asked to work as informants. Some openly and defiantly champion outlawed revolutionary groups that have been officially designated as terrorist organizations. Others—mostly young men—continue to engage in public and publicized performances of rage. How can we understand such fearless public manifestations, which flaunt the very real risk of long-term prison sentences, in a neighborhood under constant undercover police surveillance?

In this chapter, I tackle the threatening presence of undercover police surveillance in Devrimova and the various strategies Devrimovan youths use to negotiate this shadowy, fuzzy presence in the neighborhood. In his later writings, Foucault (1988, 19) critiqued his earlier works for dwelling "too much on the techniques of domination and power" and moved toward an analysis of the productive tension between what he called "techniques of domination" and "technologies of the self." The techniques of domination produce not only docile subjects but also resistance. They also conjure up an aspirational ethical position and inspire the act of ethical self-making, "a process in which the individual . . . decides upon a certain mode of being that will serve as his [sic] moral goal and this requires him to act upon himself, to monitor, test, improve and transform himself" (Foucault 1990, 28).

Foucault's (1988, 257) fascination with the masses' determined resistance to the Shah's regime during the Iranian Revolution and with the "absence of fear" he witnessed in the streets of Tehran when he visited the city after the September massacres of 1978 was influential in sparking his theoretical interest in questions related to ethical self-transformation, political will, and political spirituality (Bargu 2014; Rabinow 2009). In Iran, Foucault (2005 [1978], 201) observed the mobilizing effect of the sacrificial dead, which for him "link[ed] [Iranians] to the permanent obligation of justice."[4] He became intrigued by the relationship between the discourse of martyrdom and the role of political spirituality

(Afary 2003, 17), a force that can inspire "the subject to access truth and to criticize power in order to be governed less" (Diken 2015, 30). Foucault, however, did not put forward a refined theoretical explanation of the place of the dead in how oppression produces resistance and how the martyred dead inspire individuals to undertake ethical self-formation, thereby giving rise to political spirituality. In this chapter, I take my cue from Foucault's sporadic writings on martyrs' calls for a "permanent obligation of justice." To better understand how techniques of domination pave the way for what I call, after Foucault (1997), *the ethical making of the self*—the ethical work of forming oneself into an autonomous ethical subject who feels a permanent obligation to pursue justice—and how ethical aspirations can be translated into an overt and fearless defiance of authority, I argue in this chapter that we should take into account the agentive effect that the (martyred) dead have on the living. To put it differently, I suggest that, to understand the radical refusal of docility in these neighborhoods, we must pay attention to the affective force of past generations on present ones. As I illustrate here, the memory of suffering and resistance housed in the Alevi cultural archive and the functioning of revolutionary martyrs as the archive's contemporary sacrificial material, however noncorporal in their death, are crucial to understanding why Devrimovans insist on being visible in the streets as acting, speaking, and refusing subjects despite grave consequences. Bringing up questions related to ethical self-formation (à la Foucault 1988), such an archive of the past, inspires many Devrimovans to take an oppositional stance against the Turkish security state and helps free them from the immediacy of present fear.

Martyr as Spirit

Avery Gordon's (2008) work on ghostly matters is particularly useful in analyzing the power of the past in the present. Her approach to the ghost as a "social figure" and "an animated force of the oppressed past" (8) and to haunting as an "animated state in which a repressed or unresolved social violence is making itself known" (Gordon 2011, 5) has changed scholars' understanding of state violence, past and present injustices, and the collectively traumatic events of massacres, genocides, racial lynching, and the like. Torn from the world by traumatic forms of oppression and injustice, those who have died return in ghostly form. They stand at the threshold of life and death, both present and absent, there and not there, in the past and in the here and now (8). They continue to seep into the present and interrupt the politics of the day to demand justice and recompense (Gordon 2008): "they wander the world and cannot find rest because they have been mistreated, displaced and left unrecognized" (Frosh 2013, 45). By means of ghostly returns, a past injustice or traumatic event makes a sudden, unsettling, and often uncanny appearance on the stage of the present. But not all the dead who continue to seep through to the present have the same effects. As Sara Salem (2019, 275) argues in her work on the continuing effects of Nasserism in Egypt, haunting may have productive and liberatory effects: "haunting inspires, pushes, nurtures, and cultivates hope." Following Salem's line of thought, I refer to the hauntings of past resistance as *inspirational hauntings*.

A distinction between *ghost* and *spirit* is useful in understanding *inspirational hauntings*: the hauntings of past resistance and of rebellious and defiant subjects who seep into the present and serve as encouraging and emboldening political, ethical, and spiritual resources. Ghosts can be unsettling figures, and a ghostly haunting is a frightening experience that occurs "when things are not in their assigned places, when the cracks and rigging are exposed, when the people who are meant to be invisible show up without any sign of leaving, when disturbed feelings cannot be put away" (Gordon 2008, xvi). In contrast, spirits, as Kwon (2013, 192) argues with reference to Durkheim, can "develop a 'positive cult' through which the living can associate with the memory of the dead in socially constructive and regenerative way." Hauntings by the spirits can be a source of political spirituality. Here, I use the concept of *spirituality* with reference to Foucault (2005 [1978], 15): it is "the search, practice, and experience through which the subject carries out the necessary transformations on himself in order to have access to the truth."

The Turkish word for spirit is *ruh*. But *ruh* has a double meaning of spirit and ghost. As I unpack in the following text, this dual meaning indexes the double condition of revolutionary martyrs: they are both spirits of solidarity and resistance who encourage the dissident targets of state violence to defy their fear and preserve the relations of solidarity and the restless ghosts who continue to disrupt the efforts of the ruling elite, the police, and their allies. Whereas the ghostly presence of the undercover police works to strong-arm Devrimovans into complicity, the haunting memory of the martyrs inspires them to take defiant action. As explained in the introduction, in the left-wing Alevi and Kurdish imaginary two kinds of death can qualify people as martyrs: the loss of life while fighting oppression and the loss of life at the hands of the state or by state-backed violence.[5] Hasan Ocak, whom we saw in chapter 3 and who was disappeared after being taken into police custody soon after the Gazi incidents of 1995, is considered a martyr, as are those who lost their lives during the Gazi incidents. To sidestep the religious connotations of martyrdom and to emphasize the enduring impact of these departed community members on revolutionary activities, in the past few years certain revolutionary circles have begun to call them "immortals" (*ölümsüzler*), in addition to "martyrs of revolution" (*devrim şehitleri*). In the journals of some revolutionary organizations, *ölümsüzler* are referred as those "who are nowhere and everywhere."

Wandering Spirits in Devrimova

The spectral presence of the martyrs of revolution and *ölümsüzler* is inscribed into the space, memory, and sociality in Devrimova and in the other revolutionary neighborhoods. Photos and posters of dead revolutionaries—globally renowned figures such as Vladimir Ilyich Lenin and Che Guevara and local revolutionaries like Mahir Çayan and Hasan Ferit Gedik—gaze unswervingly at Devrimovans from the walls of buildings, cafés, associations, and parks. The images of martyrs depicted on such posters change depending on the historical significance of any given month. In the month of March, for example, posters of people who lost their lives in the "Gazi Massacre of 1995" (the Gazi incidents) appear on the walls of buildings. In July, walls are covered with photos of people who lost their lives in an Islamist arson attack that took place during the Pir Sultan Abdal Festival in Sivas in 1993.[6] Since 2016, photographs began to appear on walls and in public spaces in the month of July depicting the faces of the young people who died in a suicide bombing in Suruç, in Northern Kurdistan (see figure 5.1); the victims were traveling to predominantly Kurdish Kobanê in northern Syria in a show of solidarity for left-wing Kurdish fighters battling the Islamic State and to help rebuild the town.[7]

Gordon (2011) points out that hauntings produce a "temporal disturbance," especially when accompanied by suffering. A haunting "raises specters, and it alters the experience of being in time, the way we separate the past, the present, and the future" (2; see also Pile 2005). During my fieldwork in Devrimova, I often felt that I was immersed in a different temporal space in which the past actively bleeds into the present. Devrimovans old and young enjoy spending time chatting in parks, coffeehouses, association offices, and patisseries and reflecting on current political issues. Discussions about present-day political problems can quickly turn into debates about the roles played by leading revolutionaries and rebels in major historical events, such as the Russian Revolution or the fifteenth-century Sheikh Bedreddin rebellion against Sultan Mehmed I and the Ottoman state. A conversation about the position of Turkish social democrats vis-à-vis the current government in Turkey can soon become a discussion about German Social Democrats' complicity in the rise of fascism in Germany, the fearless struggle of Rosa Luxemburg and Karl Liebknecht, or the role of Turkish and Kurdish revolutionaries in 1970s Turkey. While listening to daily conversations in Devrimova, I was often struck by locals' sweeping knowledge of the history

FIGURE 5.1. Funerals of the young people who were killed in Suruç. The images and flags show the faces of deceased young people and the PKK leader Abdullah Öcalan. Image has been modified to protect the identities of those pictured.

Photo by Sinan Targay.

of the oppressed and the lives of revolutionaries both local and global. Their animated way of speaking about the ideas of revolutionary figures from the past and their confidence in their knowledge gave me the impression that those long-dead revolutionaries were very much alive and that my interlocutors had met them in person or perhaps even had conversations with them.

Highlighting the important role that memory plays in Jewish culture, Walter Benjamin (1969) asserts that the continuous act of remembrance makes the past a living entity in the present, but "not only as a memorial to something lost" (Frosh 2013, 64). It paves the way for the experience of both historical and contemporary events as being "compacted into one present swirl" (Stewart 2017). As discussed in chapter 1, remembering histories of oppression against Alevis and of resistance against that oppression so as to keep them alive in the present is also a central component of Alevi cultural practices. Complementing and enhancing these Alevi memory practices, revolutionary organizations play an important role in remembrance of the past and in keeping the dead alive not only in the collective memory but also in the social realm and in public spaces.[8] Monthly and weekly revolutionary journals distributed in these neighborhoods often include photographs and biographies of local and international revolutionary martyrs, celebrating their struggle and sacrificial devotion to the cause. The writers who contribute to these journals encourage readers to learn about and teach the life stories of revolutionaries, including lesser-known "proletarian heroes" with whom people from the working classes can identify. Some of these writers use pen names based on the names of murdered revolutionaries to keep their stories and struggle alive. For example, one author uses the pen name Missak Manouchian, an Armenian communist and genocide survivor born in the Ottoman Empire who lost his life fighting the Nazi occupation of Paris. Revolutionary organizations regularly organize commemorative events for local revolutionary martyrs and victims of state violence. These commemorations are often held at neighborhood associations or *cemevleri*, the latter indicative of the intertwinement of Alevi and revolutionary practices of remembrance. During these events, the life stories of deceased revolutionaries are narrated by people who knew them personally; they are eulogized for their fearless and devoted fight against oppression and exploitation (*baskı ve sömürü*). In their commemoration speeches, their comrades declare that the martyrs have not died but have gone instead to "the country of the immortals" (*ölümsüzler ülkesi*). Such tributes usually end with one or more of the following promises: "to keep them alive we will enhance the struggle" (*onları yaşatmak için kavgayı yükseltelim*); "following the path of our *ölümsüzler*, we will defeat fascism and colonialism" (*ölümsüzlerimizin izinde faşizmi ve sömürgeciliği yeneceğiz*); or "their memories will be kept alive in our struggle" (*anıları mücadelemizde yaşayacak*).

Yael Navaro-Yashin (2012, 15) argues that the phantomic can be embodied in material space and objects, "linger in a territory," generate an affect, and exert a determining force on politics. In Devrimova, *ölümsüz* martyrs are embodied both in material and social space, disseminate an affective energy, and exert a force on daily political activities. Their affective energy transforms those who learn about their stories into witnesses of their suffering and resistance. As we see, this process of becoming a witness effectively compels them to pursue ethical relationships with others and the world, raising questions about their own ethical self-formation.

Spirits of Resistance and Solidarity

Despite the rumors and suspicions on infiltration and informant activities, the spectral presence of the undercover police has not succeeded in driving all Devrimovans into inaction and seclusion. Many of my interlocutors, including but not limited to those who self-identify as revolutionaries, asserted that "keeping the spirit of resistance and solidarity alive (*direnişin ve dayanışmanın ruhunu canlı tutmak*)" against menacing undercover police surveillance, informant activities, and the antiterror laws has become a pressing matter. For these revolutionaries, defying fear, maintaining a visible presence on the streets, inspiring others to be courageous, and showing solidarity with those who have been singled out by state security forces are all primary means of achieving that goal.

Despite the increasing turn of the AKP government toward nationalist authoritarianism and its attendant suppressive police tactics, there continued to be street demonstrations and public refusals to collaborate with the police, albeit with fewer participants. A decade later, in 2020, such public refusals are ongoing and frequently circulate on social media platforms and in left-wing and pro-Kurdish newspapers. The effect of these refusals is to expose police infiltration schemes to the public. Although hundreds of youths from Devrimova and similar neighborhoods are or have been detained as "terrorists" for their alleged connections to outlawed revolutionary organizations, many still defiantly chant the names of these organizations proudly during neighborhood demonstrations.

I remember vividly how surprised I was in 2011 by the open display of revolutionary fearlessness in the demonstration I witnessed in Devrimova. It was an unusually warm November day, and I was having tea and chocolate cake with Helin, a young Alevi Kurdish textile worker from Devrimova, on her balcony overlooking the main street of the neighborhood. Helin had just returned from the trial of Haydar and his friends. She was complaining about its pace, saying it was "nerve-rackingly slow." Suddenly, chants rising up from the street interrupted our conversation. "Oligarchy, tremble with fear! The DHKP-C [Revolutionary People's Liberation Party Front] is coming," "Long live our party, the MLKP [Marxist-Leninist Communist Party]," "Killer cops will pay," and "Power comes from the barrel of a gun." I was surprised that people were chanting slogans that openly championed outlawed revolutionary organizations. I leaned over the balcony railing to get a better look at the demonstration. Around fifty people were participating. Some were holding red flags. Others carried posters with photographs of revolutionary militants who had been killed, including one young revolutionary who had lost her life while attempting to plant a bomb at a local office of the governing AKP a few months earlier. Utterly bewildered, I murmured, "They aren't even covering their faces." At first Helin did not understand my confusion. Looking perplexed, she said, "No, they aren't." "But," I responded, "there are surveillance cameras and undercover police everywhere. Aren't they afraid that shouting those slogans could be used as evidence that they're members of a revolutionary organization?" Helin replied calmly, "Well they could. If that's what the cops want. But we won't give in to fear, precisely *because* that's what the state wants. We have to inspire courage and defy fear."

For many Devrimovans, fear is a virus that penetrates the mind and body with the aim of subjugating Devrimovans and driving them to cowardice. Helin and many young revolutionaries in Devrimova see fear as an antipolitical weakness that leads to inaction and thus serves only the ends of "the enemy, the state." But this refusal to give in to fear is more than a refusal to relinquish to the state the ability to distribute the psychic roles of the affective self. Refusing to feel fear is also a major ingredient of what I call after Foucault (1994) *the ethical making of the self.* After telling me that defying fear is one of the most important revolutionary tasks, Helin continued in a sympathetic tone, "Of course, those out there [pointing out the demonstrators] are aware of the risks. But whenever I catch myself calculating the risks involved, I remember all those people who fought for and sacrificed their lives for equality, for justice. I remember all those innocent people killed by this state." As she was talking, I found myself turning to look at the building across from Helin's apartment on which were plastered posters with photos of those who lost their lives in the anti-Alevi pogrom that took place during the Pir Sultan Abdal Festival in Sivas in 1993. Helin noticed where I was looking and, pointing at the posters, she continued, "Whenever I feel dispirited, I remember the faces of those people over there, and then I tell myself that I have no right to be demoralized. I have to continue their struggle; we have to keep the spirit of resistance and solidarity alive."

As I illustrate in the rest of this chapter, revolutionaries' insistence on keeping the spirit of resistance and solidarity alive and on displaying fearless determination by being out on the streets as acting and refusing subjects stems not merely from a dogged focus on future-oriented activities designed to inspire courage so that dissent will not wither away. It is also a way to keep the martyrs and the immortals—the spirits and the ghosts—alive in the here and now. By protecting them from the dangers of the present, these revolutionaries enact Walter Benjamin's (1969, 225) warning that "even the dead will not be safe from the enemy if he wins."

Protecting the Dead from the Dangers of the Present

I met three of Haydar's NA friends—Halil, Ulaş, and Orhan—shortly after their pretrial release from prison in 2012. They had been detained together with Haydar after the police operation against the NA. We were at a dinner party organized by their friend Nesrin to celebrate their newfound freedom. When I arrived at Nesrin's apartment, they were already there, cheerfully talking about the beauty of Istanbul. After we met and greeted everyone, Nesrin invited us all to the table. As we had dinner, we continued to talk about Istanbul, gradually shifting the topic to the difficulties of living in such a crowded city. Orhan objected to the direction the conversation was taking: "Having spent four and half years in a high-security cell in isolation, I cannot complain about outdoor spaces." By mentioning his prison cell, he had opened a Pandora's box. Nesrin and I had agreed beforehand not to broach the subject unless Orhan and his friends wanted to talk about it.

In the hours that followed, they told us about their experiences in prison, both the hard times and the moments of absurdity. Aylin, a middle-class Sunni Turkish friend of Nesrin's who lives outside the neighborhood, was also at the dinner party, and she was aghast at the stories she was hearing. At one point, she turned sympathetically toward Orhan, who was sitting next to her, and said, "But, this is terrible. It's such a shame . . ." Orhan cut her off, saying, "Don't pity us. There's nothing to pity." But Aylin wanted to continue offering sympathy. "But poor you," she said. "You went through so much. It's so unfair." Orhan interrupted her. "Have you heard of Uğur Kaymaz, Aylin?" She shook her head. "Uğur Kaymaz was a twelve-year old Kurdish boy who was killed when police shot him thirteen times as he was standing in front of his house with his father." The incident Orhan was referring to happened in Mardin, a town in Northern Kurdistan, in 2004. "Or have you heard about all the revolutionaries who lost their lives in hunger strikes?" Aylin looked at Orhan wide-eyed in astonishment as he said the following:

I believe that wherever you are in this world, if you see someone being persecuted and you don't do anything about it, it means that you've become alienated from yourself. You've become alienated from your sense of humanity. There are terrible things happening in this country, especially in particular parts of these lands. There is a saying: "Not knowing something is ignorance but knowing and not taking action is unethical [ahlaksızlıktır]." This is the price we paid. Those who came before us also paid the price, and those who will come after us will pay it, too.

We all fell silent in the wake of Orhan's philosophical commentary. And soon after the dinner party, Orhan was sentenced to twenty-six years of imprisonment.

Ali, another young Alevi revolutionary from Devrimova who worked as a low-ranking civil servant at the time, eventually broke the silence:

Do you know when I decided to become a revolutionary, Aylin? When Orhan and the others were detained. Until that time, I deliberately stayed away from politics. I wanted to go to university. I wanted to leave this neighborhood and never come back again. But when I saw that they had been imprisoned solely because they had had some tiny argument with some undercover police, two con men who were trying to force people to spy on one another, I questioned my own selfish choices. I realized that if I turned a blind eye to what was happening in the world, if I went on pursuing my own interests, I would come to feel ashamed of myself. There are so many people in this country, in this world, who have sacrificed their lives fighting oppression and exploitation. Orhan and his friends followed their path.

Ali pointed at a photo of Ibrahim Kaypakkaya, founder of the Communist Party of Turkey/Marxist-Leninist (TKP/ML), staring at us from the pages of a revolutionary magazine that was open on the coffee table. Without waiting for a response, he continued on with his pedagogics:

Do you know who that guy in the photo is? He endured the cruelest torture a person can possibly bear, and yet he did not bow down to the state. If there is any hope for humanity in this cruel world, it is thanks to people like him. Our elders always say that not standing against cruelty is the same as being complicit with the oppressors. It is very important to keep that saying in mind. Do you know how cruel this state is? Just recently, they killed thirty-six [PKK] guerrillas in Kazan with chemical weapons.[9] Turkey doesn't even obey the laws of war. Chemical weapons have been banned. We are indebted to all those people who lost their lives at the hands of this fascist state. We have to hold up those noble revolutionaries as models for our own lives. We have to continue their struggle as our own.

Orhan's and Ali's responses to Aylin about their dedication to the revolutionary struggle reflect the burden of being a witness, which is experienced in working-class Alevi spaces. These spaces are haunted by the spirits of revolutionaries, guerrillas, rebels, and victims of state violence—by people whose lives and deaths do not matter in the hegemonic Sunni Turkish national(ist) imaginary. As I illustrate in the next chapter, although some young Alevi revolutionaries hold anti-Kurdish sentiments, many young Devrimovans have an ethical and political sense of solidarity with them and support the anti-colonial Kurdish struggle. Some of Ali's close friends, for instance, later went to Rojava, Western Kurdistan, the predominantly Kurdish region of northern Syria, to support the fight for the Kurdish cause of democratic autonomy. Kurdish martyrs work as a political force that challenges the ethnosectarian divides that are reinforced by provocative counterorganization and the policed "distribution of the sensible" (Rancière 2015).

Although undercover police armed with the powers granted by the antiterror laws are able to force some Devrimovans into docility and complicity, the memory of the suffering of those who were victimized by or who fought against state violence and the feeling of indebtedness raises the question how to respond ethically. And it is this question of ethics that compels those who grew up in an environment surrounded by revolutionary ghosts and spirits to defy their fear. As Chris Moffat (2018, 178), in his article on the afterlife of martyred Indian revolutionary Bhagat Singh, argues, we "should take seriously the force of the dead as entities to whom something is owed, and who might themselves conjure politics, holding the living to account." The roaming spirits of the martyrs' serve to bind history to biography, evoking feelings of indebtedness.[10] This compels many Devrimovans to transcend their fears and instead keep the spirit of resistance and solidarity alive under difficult conditions, sometimes in ways that may even be considered self-destructive.

In the winter of 2012, Ali refused an undercover police pressure campaign to work as an informant and lost his job as a civil servant in the local municipality. Along with friends and comrades who had also been pressured to work as informants, Ali organized a press conference in the neighborhood to publicly refuse the police's bid, thereby exposing them. In their statement, they recounted how immediately after their refusal to collaborate, their parents began receiving phone calls from the police accusing their children of being members of a terrorist organization. The police warned their parents that should their children refuse to collaborate, something Ali and his friends considered dishonorable, they would be imprisoned as terrorists. The press conference ended with a pledge to resist police pressure and a promise to stay on the streets of Devrimova. When I saw Ali for the last time in 2015, he had just been kidnapped and beaten by three undercover policemen. He told me that, even though he could be arrested at any moment, he had no regrets for having joined the struggle against what he called a "colonialist fascist police state" (*sömürgeci faşist polis devleti*). In 2016, some seven months after our conversation, he was arrested. As of 2020, he is still in prison, having been sentenced as a "terrorist convict."

The ruling of Turkey is well aware of the force of the martyrs over the living. NATO's *Allied Joint Doctrine for Counterinsurgency*, which as I wrote earlier was published under the signature of a Turkish major general, states, "Killing insurgents can be counterproductive if these actions cause extensive collateral damage and resentment, generating martyrs and promoting recruitment and revenge" (2011, para. 0353). Turkish counterinsurgency's way of handling this "counterproductive" effect of the killing of activists and racialized Kurds and Alevis is to erase the memory of martyrs by destroying graveyards and other memorial spaces (Aydin 2017). Since the alleged coup attempt of 2016, the Turkish ruling elite has appointed trustees to take the place of elected Kurdish mayors, all of whom were removed by emergency decree. One of the first things the trustee of the Kızıltepe district of Mardin did after assuming power was to remove the statue of Uğur Kaymaz, the martyred Kurdish boy Orhan had referenced. The trustee appointed to the Derik district of Mardin demolished Uğur Kaymaz Park. So, too, the graveyards of PKK guerrillas were routinely destroyed by the Turkish security forces. And as I write these sentences, the police snatched the body of İbrahim Gökçek, a member of the left-wing music band, Grup Yorum who had died after a 323-day hunger strike protesting government persecution and a ban on the group's concerts, while it was on its way to his funeral at a Gazi *cemevi*.[11] The destruction of monuments, memorial spaces, graveyards, and even corpses indexes once again Walter Benjamin's (1969) warning about the dead not being safe from a victorious enemy.

Rage, Revenge, and Masculinity

As we have seen throughout this book thus far, the radical refusal of docility and complicity takes as many forms as do oppression and domination: they include being a member of a revolutionary organization, working in a left-wing trade union, organizing strikes, going to demonstrations, participating in armed action against the state security forces and their alleged allies, fighting drug dealers, refusing to collaborate with the police, and organizing solidarity activities.

When the figure of the revolutionary martyr intersects with working-class masculinities, young men are emboldened to express their rage by being visible on the streets as a threatening presence, an embodiment, even, of the many martyrs envisioned as clamoring for revenge. In the context of growing rage against the oppressive security state and ongoing capitalist exploitation, both of which intersect with patriarchal structures, ethical aspirations can and do easily translate into moralistic stances. As we have seen in the previous chapter, not fighting against the drug dealers and the police can easily be considered a sign of cowardice and moral deprivation. Sexist, patriarchal behaviors can even come to be celebrated as exemplary revolutionary practices.

Studies of masculinity among impoverished male residents of those neighborhoods labeled as "dangerous" note that fear is seen as a sign of weakness and a threat to maleness (Brownlow 2005; Stanko and Hobdell 1993). As Kopano Ratele (2013, 12) observes regarding performances of fearlessness by the marginalized male youth of South Africa, "Powerlessness and performances of fearlessness are [. . .] densely entwined." Such performances operate as a coping strategy used to manage survival risk in violent areas where vulnerability attracts violence. To avoid victimization, these young men learn to become fearless. To secure their place in the public arena, the streets of Devrimova, like those in other marginalized spaces, in effect become "sites of masculinity performance and practice" (Brownlow 2005, 582) where young men can express their rage and turn their masculinity against the police specter that would seal their fates. In Devrimova, the expanded powers of the 2006 antiterror law, the menacing presence of the undercover police, and police informants' activities combine to threaten an already at-risk and materially abject working-class masculinity. It is this combined threat that turns the manifestation of male-gendered counterpower and rage by revolutionaries into a kind of revolutionary political obligation.

Every two months or so, a routine performance is enacted in the neighborhood. Masked male teenagers hold demonstrations in which they pull dumpsters into the streets, creating makeshift barricades, which they set ablaze while chanting revolutionary slogans: "Stand shoulder to shoulder against fascism," "mothers' rage will strangle the murderers," "revolutionary martyrs are immortal," and "killer cops out of Devrimova." Shortly after these barricades are set up, armored police cars arrive and use water cannons to disperse the group. The young men respond by lobbing Molotov cocktails and stones (see figure 5.2). As the armored vehicles move in closer, the group abandons its position behind the burning dumpsters, with a few young men remaining to throw stones at the police.

The first time I witnessed this performance was in December 2010, while having dinner at Nilay's home with her family. Watching from the window above, I became agitated and nervous. In contrast, neither Nilay nor her family members

FIGURE 5.2.   A young man is throwing a Molotov cocktail at the police during a police raid in his neighborhood. The poster behind him reads, "Günay Özarslan Is Immortal. People's Front." Günay Özarslan, a young revolutionary woman, was killed by the police during a house raid on July 23, 2015.

Photo by Sinan Targay.

showed any trace of alarm. For them, it was a routine event. As we headed back to the dinner table, they began to reflect on what had happened.

> Nilay's mother, Servet: See, what revolutionism (*devrimcilik*) looks like today? It has become child's play!
>
> Nilay's father, Rasim: Such an unnecessary demonstration of audacity! It is as though revolutionaries have nothing else to do. [Turning toward me.] Do you appreciate the fact that no one cares about their exploit? Did you notice the old women passing by the container with their shopping bags? They didn't even feel the need to change their pace. If they can't even scare old women, how are they going to scare the police?

Armed with Rasim's cautionary, I learned to pay attention to the passersby on the street during these kinds of barricade actions. He was right: not many seemed scared. In fact, the presence of people gathering at street corners, watching the demonstrators, and occasionally applauding them gave the impression that these demonstrations were taking place on a theater stage.

Even though Devrimovans like those in Nilay's family, middle-aged men and women in particular, viewed these acts as merely demonstrations of bravado, from an anthropological perspective we might argue that such ritualistic performances help marginalized young men manifest power. Through such performances young men can "write themselves on the street" (Koskela 1997, 317), express their anger, and turn their bodies into weapons to counter the relentless presence of the police in the neighborhood. During these ritualistic acts, young men who take over the streets become not only embodiments of fearlessness but also of the *ölümsüz* martyrs.

Chatting and eating sunflower seeds on a hot summer evening in the neighborhood park, Can and Özgür, two unemployed young Devrimovans who engaged regularly in such performances, explained to me why young men continue to make those protests. Can spoke first:

> If you were born in Devrimova, you don't have a bright future ahead of you. As a working-class person, you are exploited. You work for next to nothing, which gets you nowhere in life. As a Kurd or Alevi, you're discriminated against. The entire system is against you. The state is against you. It sees you as an enemy and a terrorist. There's a good chance you'll end up in prison at one point or another. The police in the neighborhood act like an occupying force [*işgal gücü*]. They harass us, the youth, all the time. They force us to work as informants and threaten us. When you go out onto the streets, when you turn garbage dumpsters into barricades, you're saying to the police, "This place belongs to us. Go away." The state wants us to be fearful. We refuse that. We refuse to be intimidated by them. It is our way of saying, "We're here, and we're not afraid of you."

Özgür chimed in immediately:

> That's so true. The neighborhood is full of undercover police. I'm sure there are several of them here today, watching us. They act like they can do anything they want. I know that some people in the neighborhood see that kind of defiance as unnecessary shows of bravado. But what they don't understand is that if we submit there will be even more police in here; they will do whatever they want to do. They are behind the gangs. More police mean more drugs, more crime. If the neighborhood residents [*mahalleli*] can still go out safely in the neighborhood, if we can sit and eat sunflower seeds here, if we can still organize demonstrations and marches in the neighborhood, it is thanks to such barricade actions. Otherwise, it would be under total occupation. You showed us

that French movie [*La Haine*, a movie about the life of racialized working-class youth in a Parisian banlieue].[12] If we [the neighborhood residents] are disorganized, if the police feel safer in our neighborhoods, our neighborhoods will be like that [the banlieues in the movie]. There would be more police harassment, more drugs, more prostitution, and less hope for the future. Just like the neighborhoods of the laborers in Paris. If there's no resistance, there's no future.

Can jumped back into the dialogue with an excitement he did not hide:

That's true. If you look at the history of this neighborhood, there has always been resistance. The revolutionaries fought to their deaths to build these neighborhoods. And some revolutionaries lost their lives building Devrimova. If you don't do anything, if you obey the police, you have no dignity. You are betraying them. To be honest, when I see the police, I see the murderer state. I see the potential murderer. They should know that they are not wanted in here. When you go out to clash with the police, you are telling the police, "Go away, you are not wanted in here." But at the same time, you also keep the struggle of those people who sacrificed their lives for us, for building these neighborhoods for us, alive. I don't know if it will make sense to you, but when I go behind the barricade and clash with the police, I feel like I am doing what those revolutionaries wanted me—us—to do. I feel like you become one with them. It's like I'm taking revenge for all those revolutionaries who were tortured and killed by the state. When I take a stone in my hand to throw at the police, I say, "This stone is coming to you from the revolutionaries you killed." The moment I move my hand to throw it, I say, "This is," let's say, "for Gülay Kavak [a revolutionary who lost her life in 2001 during hunger strikes]. This is for Hasan Ocak." In that moment, I feel like Hasan Ocak comes alive in my body. And it makes me feel stronger, undefeatable. At the end of the day, we are indebted to those who paid the price [*bedel ödemek*]; we're obliged to keep their struggle alive and stand strong against the state's attacks.

Subjects can and do resist, react, and refuse the policed distribution of the sensible through their use of the space (Kennedy 2013; Rose 1993). People's insistence on being present in spaces deemed inappropriate for them—for example, women's presence in the "dangerous" city streets at night (Koskela 1997), elderly people's presence in places associated with youth (Laws 1997)—can challenge the policed distribution of roles. Devrimova's young men's routinized public performances of fearlessness are also acts of refusal to be distributed as weak or intimidated subjects. The menacing undercover police presence in the neighborhoods evokes this subject position's counterpart—a subject who refuses to be afraid, a subject who asserts ownership over the streets and expresses rage in response to the unremitting presence of the police. As Can's words illustrate, the police are also a ghostly reminder of past state crimes as well as the violence yet to come: "When I see the police, I see the murderer state. I see the potential murderer." During these ritualistic street actions, the martyrs who have "paid the price" (bedel ödemiş) are conjured up as restless spirits demanding revenge. Resurrected in the bodies of the revolutionary youth during clashes with the police, martyrs become an invigorating force of street action. In this way, manifesting rage against the state becomes a way of paying back the debt owed to those who sacrificed their lives in the struggle to build a better life for the racialized and dispossessed working classes.

Aware of the above mentioned agentive effects of martyrs, some revolutionary organizations feed the feeling of indebtedness when calling the youth into the streets and into clashes with the police. In their journals, they tell young people to always keep the revolutionary martyrs in their minds. They recount how martyrs fearlessly sacrificed their own lives to put an end to the exploitation of the working classes: "Those who built the *gecekondu* houses in your neighborhoods sacrificed their lives for you"; "those who sacrificed their lives in hunger strikes did so to build a better country." Some of these organizations employ an overtly masculinist language, directing young militants to prove themselves as true and fearless *delikanlı* (tough guys, literally "crazy-blooded") by not shying away from confrontations or clashes with the police.[13] In their journals and social media pages, these organizations also accuse those revolutionary or socialist organizations that do not support confrontations and clashes with the police of cowardice and of not being real revolutionaries. By championing fearlessness as the highest moral value, these organizations exert moralistic pressure on young men, something akin to a form of policing of the proper moral revolutionary order.

As Clara Han (2017, 181) points out, policing is "tightly aligned with the other conditions of life" such as poverty and racism. In marginalized neighborhoods that are under occupation, the panoptic gaze of the police is accompanied by impoverishment, feelings of despair, and various forms of racist violence. These young men live their lives trapped under an oppressive form of rule that threatens the presents and futures of racialized working-class Alevis and Kurds. They survive while being pinned down under the all-pervasive gaze of the undercover police, who attempt to force them into complicity and inaction. The *inspirational hauntings* of those who sacrifice their lives fighting oppression are a source of political spirituality (*à la* Foucault) and encourage others to translate their ethical concerns into undisguised defiant acts. But their aspirations for ethical self-making do not always escape a devolution into self-destructiveness or moralistic pressure that does not go against the grain of the patriarchal distribution of the sensible. Devrimovan youths' refusals to be fearful demonstrate the complexities of the Rancièrian binary of policing/politics: in the places where multiple forms of structural violence convolute, it is impossible to sort them neatly into separate spaces or stances.

As we have seen in this chapter, in one sense, Devrimovans youths' refusal of fear and insistence on being in the streets as defiant subjects are important political acts. These acts work against the grain of the policed assignment of their roles as fearful, docile, and complicit subjects of the Turkish security state. In an environment where undercover policing compels Devrimovans to spy on one another, thereby provoking mistrust and disturbing community relations, public refusals to work as informants serve to keep the spirit of resistance and solidarity alive. But in another sense, such refusals serve the ends of policing in that being on the streets defiantly championing revolutionary organizations, publicly exposing the police's bids to recruit them as informants, and clashing with the police all work as means of informing on oneself. Gary Marx (1974, 405) has demonstrated how one of the primary tasks of informant agents provocateurs who had infiltrated Black Panthers in the United States was to encourage the use of violence by the group. Although it is impossible to know much about the infiltration of *agents provocateurs* in the revolutionary groups of contemporary Istanbul—such knowledge usually is gained only in hindsight when archives and the remorseful testimonies of the agents themselves become available—it is possible to conceptualize the police in the neighborhood as *provocative agents*. The unrelenting police presence in the neighborhood, surveillant and violent, provokes the desire to manifest rage against it. When Devrimovan revolutionary youths' fill the streets to express their rage and display their commitment to the revolutionary cause, the police are easily able to pick out the most devoted among them. The slogans they chant to champion revolutionary organizations and their performative participation in street violence are used as legal evidence in later trials that will put them behind bars as "terrorist" convicts. Such acts contribute to the disappearance of dissident citizens, activities, and voices from the streets and the community. At one level, then, these performances of rage and devotion to the cause serve the ends of counterinsurgency. But as Özgür suggests, at another level, the very same acts also prevent the "total occupation" of the neighborhoods. By making the neighborhood a dangerous place for the police and the drug gangs, they open a space for various forms of dissident activities and voices.

The same is true for the desire for the *ethical making of the self* and the performative manifestations of masculinist rage. Inspired by the haunting histories of resistance and oppression, the desire to form oneself into an autonomous ethical subject in the mold of the fallen *ölümsüz* encourages many to fight for and demand justice, lest those histories be erased from social memory. On the one hand, such aspirations are a major source of political will and, in Foucault's words, "political spirituality" (2005). On the other hand, because the feelings of rage, the desire for revenge, and the loyalty to the memory of suffering and resistance intersect with patriarchal social formations of masculinity, the aspiration to *ethical-making of the self* in certain contexts translates into an act of policing by going with the grain of what has been policed as sensible. Such acts pave the way for moralistic stances that reproduce already existing gendered roles. The practice of a Rancièrian politics as neatly distinct from policing is an impossible task for those who live in racialized working-class spaces within contemporary capitalist security states. As I illustrate in the next chapter, when ordinary emergencies are replaced in such spaces with extraordinary emergencies, figuring out the best political stance and practice becomes even more challenging.

GEZI UPRISINGS

The Long Summer of Solidarity and Resistance,
and the Great Divide

On May 28, 2013, a seemingly unremarkable protest against the demolition of
Istanbul's downtown Gezi Park quickly turned into what would become known
as the Gezi uprising. Begun as a small-scale sit-in to prevent the park's destruction and transformation into a shopping mall, the protest drew several tens of
thousands of Istanbulites from diverse backgrounds—members of the working
class, middle, and upper-middle classes; Armenians, Kurds, Turks, and Alevis;
anticapitalist Muslims, socialists, and LGBTQ activists; and more. Despite the
riot police firing water cannons and tear gas, the protesters were determined to
remain in the park and in the adjoining Taksim Square. They set up makeshift
barricades around the entrances of the square to cordon off a police-free zone.
Functioning as ghostly reminders of past state violence and resistance to it, some of
the barricades were named after deceased revolutionaries—among them the
journalist Metin Göktepe, killed in police custody in 1996, and Mahmut Murat
Ördekci, killed in prison by state security forces during an operation against
hunger strikers in 2000.[1] During a two-week period in June 2013, Gezi Park became the site of the Gezi Commune. Hundreds of people pitched tents in an
Occupy-style symbolic space of uprising, prompting the spread of resistance
across the country. For a short but powerful time, the Gezi Commune created a
sense of joyful and creative rebellious community that transcended ethnosectarian and class divisions. This coming together of seemingly incongruous
groups, including Kurds and Turkish nationalists, football fans and feminists,
generated an "anti-depressant effect" (Gambetti 2014, 89) among those dissatis-
fied with the AKP government. In that atmosphere of resistance and solidarity,

protests erupted in other parts of Istanbul and Turkey as expressions of dissent against the AKP government.[2] In mid-July, the police forcibly drove everyone out of both the park and the square.

The uplifting effects of the Gezi uprising were felt in Devrimova and other Alevi working-class neighborhoods. Soon after the Gezi sit-in expanded into a broader protest, Devrimovans of all generations began traveling to the city center to participate in demonstrations. On the night of June 2, 2013, around a thousand Devrimovans poured onto the streets of the neighborhood, blocking off the nearby highway and walking on foot for several hours to Gezi Park. Accustomed to clashing with the police in their neighborhoods, the youth of Devrimova and other neighborhoods were at the forefront of the uprising at the city center. Guiding middle-class protesters who had no experience in such direct conflict, they taught them how to build barricades, respond to water cannons, mitigate the effects of tear gas, and throw tear gas canisters back at the police. They were major actors in the uprising and came to be respected by the middle-class participants of the Gezi Commune, who had previously known little about them, for their skills in resisting police violence.

This happy alliance was short-lived. Devrimovans and residents of other Alevi neighborhoods would soon find themselves embroiled in an outbreak of police violence closer to home, one that would rock their neighborhoods and force them to take up their own fight. Less than a month after the start of the Gezi uprising, escalating police and gang violence in Devrimova and other working-class Alevi neighborhoods prompted residents to retreat from the central areas of the city where demonstrations were still ongoing and to defend their home turf. Special operations forces sealed off the boundaries of the neighborhoods and, standing next to their armored vehicles, checked identity cards, using intimidation tactics to limit the movement of people in and out. My interlocutors repeatedly juxtaposed the spatialization of events, saying that while the Gezi uprising continued in affluent neighborhoods, working-class neighborhoods were again being turned into occupied Gazas. In an attempt to drive the police and gangs out of their neighborhoods, local youths donned masks and took up arms. Like hedgehogs curling into an armored ball to protect themselves from life-threatening danger, the neighborhoods became impermeable. At the same time, members of the government and pro-government journalists attempted to "Alevize Gezi" (Karakaya-Stump 2014) by claiming that it was Alevis who had instigated the uprising. Echoing racist discourses, they portrayed Alevis both as a belligerent people and as gullible dupes easily manipulated by "foreign forces" (*dış mihraklar*) into rising up against the state.[3] Why was it that the moment the Gezi uprisings began police violence became concentrated so quickly in those neighborhoods? Why was it that Alevis found themselves almost immediately the subject of a heated media debate about the origins of a nationwide uprising?

In this chapter, I provide numerous examples of the ways in which the violence unleashed on Alevi working-class urban spaces and bodies at the height of the nationwide Gezi uprising proved to be effective provocative counterorganization. Police intervention at Gezi focused on *countering* the organization of anti-AKP dissent and partitioning it along ethnosectarian and class lines. Fueled by racist anti-Alevi discourses, the violence unleashed in working-class Alevi spaces and on working-class Alevi bodies ended the uprising's short-lived antidepressant effect by stoking sentiments of fear, insecurity, and mistrust. Similar to the counterinsurgency operation that took place in Gazi in 1995, counterinsurgency interventions in Gezi in 2013 not only strengthened what Nosheen Ali (2010, 739) calls a *sectarian imaginary*, "a normalized mode of seeing and interacting with the sectarian other through feelings of suspicion and resentment."[4] It also increased defensive counterviolence and internal conflict in the neighborhoods. Both operations show the significance of working-class Alevi neighborhoods as "spaces of intervention" (Dikeç 2006) in the ruling elite's attempts to *counter* the existing or emerging forms of alignments within Turkey's left-wing, dissident block.

Back to the Neighborhoods

The escalation of violence in the neighborhoods occurred in parallel with police action to reenter Taksim Square and clear Gezi Park and the commune of protesters. On June 15, 2013, the police successfully retook control of Gezi Park using water cannons and large amounts of tear gas to drive the protesters out of the park and the square. The next morning, I met my friend Nalan, also an academic, in Beşiktaş, a central district near Taksim, to go see what was happening. However, news had spread on Twitter that the police were not letting anyone into the square and were taking people into custody if they tried to get in. While standing in front of an independent bookstore near the stand for the Taksim-Beşiktaş *dolmuş* (a large, shared taxi that carries around ten passengers) and talking about what to do, we ran into three of my young Devrimovan interlocutors, Ahmet, Ercan, and Helin. Like us, they were going to Taksim Square that morning. But when they saw the police taking people into custody in the area, they walked back to Beşiktaş. After a short chat in front of the bookstore, we decided to have breakfast at a café and wait to see what would happen so we would not miss a spontaneous protest if one broke out.

While drinking our tea and eating our *simit* (bread rings) at an outdoor café with small wooden stools and tables, we began to discuss the recent turn of events. It was upsetting, they said, to see that the park—which for two weeks had been home to hundreds of peaceful people and the site of numerous educational events, including yoga classes, sexism and gender workshops, and discussions on social memory and state violence—had been taken over by the police. Yet they were sure that the commune and the demonstrations would not come to an end simply because the police had retaken control of the park. "I'm sure thousands of people will pour into Taksim today," Ercan said. "It *cannot* end like this," he added. Helin continued, "The resistance proved that the AKP has lost its power and legitimacy." Nodding approvingly, Ahmet went further: "Even the bourgeois Turks have been out protesting. After this, it's going to be really hard to drive everyone back into their homes." Ercan chimed in to recount how he had taught some "bourgeois guys" how to throw tear gas canisters back at the police. When we commented on their seeming fearlessness, Ercan responded, "This is a piece of cake. It's not even worth mentioning when compared to the state's attacks in [Northern] Kurdistan and the people's resistance there." With the mention of the brutal forms of state violence in Northern Kurdistan, the atmosphere suddenly grew tense. Nalan broke the silence by saying, "A friend of a friend of mine was filming a documentary about Gezi and this guy came and said to the camera, 'I always thought that the Kurds and the PKK were our enemy, but now I understand that they were actually our friends. Our real enemy is the police.' It's so strange."[5] Ahmet responded right away: "It's not strange at all. It's the truth. People believed what the TV told them, what the state said. Now they come to Taksim, they see the Kurds, they see who is the real friend, and who is the real enemy. That's why this Gezi uprising is so important." Perhaps in an attempt to return some lightness of spirit to the uprising, Helin started joking about the unremitting *halay* (folk dance) that had taken place for several days in Gezi Park beneath a huge post of PKK leader Abdullah Öcalan. This cheered us up. "Kurds and *halay*," Ahmet said wistfully. "No force on earth can keep Kurds from *halay*."

Ahmet then stopped our conversation to answer his phone, and his countenance changed, his optimism gone. He sprang to his feet, muttered a few words, and hung up. "The police attacked Okmeydanı," he said, referring to an Alevi-populated working-class neighborhood where his cousins lived. "Some people may have been killed." Then, turning his gaze to Ercan and Helin, he said, "Come on! We should go! We have to go!" They left in a hurry. They did not ask us if we wanted to go, nor did we think that we could. That phone call separated them from us. It reminded us of the reality: we could peacefully march, resist, and demonstrate together in the city center, but we could not protest together in those neighborhoods. Dissent in those neighborhoods was too dangerous for middle-class solidarity.

That morning, while patrolling the empty streets, a group of armed riot police shot Berkin Elvan, a fifteen-year-old boy, in the head in Okmeydanı. After lying in a coma for 269 days, Berkin died in March 2014. A video later leaked on YouTube shows that the neighborhood was quiet at the time of the shooting.[6] A policeman shot directly at Berkin while he was waiting at a street intersection and was watching the police (Akıncı 2017). In the days to follow, Berkin became a "martyr" of the Gezi resistance, another spirit of resistance whose inspiration would propel his contemporaries and the coming generations into ethical self-formation (Foucault 1990) and resistance against oppression.

After that morning, I didn't see Ahmet, Ercan, or Helin in Taksim again. Like many other young Devrimovans, they spent the rest of the summer and fall going from one neighborhood to the next, trying to defend each area against escalating police and gang violence and participating in meetings, demonstrations, and marches. While the residents of Devrimova and other neighborhoods grew more concerned about the intensifying police and gang violence in their own communities, the middle-class participants of the Gezi uprising went back to their own neighborhoods to establish assemblies in the local parks and organize public discussion forums and workshops throughout the summer and fall of 2013. The demonstrations in the central areas of the city such as Taksim, Beşiktaş, and Kadıköy continued, but with less participation and intensity. The increasing gang and police violence and the defensive counterviolence that it provoked made it difficult for me to be present as a researcher. True to their design, the identity checks and interrogations at the neighborhood entrances—conducted by both the police and various revolutionary groups—were also a barrier. To avoid police attention and violence, I made only infrequent visits to Devrimova and several other neighborhoods throughout the rest of 2013 and again in 2014, 2015 and 2016. I made sure beforehand that no clashes or police raids were ongoing at the time of my visit. My interviews and discussions took place either in houses or outside the neighborhoods.

Intensification of Violence in the Neighborhoods

During that summer of 2013, it was in Okmeydanı and Gülsuyu that gang and police violence became the most intense and attracted the most media attention. Like several other working-class neighborhoods of Istanbul, these two neighborhoods had been targeted by AKP-led neoliberal urban transformation projects. The aim was and it still is to transform them into affluent neighborhoods by moving their current residents out, demolishing existing houses, and building luxury apartment buildings in their place (Karasulu 2016). Throughout the summer and fall of 2013 in the streets of Okmeydanı, there were relentless clashes between the police and masked youth, the vast majority of whom were young male teenagers from the neighborhoods who would throw stones at the police.[7] Residents of Okmeydanı who tried to march peacefully in the streets to protest the police violence often faced tear gas and plastic or real bullets that were fired into the crowd.[8] Routinized security interventions aimed at breaking up the marches deployed large numbers of police, tanks, and helicopters in what the media and government officials termed "antiterror operations" (see figure 6.1).

Whereas in Okmeydanı the problem was one of overwhelming police presence and violence, in Gülsuyu the problem was the police's simultaneous presence and absence. The police were absent when they were needed to provide security against gang attacks, but at the same time and as part of the same process they made themselves present by carrying out several antiterror raids on leftist residents. As in Devrimova, drug dealing in Gülsuyu had become a significant issue by the early 2000s. Despite local residents' attempts to put an end to drug-dealing activities, dealers continued to be active in the neighborhood (İşeri 2014). In the summer of

FIGURE 6.1. Military vehicles in a predominantly Alevi-populated working-class neighborhood of Istanbul on a summer day in 2013.

Photo by Sinan Targay.

2013, with a conspicuous lack of state security forces in the neighborhood to stop them, the dealers became even more violent—targeting pro-Kurdish and revolutionary activists who had taken an active part in the Gezi uprising by perpetrating a series of gang attacks on Gülsuyu's streets.[9]

A brief listing of the gang attacks that took place in Gülsuyu that summer gives an indication of their targets and scope. On July 14, 2013, gang members who had been terrorizing residents for years and who were well known by the residents and the police fired on a group of Kurdish people, among whom were members of the pro-Kurdish Barış ve Demokrasi Partisi (Peace and Democracy Party, BDP).[10] Ten days later, the same gang members shot a young revolutionary in the stomach; he was friends with Devrimova's NA's active members, an active participant in the Gezi uprising and a member of the Sosyalist Gençlik Dernekleri Federasyonu (Socialist Youth Associations Federation, SGDF). This young revolutionary survived the gang attack only to lose his life in the Suruç bombing of July 2015, along with thirty-two other SGDF members who were planning to cross the Turkey–Syria border to help with rebuilding efforts in solidarity with the residents of predominantly Kurdish Kobanê in northern Syria.[11] Less than two weeks later, on August 7, two young revolutionaries who were hanging up posters for Gülsuyu's Art, Life and Culture Festival were shot in the feet by gang members. The same day, these same gang members fired on the office of a socialist party known for its collaboration with the Kurdish liberation movement, wounding three members.[12] Later that day, they fired on the crowd that had gathered to protest the shooting, wounding nine more people. And on September 29, Hasan Ferit Gedik, whom I introduced in the opening vignette of this book, was shot to death by the same gang members while walking in a public march to protest the neighborhood's escalating gang violence.

The dramatic killings brought media attention to the neighborhood. But by detaching the issue from the long-standing problem of drug dealing in the neighborhood and by diverting attention from the targets of the gang violence— pro-Kurdish and Alevi activists who had participated in the Gezi uprising—the mainstream media reduced the issue to an ordinary crime story. In their telling, the "mafia" and "mafia-like revolutionary organizations" played equal roles, much in the same way that Donald Trump would later equate those protesting neo-Nazis with the Nazis themselves.[13] Newspapers ran stories about the event with headlines such as "[Socialist Party] Organization-Drug Dealer War," "Gang Terror," and "The Mafia Is Back in Istanbul."[14] In the following days, tensions between revolutionaries and gang members continued in Gülsuyu, and to a lesser degree in Devrimova and other neighborhoods, giving rise to an increasing feeling of insecurity. Yet for middle-class participants of the Gezi uprising, the developments in Gülsuyu, treated as altogether isolated from those in Gezi, went unnoticed that summer.

As mentioned, the police in Gülsuyu were curiously absent when needed as a security force against the drug gangs; yet immediately following the gang shootings they carried out a series of antiterror raids not on the gangs but on Alevi and Kurdish activists, taking dozens of young revolutionaries into custody. As discussed in chapter 4, the urban poor often complain about police reluctance to provide security in their neighborhoods. Viewed as "undeserving" by the ruling elite in contemporary capitalist societies, racialized populations of the urban poor are often left to police themselves—that is, as long as they remain in their own spaces and do not pose a threat to privileged citizens and their properties. When gang violence increased in the summer of 2013, many of my interlocutors, activists and non-activist neighborhood residents alike, noted the implications of the timing of the gang attacks and police raids. They saw the confluence of events not simply as police reluctance to get involved but as part of a "state project" aimed at creating "disorder" (kargaşa) in the neighborhoods. For many people, the goal of creating this kargaşa was to punish the residents of dissident neighborhoods and keep the locals preoccupied in their own spaces. Jiyan, a young Kurdish woman who worked as a secretary in a small firm and who often visited Gülsuyu to see her cousins there, told me as we sat in her apartment in Devrimova on a hot September day in 2013:

> No one can convince me that there is no connection between the gang attacks in Gülsuyu and the Gezi uprisings. The state knows very well that the main sources of dissent in Turkey are the Alevis and Kurds. They know that if we don't go to Taksim Square, the others will not be able to handle the police's repressive actions. Who fought at the forefront in Gezi? The youths from our neighborhoods. Now, the state is punishing us with gangs in Gülsuyu! They punish us by shooting directly at our people in Okmeydanı! Whether the state or the gangs, they are all the same, they are all together in this! The state wants to keep us preoccupied in these neighborhoods.

Jiyan's analysis of the combined effects of the gang and police violence turned out to be accurate: as the youth of Devrimova and other similar areas became preoccupied with their own struggles in the neighborhoods, the demonstrations in the city center petered out.

Media-Driven Interference

Police and gang violence were not the only causes of insecurity in the neighborhoods. At the time, Alevis were at the center of heated media debates on a possible sectarian conflict overtaking the country. On May 29, 2013, one day after the start of the Gezi uprising, Prime Minister Erdoğan and President Gül made a widely publicized announcement: the new bridge to be built over the Bosporus Strait would be named after Yavuz Sultan Selim, the sixteenth-century Ottoman sultan responsible for the massacre of thousands of Alevis. Reacting to the criticisms of Alevi community leaders, Erdoğan defended his choice by describing Sultan Yavuz as an "excellent warrior" and a "brilliant commander," further emphasizing his violent acts.[15] The effect was to provoke Alevis' historical fears of massacres and to invigorate sectarian tensions.

In the following days and months, members of the government, including Erdoğan and pro-government journalists, attempted to "Alevize Gezi" (Karakaya-Stump 2014) by blaming the Gezi uprising on Alevis, claiming that it was Alevis who had instigated them and that Alevis were being used and provoked by foreigners and "leftist extremists" who wanted to sow chaos in the country.[16] They argued that Alevis would draw the country into a civil war like the one in Turkey's southern neighbor of Syria.[17] Some even argued that the Alevis were getting ready for a major armed rebellion.[18]

As leading counterinsurgency strategist David Kilcullen (2006a) argues, "media-driven political interference" in dissent is key in counterinsurgencies. The task of the counterinsurgent is to come up with an "easily expressed story or explanation that . . . provides a framework for understanding the event" (Kilcullen 2006b, 33). Echoing British counterinsurgency practices in Malaya that "mobilized ethnic cleavages to ensure quashing of unified support for the guerrillas" (Khalili 2012, 178), Kilcullen suggests that counterinsurgents "use nationalist narrative," "ethnic historical myths," and "sectarian creeds" to marginalize insurgents. Providing guidance on how to use those tactics, the *US Army/Marine Corps Counterinsurgency Field Manual* (Petraeus et al. 2010, 32) advises counterinsurgents to learn "how culture, interests, and history inform insurgents [and] to understand links among political, religious, tribal, criminal, and other social networks." The 2006 edition of the manual, introduced to the Turkish public in 2008 as a highly informative guide by the pro-military journalist Mehmet Ali Kışlalı in his newspaper column in *Radikal*,[19] also suggests that counterinsurgents should exploit insurgents' fear of persecution.[20] As we have seen in chapters 2 and 3, in addition to being familiar with the US manual, Turkish counterinsurgent officers also followed the examples of British counterinsurgency practices in Malaya and Belfast (Kışlalı 1996). Within this frame, the anti-Alevi media and official discourses worked hand in hand with the violence directed at Alevi bodies and spaces as affect- and-emotion-generating provocative counterorganization techniques whose aim was to crush any form of unified antigovernment dissent and turn dissident communities against one another.

On the one hand, these discourses and violence communicated to Sunni populations that Alevis were a "threat" (*tehdit*) to the security of the nation. On the other hand, by threatening the security of Alevis, they made it possible for past Alevi massacres to seep into the present and intensify everyday fears and feelings of insecurity. As David Altheide (2006, 18) argues "fear does not just happen; it is socially constructed and managed by political actors to promote their own goals." The Turkish governing elite were able to benefit from inducing historical Alevi fears of massacres precisely because of the context of the nationwide uprising. In effect, they placed the ongoing everyday terror in the neighborhoods into a larger historical frame of violence and fear. This fear was effective in splitting up the unified dissident bloc and paving the way for intercommunal violence.

Sectarian Imaginary 2.0: Resurrecting Alevi Insecurity

As we saw in chapter 3, the provocation of fear by governing elites secures and highlights the boundaries between diverse groups of people, dividing them into "us and them" (Ahmed 2003). Precisely for that reason, the provocation of fear is central to techniques of modern counterinsurgency (Green 1999; Masco 2014). Not unlike what happened during the Gazi events of 1995, an intensifying atmosphere of fear and insecurity after the Gezi uprising became a divisive force that reinforced the sectarian imaginary both within and outside the neighborhoods. That all eight young people who had lost their lives during the Gezi uprising of 2013 were Alevis further strengthened this imaginary.

Many of my Alevi interlocutors perceived the concurrence of police and gang violence and the public government and media focus on Alevis as the punitive message of an anti-Alevi sovereign power. The message to them was clear: Alevis are killable subjects. Doğan, a young Devrimovan who had emphasized in our earlier meetings that he identified above all as a revolutionary, had changed his mind by that winter of 2014:

> These people [pro-government journalists] follow the orders of the AKP. They write what the AKP tells them to write. Some may even sound sympathetic to Alevis. They wrote about the Alevi massacres. They acknowledge the fact that the Sunnis of this country have killed Alevis. Yet the very same journalists who seem to recognize the past violence against Alevis also say that there will be an armed Alevi rebellion. If you read the articles of these people carefully, you understand that their words are all threats. They are actually telling Alevis, "Behave yourself!

There were Alevi massacres in this country before, and there could be more massacres." They tell the Alevis that they are not wanted in this country. They also tell the Sunnis that Alevis are dangerous. This is provocation. They are all provocateurs. They say, "Alevis are arming themselves. Watch out!" For them, murdering us is permissible [*katlimiz vaciptir*]. They believe that if they kill Alevis, they will acquire merit in God's sight. You know, that's how it was in the Ottoman era. They want to bring those days back. Actually, my mom always told us that if the Sunnis had the opportunity, they would kill us all. I always thought that she was exaggerating. But now I see Alevis are the biggest scapegoats in this country. I have always been on the side of the oppressed, but apparently, I did not take the oppression of Alevis seriously.

As in 1995, growing numbers of young revolutionaries who had not previously identified as Alevi began to attend to their Aleviness and to review the annals of historical Alevi suffering. I increasingly began to hear accounts of how Alevis were the most long-suffering group in Turkey. In the years that followed, the targeting of Alevi spaces and bodies by state security forces heightened these sentiments, as when police forces murdered Uğur Kurt in the garden of Okmeydanı *cemevi* where he was attending a funeral in 2014,[21] or when antiterrorism units conducted numerous *cemevi* raids in Alevi neighborhoods in 2015, 2016, and 2018.[22]

To return to Hannah Arendt's insights concerning violent interpellation— "If one is attacked as a Jew, one must defend oneself as a Jew" (Arendt and Gaus 1964)—being attacked and insulted as an Alevi by a sectarian other elicits a defense of one's Aleviness, even in those previously reluctant to identify as Alevi. Being targeted as Alevis reminded those born into Alevi communities that, despite their self-identification, ruling elites considered them first and foremost as Alevis. Labeled as "belligerent," "extremist," and "easily exploited by enemies of the state," they had become killable subjects: Giorgio Agamben's (1988, 53) *homo sacer*, people who can be killed without having committed a crime and "with respect to whom all men act as sovereign." Their murderers would not be found guilty; on the contrary, they would be awarded by the original sovereign—God. In Doğan's words, "For them, murdering us is permissible [*katlimiz vaciptir*]. They believe that if they kill Alevis, they will acquire merit in God's sight. You know, that's how it was in the Ottoman era. They want to bring those days back."

The ghostly reappearance of the Alevi-massacring sultan on the lips of the prime minister was effective not only in bringing the Ottoman fatwas that had ordered the murder of the Alevi communities back into communal memory. It also recalled the historical partnerships that had been forged between the Ottoman ruling elites and Kurdish local elites in suppressing Alevi rebellions (Kieser 2003, 183). In contrast to the mid-1990s, when the PKK was fighting actively against the Turkish state and its military, there were peace negotiations between the PKK and the Turkish state in 2013. That the Kurdish liberation movement had refrained during the fragile peace process from calling on Kurds to participate in the Gezi uprising protests further strengthened the idea of Kurds as the allies of a Sunni state. For many Alevis I spoke with, it was very similar to what happened after Gazi incident, "history engaged through memory" (Green 1999, 65) became a divisive social force that transformed "the Kurd" with whom many working-class Alevis shared common spaces and political organizations into a potential persecutor. This exacerbated already existing conflicts and ethnosectarian cleavages between Alevis and Kurds within and outside the neighborhoods.[23] I often heard people say things like "The state would make peace with anyone but Alevis," and "At the end of the day, the majority of Kurds are Sunnis, and they worked with the Ottoman Empire."

As the ruling elite's provocative counterorganization campaign stirred up sectarian tensions, and memories of Alevi massacres and Sunni Kurd collaboration with the Ottoman ruling elite were invoked, another history bubbled up into the collective memory. The history of Alevi resistance, revolutionary solidarity, and the political struggle to counter provocative counterorganization campaigns conjured up the spirits of those who had worked to challenge ethnosectarian divisions. One spirit in particular, that of Hasan Ocak (see chapter 3), sprang to life. His legend began to surface in the neighborhood, powerfully haunting certain circles, compelling young revolutionaries to bridge the quickly yawning ethnosectarian divides and defy the policed distribution of the sensible (Rancière 2001).

Despite the police and gang violence that had been unleashed in the neighborhoods, in the summer of 2013 residents of Istanbul's Alevi working-class neighborhoods managed to organize public discussion forums in the spirit of the Gezi uprising. On a tranquil August evening in 2013, I attended one of these forums in a neighborhood park in Devrimova named like parks in other such neighborhoods after a deceased revolutionary. Around two hundred men and women of all generations were gathered around a stage located at the park's center, leisurely eating sunflower seeds and listening to the speakers share their ideas about recent developments. As is customary during special events held there, the interior margins of the park were surrounded by several stands belonging to revolutionary groups and adorned with the posters of deceased revolutionaries.

While I was entering the park with Helin, we ran into Orhan, one of the incarcerated NA members featured in the previous two chapters who was at the time on pretrial release. He was waiting for his turn to give a short talk. Normally a serene person, Orhan looked nervous. "Things are getting very serious," he said. "The state wants to stir up tensions between Alevis and Kurds. We have to do something to stop them. Otherwise, things will become difficult in the neighborhoods." Helin nodded apprehensively. "To make matters worse, some revolutionary organizations cannot see this. How can they not see the state's games?" Orhan responded right away. "Don't be so naïve Helin, *arkadaş* [friend]. What else do you expect from the state's revolutionary organization?" He was implying that some revolutionary organizations were being sponsored by the state. As I have noted before, this is not an uncommon view among certain neighborhood circles. At that moment, Orhan was called to the stage. He ran to the front, took the microphone, and after greeting those gathered with a confident tone, he began his short speech:

> Comrades, with the Gezi uprising, the government realized that it was losing legitimacy. Now, to distract us, the state wants us to turn against one another. We, the poor laborers [*yoksul emekçiler*], the Alevis laborers [*Alevi emekçiler*], the Kurdish laborers [*Kürt emekçiler*], know better than anyone else the tricks of this state. Today, perhaps more than ever, we must remember Hasan Ocak. We must remember his legacy. We must remember what the state wanted to do in Gazi in 1995. The state wanted to provoke Alevi–Sunni conflict. Comrade Hasan quickly identified the provocateurs and spoiled their game. Remember what those provocateurs were trying to do. They were calling people to march to the mosque. What did Comrade Hasan do? He led people to the police station to show them that our problem is not with the people [*halklar*] but with fascist state terror. Comrades, we shall never forget that our sole enemy is this fascist colonial state [faşist sömürgeci devlet] and its capitalist order. Let's not be manipulated by the state. The state wins by making us enemies of one another. We must remember those who sacrificed their lives for the brotherhood of the people [*halkların kardeşliği*]. We must remember the martyrs of the revolution. We must remember Hasan Ocak. Today, we must all be Hasan Ocak!

Orhan's talk ended with loud applause, though I noticed that certain anti-Kurdish groups did not applaud him. That summer, without knowing that he would soon be sentenced to twenty-six years' imprisonment, Orhan and his comrades from the NA devoted themselves to reminding everyone about Hasan Ocak's struggle against the state's provocative counterorganization attempts to trigger ethnosectarian tensions among Alevis and Sunnis in Gazi. But for certain revolutionary groups, as well as for some Turkish Alevi residents, Kurds were, first and foremost, Sunnis and therefore could not be an ally to Alevis.

Counterviolence and a Moral Dilemma

As we saw in previous chapters, the fear provoked by state security forces is not always debilitating. The memory of past resistance and suffering may encourage those familiar with these revolutionary life and death narratives to confront their fears and engage in defiant action. In the context of the fear of massacres provoked by state-initiated or state-backed violence against historically persecuted communities, fear may also give rise to "countering fear by the right of self-defense" (Yassin 2010, 7). As Chrissie Steenkamp (2005, 264), drawing on the case of state violence in Northern Ireland, puts it "People's fear of victimization . . . can lead them to use violence to restore order and security." Such fear and the various forms of desire it gives rise to—the desire for self-defense, security, control—are productive forces that intervene in local space and inform the manner and forms of dissent.

In the summer of 2013 and in subsequent months and years, my interlocutors from the neighborhoods became preoccupied with the question of defensive counterviolence or, as they put it, "revolutionary violence." Families, friends, comrades, and revolutionary groups divided into two camps: those who believed that counterviolence would do more harm than good and those who believed that nothing else would work. But because the issue was complex, it was not easy to advocate wholeheartedly one position over the other. New developments and the scale of the violence wielded by police, gangs, and revolutionaries led to confusion, forcing people to change positions frequently.

When the shootings began in Gülsuyu in mid-July 2013, Tarık, a Devrimovan university student and construction worker in his early twenties who had friends in Gülsuyu, visited there frequently in the spirit of solidarity. Sitting in a café in Kadıköy (a central Istanbul district) at the height of the gang violence, he shared with me his concerns about what he and his friends called revolutionary violence:

> Using revolutionary violence is not right at this point. There's a massive mobilization going on throughout the country. If we use violence, we'll lose legitimacy. The state would use it against us. The state would circulate pictures of armed revolutionaries in the media and say that revolutionaries and Alevis are using arms. You know how Devrimovans blame the revolutionaries for bringing violence into the neighborhood. In a way they're right. We've done a great job in the neighborhoods. We came together and marched all the way to Gezi. Gezi brought people together. Revolutionary organizations that had had problems with one another managed to come together. We have to be sensitive,

and we should try our best to keep these people united. We can't win this battle unless the Kurds, Alevis, revolutionaries, Turks, working classes, and all of the oppressed groups come together. We should try our best to keep together and stay united. That's the primary task of us, the revolutionaries. The only way to push the police and gangs out of the neighborhood is to fill the streets with people. Then the state and the gangs would not do anything against us.

Within a few weeks of our conversation, on August 7, both Tarık and I saw firsthand that the gangs were willing to shoot at people who were peacefully marching in the street. They wounded nine people. That night, a number of masked men who called themselves the revolutionary militia went into the streets of Gülsuyu with long-barreled guns and fought the gang members. I wanted to hear Tarık's analysis of these events but was unable to meet up with him again. Along with the houses of several other young revolutionaries from Devrimova, Gülsuyu, and other Alevi neighborhoods, his house was raided by special operations forces a couple of days after the shootings. He was sent to a high-security prison as a terrorist suspect. Threatened with more than fifty years of imprisonment and held in pretrial detention for two years, he was finally granted pretrial release in 2015, whereupon he left Turkey.

In 2015, Kurdish forces in Rojava in Western Kurdistan, a predominantly Kurdish region in northern Syria, began to attract international attention for their fight against the Islamic State and for their attempts to build a democratic confederalism there. I heard from Tarik's friends that, as soon as he was released from prison, he went to Rojava to join the ranks of the socialist and anarchist International Freedom Battalion and to contribute to the people's struggle there.[24] As I write these sentences, I have heard no more news about Tarık's life in Rojava. But many of his friends who went there in those years, including a young woman who had been shot at by the drug gangs during the march in Gülsuyu in the summer of 2013, lost their lives. Although their stories did not attract public or media attention and for the most part remain unknown, their faces continue to appear on the neighborhood walls, their stories are printed and reprinted in the revolutionary journals that circulate in the neighborhoods, and they are regularly commemorated during the second week of May, which since 2017 has been celebrated by some revolutionary groups as the week of the immortals (*ölümsüzler haftası*). Despite their invisibility in mainstream Turkish circles, they, too, have been reanimated as spirits urging their contemporaries to keep the spirit of resistance and solidarity alive.

In the summer of 2013, the ongoing police violence, the antiterror operations against young revolutionaries, the house raids and arrests, and the reluctance of the police to prevent gang violence increased the feeling of insecurity in the neighborhoods and made otherwise nonviolent activists more sympathetic to the idea of armed self-defense. A month after Tarık's arrest I talked to one of his friends, Erhan, a schoolteacher whom I also knew from the neighborhood. When I had spoken with him in July 2013, Erhan, like Tarık, opposed revolutionary violence. But, six months after his friends' arrest and while waiting for the punishment he knew must also be awaiting him, Erhan was working from a different logic:

> At this point, maybe revolutionary violence is inevitable. Maybe we were wrong. We're in a new phase now. To be honest, we didn't understand how fascist this state had become. We thought that they wouldn't go this far with a large-scale uprising in the country. Right now, the state doesn't leave us with any choice. I know that violence begets more violence. But how do we defend the neighborhoods now? How do we defend the people? If there were to be a Gazi-like massacre, how would we look them in the face? We have to prepare for the worst. People in the neighborhoods are afraid. And they have every right to feel that way. These people have witnessed massacres. These people saw what happened in Gazi, Sivas, Maraş . . . Those who came from Kurdistan suffered the most brutal forms of state violence there in the 1990s. You cannot offer a guarantee to anyone that there will be no more events like what happened in Gazi in 1995 or Cizre in 1992.[25] You can't tell the people to not be afraid if you are not going to do anything to protect them. Every day there are new debates on TV about Alevis. People listen to these debates and they get scared. And then there are the gangs. Since they have the state on their side, the gangs have no fear. The state attacks on one front, the gangs attack on another. And then there are these so-called revolutionaries, who rely on fourteen-year-old, fifteen-year-old kids. They go out with guns. Someone has to control them, too. They're as dangerous as the police and gangs. If you let those guys out onto the streets alone, then things will get even more dangerous. This is the irony: you need to take up arms to prevent the armed violence and attacks coming from so many different fronts.

The moral dilemma Erhan articulated so succinctly pervaded the neighborhoods during and after the summer of 2013. During my visits, discussions about the violence affecting family members, friends, and comrades seemed to reach no conclusion. The dominant feeling was that there was no solution. Disagreements and mutual distrust between revolutionary groups, suspicion about police infiltration and provocation, and the reluctance of some groups to collaborate with others, especially with the Kurds and their revolutionary Alevi allies, made many people worry about the use of defensive violence: "Once guns become part of the picture, people may turn against one another. That's exactly what the state wants us to do; turn against one another." Aware of the nationalist and anti-Kurdish tendencies of some revolutionary groups and having suffered violence from them in the past, Kurds were especially worried about revolutionary violence in the neighborhoods. The Kurdish youth in neighborhoods like Devrimova, where the Kurdish population is small, were particularly worried that they could easily become targets.

Residents repeatedly lamented the fact that the most respected and community-minded of the young revolutionary cadres, those who had worked to heal ethnosectarian divisions and mediate conflicts, were the ones targeted by the antiterror laws. NA members of the early 2000s, including Orhan and his friends, and later Tarık and his friends were imprisoned on charges of terrorism or had to leave the country to avoid long prison sentences. As operations against the most community-oriented revolutionaries escalated, the question arose: If self-defense had become necessary, who would organize the people to prevent counterviolence from spinning out of control? Despite the need for self-defense, counterviolence had not been effective in reducing anxieties. On the contrary, it had increased them.

"Speech Has Lost Its Capacity for Action"

While these debates about counterviolence were taking place in the neighborhoods, a new poster began to appear on the walls of the neighborhoods. Issued by an outlawed revolutionary organization, it read, "Our people (halkımız), hand over your arms to us." One of the posters had graffiti written across it: "Speech has lost its capacity for action, now is the time for weapons to act" (Söz eylemini yitirdi, silahın eylemidir şimdi). At the same time, more and more masked and armed revolutionary youth began to appear in the neighborhoods, patrolling the streets (see figure 6.2). As many of my interlocutors predicted, the existing ethnosectarian tensions within the neighborhoods burgeoned into outright conflict between pro-Kurdish groups, their revolutionary Alevi allies, and anti-Kurdish revolutionary groups. Reminiscent of the logic of the Nixon doctrine formulated toward the end of the Cold War—"Asian boys must fight Asian wars" (Mamdani 2002)—in the months following the large-scale Gezi uprising that reverberated powerfully across the country and in which they had taken an active role for a short time, the working-class Alevi and Kurdish youth of Istanbul's dissident neighborhoods now found themselves fighting against one another.

FIGURE 6.2.   A revolutionary militant.

Photo by Sinan Targay.

The solidarity of people during the Gezi uprising, their unity in action and speech at the protest's peaceful outset, represented a threat to AKP rule. By selectively targeting Alevi spaces and bodies, the government sought to reaffirm its power through violence. Colonizing the space for politics, for action, and for speech, state violence facilitated its mimetic twin—counterviolence—and to feel powerful, some revolutionary youth groups once again opted to become mimetic rivals of the state by adopting violence. Such mimetic actions allowed no space for dissensus, "a dissociation introduced into the correspondence between ways of being and ways of doing, seeing, and speaking" (Rancière 2010, 15). In many ways they actually contributed to the police distribution of the sensible and the state's attempts at provocative counterorganization.

As we saw in chapters 4 and 5, engaging in armed and masked extralegal security activities was particularly attractive for those young male teenagers who were also the main targets of police and gang violence. Such activities were a way to cope with the very real threats to themselves and their future and gave them a sense of having salvaged their agentive dignity in an environment where state security forces constantly threatened their bodies and agency.

Unlike the mid- and late-1990s, when the counterviolence by and large targeted the people, places, and things that were associated or allegedly associated with the state, this time violence in the neighborhoods also had an intercommunal dimension. The exacerbated ethnosectarian cleavages over the years, the availability of guns, and the experience of armed vigilantism paved the way for armed conflicts within the neighborhoods. As Orhan and many other of my interlocutors predicted, the existing ethnosectarian tensions burgeoned into outright conflict between pro-Kurdish groups, their revolutionary Alevi allies, and anti-Kurdish revolutionary groups. Focusing their defensive action on the Kurds, some groups worked to prevent Kurdish political activities from taking place in the neighborhoods. On July 29, 2014, for instance, a group of young revolutionaries in the Nurtepe neighborhood tried to remove a presidential election campaign stand that had been set up by the pro-Kurdish umbrella party, the Halkın Demokrasi Partisi (People's Democracy Party, HDP). Clashes occurred between the two groups, and then the conflict spread to other neighborhoods. Such clashes continue to occur sporadically in the neighborhoods. Both the violence of these anti-Kurdish revolutionary groups against Kurds and their revolutionary Alevi allies and the counterviolence it generates mimetically reproduce government efforts to police dissent.

Built on the logic of the low-intensity conflict doctrine, provocative counterorganization enables ruling elites to intervene in the organization of political dissent in such a way as to both counter existing alignments among dissident populations and prevent those that are emergent. They do so by provoking conflict among actually and potentially rebellious populations. Despite certain revolutionary youths' efforts to prevent such intercommunal conflict, the feelings of insecurity that cluster around the resultant "sectarian imaginary" have become so powerful that some segments of the revolutionary groups acted on those feelings. By reifying and accentuating the differences between the Alevi and

Kurdish working classes and by targeting Kurds and those revolutionary Alevi groups who have worked together with them, these anti-Kurdish groups became mediators of government efforts to police dissent and divide dissident forces during a large-scale uprising. Once again distributing security as the main concern, the escalating violence in the neighborhoods kept residents and revolutionary youths busy with intercommunal conflict and matters of security. The confinement of the violence to the neighborhoods served to reaffirm the roles these neighborhoods played in the police distribution of the sensible (Rancière 2001) as places of "terror" and "the unruly," thereby marginalizing Alevis and Kurds in the eyes of the wider public as "violence-prone" sectarian subjects.

For the middle-class liberals of the Gezi uprising, the Alevis became the population that had been duped by "radical, extremist" organizations. The street fights between Kurdish and Turkish Alevi youth sparked heated debates within middle-class leftist circles about the Kurdish movement's position on religion. Some suggested that it was a Sunni-dominated movement and not a secular movement. Others alleged that Alevis were "imprisoned" in their sectarian identity, which amounted to little more than a non-class-based identity politics. Together, these events and processes were effective in rapidly partitioning the millions who had risen up against the government in the Gezi uprisings.

EPILOGUE

Policing as the Generation of (Dis)Order

In 2014, the Italian political philosopher Giorgio Agamben argued that in the era of the "war on terror," the police are no longer concerned with providing order.[1] Instead, the police now manage disorder. But given what I observed in the predominantly Alevi working-class neighborhoods of Istanbul, this important point does not go far enough. I argue throughout this book that, in its war on politics, policing is also concerned with generating disorder. Generating disorder through what I call *provocative counterorganization* enables ruling elites to intervene in the organization of dissent in a way that counters existing assemblages and alignments among actual or potentially dissident populations and is not unique to the age of the global "war on terror." Police attempts to maintain capitalist, racist, colonial, patriarchal, nation-state order by generating and managing disorder is in fact an enduring legacy of Cold War counterinsurgency doctrine of low-intensity conflict, itself informed by the colonial school of warfare.

Both counterinsurgency and politics have as their goal the transformation of populations. But if politics aims to work against the grain of policing so as to open up new spaces, roles, and relations via practices of world-building, the aim of counterinsurgency, as policing, in national security states is to reproduce populations both as compliant and as ready to be mobilized against a real or imagined enemy. Counterinsurgency therefore is both a project of docility (Foucault 2012) and of animosity (Schmitt 2007). To achieve its goal, counterinsurgency focuses on the separation of populations and their distribution into separate spheres (Rancière 1999, 2001). By encouraging and fostering ethnoreligious and ethnosectarian cleavages and racialized animosities, counterinsurgency promotes the rigidification of boundaries between various groups. To this end, it not only stigmatizes dissident groups as security threats in the eyes of the wider public. By actively encouraging violence among dissident groups and opening fissures between groups and their bases of supporters, it also makes possible their transformation into actual security threats to their constituency. As the stories in this book illustrate, Turkish state policing of dissident working-class Alevi populations has involved each of these techniques in service of a logic of counterinsurgency as provocative counterorganization with the ultimate aim of a bottom-up destruction of the political.

Since the mid-1990s, various overt and covert policing instruments of counterinsurgency have been applied in the neighborhoods: theatrical forms of state violence, inflammatory police presence, devastating police absence as a security provider, ethnosectarian triggering, counterviolent provocation, coercive turning of dissidents into police informants, and selective targeting of the most respected and community-minded revolutionaries by antiterror laws. All the while, such techniques have managed to contain revolutionary violence and energy in the neighborhoods. Yet, although these techniques were effective in partitioning left-wing dissent in Turkey along ethnosectarian and class lines, they were not enough to fully cut the ties between the revolutionaries and their popular base. Nor were they even fully effective in driving a wedge between the Kurdish liberation movement and the revolutionary Left. In 2015, only two years after the suppression of the Gezi uprising, the pro-Kurdish People's Democracy Party (Halkın Demokrasi Partisi, HDP), cochaired by Figen Yüksekdağ, the former chair of the Socialist Party of the Oppressed (Ezilenlerin Sosyalist Partisi), and Selahattin Demirtaş, a Kurdish politician and human rights activist, received 13.12 percent of the vote, six million in total, thereby passing the 10 percent electoral threshold for representation in parliament and gaining 80 seats in the 600-seat Turkish National Assembly. Along with many other members of the People's Democracy Party, including elected mayors and members of parliament, both Yüksekdağ and Demirtaş are now in prison for allegedly distributing "terrorist propaganda." Despite decades-long state violence and counterinsurgent policing, the Turkish ruling elite has never successfully managed to snuff out the spirit of left-wing dissent in Turkey.

As elaborated on in chapter 5, there is one major political force that resists all manner of counterinsurgency techniques and inspires many into ethical self-formation and defiant action. That is the force of the revolutionaries and rebels who sacrificed their lives while fighting oppression and those who lost their lives at the hands of the state or state-backed violence; in other words, the memory of the resistance and suffering. The weakness of state violence, whether overt or covert, is its tendency to generate backlash in two temporally contiguous forms:

feelings of absolute injustice in the here and now are transformed into an actionable rage that draws on the resurrection of past oppressed generations as a powerful force of inspiration. As long as the violence of the security states continues, the inspirational hauntings of those buried on the margins of history will continue to bubble up into the present to feed the spirit of resistance and encourage political action.

In contrast to counterinsurgency, politics requires a very different kind of transformation of the population. Political action entails challenging the policed fostering of separations, animosities, and rigid boundaries between groups, most specifically among the oppressed populations, whose togetherness has the potential to transform the established order. Politics disassociates populations (Rancière 2010) from their predetermined social roles and transforms these roles and their spaces, all the while liberating and transforming them. Making contentious the givens of participation, politics allows previously unheard voices to be heard and the invisible to become visible; it allows those rendered invisible and unheard to enter the sensible. It makes them actors on the world-historical stage. If by spreading feelings of insecurity in the name of security, counterinsurgency, as policing, invite (or strong-arm) populations to seek shelter in the familiar and identify with their predetermined roles and social identities, then politics demystifies the familiar and reformulates social identities and roles.

In negotiating the policing effects of the Turkish state's counterinsurgency apparatus that intervenes in and predetermines the distribution of roles and types of participation à la Rancière, certain segments of Turkey's racialized Alevi and Kurdish populations continue to make contentious the givens of their situation. Refusing to assent to their ascribed roles and identities and the distribution of the population within rigidly contained boundaries, they dare to replace the question of security with a demand for justice, equality, and heterogeneous coexistence.

The persistent insecurity in these neighborhoods, more or less constant over the past sixty years since their establishment, produces a complementary desire for security and a need for vigilance over the sources of insecurity. In practical terms, each person is driven to seek safety in the familiar—in longtime friends and allies and within family and ethnosectarian networks. But such long-term insecurity also drives people to find malice in others outside the familiar, in those belonging to other friendships and alliances, other familial and ethnosectarian networks. Even if the vast majority of Devrimovans agree—logically, amicably— that the main source of insecurity in the neighborhood is the state security apparatus, the affective force of their fears can still have the effect of projecting the source of insecurity onto those fellow residents in their everyday relations who are outside their personal networks. Fueled by historical fears of persecution, these sentiments of animosity toward sectarianized ethnic others allow some—including some segments of the revolutionary youth—to contribute to the separationist police order.

In this book, I have defined counterinsurgency not solely as a project of pacification but also as a productive and permanent war on politics. If politics works against the grain of the established order to open up new possibilities and spaces, then counterinsurgeny wages a preventive and provocative war on such openings and possibilities. The paradox is that counterinsurgency is dependent on political struggle. Indeed, the presence of counterinsurgency in an area is the very proof of the existence of political struggle there. But counterinsurgency is also productive of political struggle precisely because its dirty techniques exacerbate the injustices already present in society. As long as the root causes of dissent exist—domination, exploitation, inequality, injustice—so will counterinsurgency and its antithesis in politics.

Although counterinsurgency cannot end dissent and rebellions altogether, it is successful in making the world a more malign place. It creates its own monsters. The global "dirty war" of counterinsurgency waged in the name of security has made the world a more insecure place, most especially for oppressed populations whose living spaces have been transformed into places of permanent conflict, crime, and violence. In this highly securitized context of the global present, it is only by seeing counterinsurgency for what it is—a provocative counterorganizational police war on politics—that we may be able to more fully grasp the workings of civilian and nonstate-actor violence enacted in such spaces.

Notes

PREFACE

1. The Kurds' homeland, Kurdistan, is partitioned between four nation-states. Northern Kurdistan (*Bakur*) is in southeastern Turkey, Southern Kurdistan (*Bashur*) is in northern Iraq, Eastern Kurdistan (*Rojhelat/Rojhilat*) is in northwestern Iran, and Western Kurdistan (*Rojava)* is in northeastern Syria (Gardi 2017). I refer in this book to Kurdish southeastern Turkey as Northern Kurdistan, as the Indigenous population of Kurds themselves do.

INTRODUCTION

1. On May 28, 2013, a small, mostly middle- and upper-middle-class protest against the demolition of Istanbul's downtown Gezi Park quickly and spontaneously turned into what would later become known as the Gezi uprising.

2. Although Alevis (then named as Kizilbash) were persecuted during the Ottoman era, as Hamid Bozarslan (2003) notes it is ahistorical to talk of a *longue durée* as there have been discontinuities in the Ottoman history.

3. In this book, following Steve Garner and Saher Selod (2015, 12), I approach racialization as a process that "entails ascribing sets of characteristics viewed as inherent to members of a group because of their physical or cultural traits." The effects of racialization include "name-calling, blaming, demonization and other forms of stigmatization;" "discrimination, segregation, eviction and other forms of exclusion from the society of the racial dominants;" "harassment, persecution, prosecution, incarceration and other forms of punishment, including the ultimate one: lynching." (Gans 2017, 346).

4. See also Yilmaz 2020.

5. Drawing on the case of Belfast, Allen Feldman (1991, 85) defines endocolonization as "the occupation and infestation of insurgent and delinquent communities by systems of surveillance, spatial immobilization, and periodic subtraction of subjects from homes and communities."

6. It is impossible to determine the exact size of the population of Istanbul's predominantly Alevi-populated working-class neighborhoods. In the early 1990s, many of them were divided into three or four different administrative units and were officially incorporated into other neighborhoods. To estimate the population of Devrimova, I consulted neighborhood *muhtars* (administrative heads) in the four neighborhoods into which segments of Devrimova had been absorbed, thus arriving at the approximate number of residents in the area formerly known as Devrimova. Most Devrimovan residents do not use the official names of the new neighborhoods but prefer instead to call the neighborhood by its original name. Devrimova literally means "revolution plain." I chose this pseudonym to emphasize that the neighborhood is known as Istanbul's one of several revolutionary neighborhoods. All persons and organizations in this study have been pseudonymized. In the first four chapters of the book concerning the 1970s through the 1990s, I disclose the names of revolutionary organizations active in the neighborhoods. However, in the ethnographic chapters covering events closer to the present day, I do not reveal the names of organizations, except in a few publicly known incidents. None of the photos and video recordings cited in the book are from Devrimova.

7. For police and gang violence and insecurity at the urban margins and the "punitive management of poverty" (Wacquant 2009), see Auyero et al. 2015; Comaroff and Comaroff 2016; Fassin 2013; Gledhill 2015; Ralph 2014, 2020; Rios 2011; LeBrón 2019; Samett 2019; Silverstein and Tetreault 2005; and Willis 2015.

8. The PKK was established in 1978 as an anticolonial, Marxist-Leninist guerrilla organization. Its initial aim was to build an independent socialist Kurdistan. In 2005, the PKK adopted the view of autonomous radical democracy and redefined its aim as the establishment of democratic confederalism and autonomy (Öcalan 2017).

9. On current security strategies for producing docility and their links to Cold War counterinsurgencies and colonial warfare, see Harcourt 2018; Kelly 2010; Kelly, Jauregui, Mitchell, Walton 2010; Khalili 2012; Masco 2014; and Neocleous 2011.

10. For an analysis of how colonial warfare techniques and Cold War counterinsurgencies travel across time and space, see Harcourt 2018; Khalili 2012; Masco 2014; Schrader 2019; and Tullis 1999.

11. A stay-behind covert intelligence and armed operations network established to counter the "communist threat" in several NATO member states and destroy left-wing dissent.

12. Cihangir Akhsit.

13. As Martha Huggins explains, "The most ambitious efforts by the U.S. military to reorganize foreign police were carried out in occupied Germany and Japan and the reoccupied Philippines; and in Greece and Turkey, where Truman's Greek and Turkish program provided funding for the training of police" (1987, 157).

14. Persecution of Alevis dates back to the sixteenth century. Alevis were then known as Kizilbash (Karakaya-Stump 2018).

15. For Sunni supremacism in Turkey, see Akyildiz, forthcoming.

16. Since the establishment of the Republic of Turkey, there have been several waves of massacres against Kurds in various parts of Northern Kurdistan (see Bozarslan 2008; Van Bruinessen 1994a). Violence against Kurds still continues. One of the cruelest acts of violence against Kurdish Alevis is known as Dersim Genocide (Deniz 2020), took place in the Dersim region of Northern Kurdistan in 1938. Around 13,000 people from Dersim lost their lives in the air bombings, and an additional 3,470 people were deported to western provinces of Turkey (Van Bruinessen 1994b, 2). Throughout the 1960s and 1970s, small towns and cities such as Malatya, Corum, Sivas, Tokat, and Maras witnessed a series of anti-Alevi pogroms organized by Islamists and nationalists. The anti-Alevi pogroms continued in the 1990s (Massicard 2013). Remaining non-Muslim populations were forced to leave the country by various means (Bali 2008). There were anti-Jewish pogroms in June and July 1934 and anti-Christian and anti-Jewish pogroms on September 6–7, 1955. About 1.5 million Greek citizens of Turkey were forced to leave the country in 1923 during compulsory population exchanges between Greece and Turkey (Hirschon 2003). On November 12, 1942, the Turkish legislature passed the Capital Tax Law, which mandated the formation of committees to determine the amount of taxes that the country's citizens would be obliged to pay. The rate at which non-Muslim professionals, merchants, and industrialists were to be taxed was set at four times that of their Muslim counterparts. In the event that they were unable to pay the full amounts assessed, they would be legally obligated to work off their outstanding debt through physical labor. This consequently led to the massive emigration of the remaining non-Muslim citizens of Turkey from the country (Ahmad 1993).

17. Like the Alevis, Kurds also make up approximately 20 percent of the population in Turkey (Koc et al. 2008). In 1965, the percentage of the non-Muslim population in Turkey was estimated at 0.8 percent, with the number dropping to 0.3 percent in 1990 and to 0.2 percent in 2005 (İçduygu et al. 2008, 363). The majority of Ottoman Arme-

nians lost their lives during the genocide that took place in 1915. In the modern period, the Jewish population of Turkey has remained small (Bali 2012).

18. A Turkish fascist and racist party, the Nationalist Action Party (Milliyatci Hareket Partisi: MHP), which was founded in 1969, played a crucial role in inciting right-wing paramilitary organizations to fight against leftist activists. In 1990, the journalist Uğur Mumcu (reprinted in Mumcu 1997) revealed official court documents proving Turkish security collaboration with far-right paramilitary groups in the 1970s. "In late 1970s, on average twenty-two people died a day because of political violence" in Turkey (Kumral 2017, 236).

19. See CIA's publicly available report on the left-wing dissent in Turkey in the 1970s: https://www.cia.gov/readingroom/document/cia-rdp82m00786r000104630001-5 (last accessed May 29, 2021).

20. In 1991, the Social Democratic Populist Party (Sosyal Demokrat Halkçı Parti), largely supported by Alevis and secular Sunni Turks, made an alliance with the pro-Kurdish People's Democracy Party. This alliance resulted in the entrance of twenty-two Kurdish politicians into the Turkish National Assembly. However, these pro-Kurdish parliamentarians did not remain in parliament for long. The deputies were accused of supporting "terrorism," and in July 1993, the People's Democracy Party was shut down by the constitutional court (Güneş 2013). In the following decades, several pro-Kurdish political parties were established under different names, only to all be dissolved by the constitutional court on charges of separatism.

21. One of the major sources of tensions between the Left and the Kurdish liberation movement stems from the "Turkishness contract"—a term sociologist Barış Ünlü (2016) coined, inspired by Charles W. Mills's (2014) "racial contract." The "Turkishness contract" is based on the privileging of Turks in various spheres of social life and on discrimination against Turkey's many non-Turkish populations. Although Turkey was established as a secular nation-state, the "Turkishness contract" also includes the privileging of Turkey's Sunni Turkish Muslim populations over non-Muslims and Alevis, who are not considered "Muslims proper" in the Sunni Turkish imaginary. Although there is a colonial relationship between Turkey and Northern Kurdistan, the majority of Turkish leftists have failed to address it and have instead contributed to the reproduction of colonial power relations and racialized hierarchies between Turks and Kurds. For a detailed discussion on the Turkish left and the Kurdish question, see Yegen 2016. For the condition of Kurdistan as an international colony and Northern Kurdistan as an internal colony, see Beşikçi 2004 and Kurt 2019.

22. For the Turkish counterinsurgency's promotion of paramilitary forces and local rivalries in Northern Kurdistan against the PKK, see Jongerden 2007; Aydın and Emrence 2015 and Kurt 2017. For the British counterinsurgency's support of paramilitary forces in Northern Ireland against the IRA, see Sluka 2000 and McGovern 2013. For the British counterinsurgency's provocation of ethnosectarian cleavages in Malaya against communist guerrillas, see Khalili 2012. For South African ruling elites' encouragement of violence within Black communities during the anti-apartheid struggle, see Haysom 1989. For US security agents' provocation of counterviolence by the Black Panthers, see Marx 1974. For the US support and armament of Islamist jihadist groups against communists in the Middle East during the Cold War era, see Mamdani 2018.

23. The article was meant to circulate only within the army. Akyol was furious about the leak.

24. According to the *Allied Joint Doctrine for Counterinsurgency*, counterinsurgency "is an intelligence driven activity" (NATO 2011, para. 0327). Collusion, including "implement(ing) initiatives promoting the switching of sides," and "promot(ing) denunciation and betrayal by the fellow insurgents or by the populace" (para. 0354) are

important intelligence activities that help create divisions within and between insurgent groups and communities.

25. "Subaltern counterpublics have a dual character. On the one hand, they function as spaces of withdrawal and regroupment; on the other hand, they also function as bases and training grounds for agitational activities directed toward wider publics. It is precisely in the dialectic between these two functions that their emancipatory potential resides" (Fraser 1990, 68).

26. The *Allied Joint Doctrine for Counterinsurgency* suggests physical isolation and the sealing of borders surrounding "insurgent territories" as techniques for reducing the provision of external support to insurgents (NATO 2011, para. 0356).

27. Mahir Çayan was a legendary revolutionary leader in the 1960s killed by state security forces in Kızıldere in 1972 along with nine of his comrades.

28. Pir Sultan Abdal was a sixteenth-century Alevi rebel and poet.

29. Sibel Yalçın was a revolutionary militant killed by the police in 1995 at the age of eighteen after taking part in an armed action that resulted in the killing of a policeman. Berkin Elvan was a fifteen-year-old boy shot in the head in 2013 by a policeman in the predominantly Alevi working-class Okmeydanı neighborhood of Istanbul. A video later leaked on YouTube shows that the neighborhood was quiet at the time of the shooting. A policeman shot directly at Berkin while he was waiting at a street intersection watching the police.

30. See, for instance, Cunningham 2004; Masco 2014; Price 2016; and Weld 2014.

31. RAND Corporation is a US government-funded defense policy think tank. It was "originally formed as an outgrowth of the research wing for the US Air Force" and worked with the Pentagon and other intelligence agencies to craft new warfare paradigms (Harcourt 2018, 19).

32. In his book *Kontrgerilla* (Counterguerrilla), Cihat Akyol (1990) fiercely criticizes journalists who attempt to reveal the Turkish state's elusive counterinsurgency techniques. He also adds that, out of fear that these strategies may be used by insurgents, books on the techniques of irregular counterinsurgency warfare are banned in Turkey (169).

33. Ismet is a pseudonym I gave to this high rank police officer. Müdür means director in Turkish.

34. For an analysis of the Ergenokon trials, see Ertür 2016.

35. In 2007, the AKP government launched the "Alevi opening" with the alleged aim of responding to Alevi demands for equal citizenship and inclusion, Yet, as Lord (2017) argues, the opening was not a step toward democratization; in practice it focused on reshaping Alevi identity and intervening in the organization of Alevis.

36. In practice the so-called opening "aimed at containing the Kurdish movement and wresting back political control of the region" (Casier et al. 2013, 137). Thousands of Kurdish politicians, including elected mayors and members of parliament, were in fact imprisoned during the "opening process" (Ercan 2013).

37. Turkey's antiterror law originally passed in 1991. In line with global trends in terror legislation it has very vague and broad definitions of terror. The 2006 amendments retained these broad, vague definitions while increasing the number and scope of crimes that can be considered to be terrorist offenses. They also made it much easier to apply the law, increased the length of punishments for alleged terrorist acts, legalized breaches of rights to a fair trial, and paved the way for the categorization of political crimes as terror crimes. With these amendments, the number of prisoners convicted on terrorism charges increased dramatically in Turkey: in 2005, there were 273 terror convicts in Turkey's prisons; that number reached 12,897 by 2011 and 18,173 "terror" suspects by 2016. Information available at the webpage of the Ministry of Justice: http://www.adlisicil.adalet.gov.tr /Istatistikler/1996/2016acilanozel.pdf (last accessed August 13, 2019).

38. For my analysis of the stigmas attached to working-class spaces in Istanbul, see Yonucu 2008 and 2013.

39. See Yonucu 2008.

40. For the uses and abuses of anthropology during and after Cold War, see Price 2002, 2011, 2016 and Perugini 2008.

41. For an excellent analysis of the ethical and political responsibilities of urban ethnographers see Ralph 2015.

1. THE POSSIBILITY OF POLITICS

1. For Alevi engagement in left-wing political activism in the 1960s and 1970s, see also Ertan 2019.

2. For the socialists' production of space and "spatial politics" in Istanbul in those years see Houston 2020.

3. For details on Edip Solmaz's brief mayorship and violence against Kurdish politicians, see Güneş 2013.

4. For the people's committee experience in Fatsa and the Turkish ruling elites' reaction to it, see Elicin 2011.

5. For the people's committee experience in the neighborhood of Bir Mayis, see Aslan 2008.

6. The five pillars of Islam are belief in God and in Muhammad as the messenger of God, daily prayer, fasting during the holy month of Ramadan, almsgiving, and pilgrimage to Mecca. Alevis only observe the first obligation.

7. For an analysis of how past Alevi massacres in Karbala' are connected to contemporary discrimination and violence against Alevis in Turkey, see Yıldız and Verkuyten 2011 and Tambar 2014.

8. Alevis whose ancestral lineage can be traced to Ali. Some *dedes* also serve as community leaders and lead congregations.

9. Hüseyin İnan, whose ancestral lineage could be traced back to Ali, was addressed and referred to deferentially as *dede* among his friends.

10. In his work on the committee experience in Fatsa, Ünal (2014) also argues that the people's committees were political spaces in the Arendtian sense.

11. For the contradictions of Hannah Arendt's political thought see Margaret Canovan, "The contradictions of Hannah Arendt's political thought" (1978).

12. As Dikeç (2013, 28), citing Rancière, argues, the word *proletariat*, in Latin *proletarii*, originally refers to "people who make children, who merely live and reproduce without a name, without being counted as part of the symbolic order of the city" (Rancière 1995, 67). For a critique of Arendt's approach to the poor and the proletariat, see Bayat 2015; Dikeç 2013; and Rancière 1995.

13. For details, see Aslan 2008.

14. Isaac Işıtan's documentary on the demolition of the Bir Mayıs neighborhood on September 2, 1977, not only demonstrates how the state security forces shot at the crowd who were gathered to protect their neighborhood but also how men, women, and children came together to collectively rebuild the houses shortly after the security forces left.

15. Işıtan's documentary presents live footage of tens of Bir Mayıs neighborhood men, women, and children passing bricks from hand to hand while singing a song and chanting about collective production after the demolition. Isaac Işıtan, "2 Eylül Direnişi Belgeseli."

16. In Turkey's working-class circles kinship terms such as *Amca* (uncle), *Abi* (elder brother), *Teyze* (aunt), *Abla* (elder sister), *Dede* (grandfather) and *Nene* (grandmother) are used to address middle-aged or elderly people, regardless of one's level of familiarity with them.

17. In those years, anarchist (*anarşist*) was the conventional Turkish derogatory term for any and all socialists and communists.

18. In his book *Kontrgerilla* (Counterguerrilla), Akyol (1990) fiercely criticized journalists who cited segments of the article in their columns, maintaining that the article was meant to circulate exclusively among army personnel. He also added that the fear that such counterinsurgency techniques might be used by insurgents led to the banning in Turkey of manuals on the techniques of irregular, counterinsurgency warfare (169).

19. The School of the Americas, the infamous training center for special forces, was also located in Fort Benning. Latin American security personnel received training at this school (Gill 2004). The Special Warfare School at Fort Bragg, North Carolina, was created in 1956 with the aim of developing US counterinsurgency doctrine and training special forces and psychological warfare unit personnel. Fort Bragg and Fort Benning are notorious for training perpetrators of human rights violations.

20. Because the meetings were held in Turkish, Kurdish female Devrimovans who did not speak Turkish could not take part.

21. The punishment of expelling a person deemed guilty of a severe crime from the community is commonly used within Alevi informal justice.

22. Named for the German playwright Berthold Brecht, Brechtian theater is a didactic political theater designed to provoke critical reflection, an awareness of the roots of social injustice, and the inspiration to effect sociopolitical change.

23. For a discussion of the "revolutionary ethics" of revolutionary students in Turkey, see Houston 2017.

24. "DHKP-C Halk Meclislerine El Attı," *Zaman*, October 18, 1997. DHKP-C is an outlawed revolutionary organization considered to be a terrorist organization by Turkish law enforcement.

25. For the encouragement of vigilantism by the ruling elites see also Abrahams 1998; Godoy 2006.

26. See Buur and Jensen 2004; Bruce 1992.

27. According to retired staff colonel Talat Turhan's testimony in the Turkish National Assembly, the military officers trained at the Fort Bragg took part in these incidents (Meclis Darbe Araştırması Komisyonu 2012 [Turkish National Assembly Coup Investigation Committee 2012], 21). Meeting date: June 26, 2012.

28. In his own counterinsurgency book, *Kontrgerilla* (Counterguerrilla), Cihat Akyol (1990), then commander of the Special Forces Unit of the Turkish Armed Forces, invokes the authority of Kitson's works. In his angry response to the Turkish journalists who criticized him for using paramilitary forces to suppress left-wing dissent and for advocating the use of state-sponsored covert groups to carry out violent acts that could then be blamed on left-wing groups, he complains that Kitson's books never received such critiques from the British public (Akyol 1990, 169). Later in 1995, a military-affiliated Turkish journalist would also object to the Turkish military being criticized for employing Kitson's techniques (Kışlalı 1996, 99). Journalist Uğur Mumcu, who exposed Akyol's article on the creation of covert groups, fake operations, and blame-it-on-the-communists techniques in his column in *Cumhuriyet* (1990; reprinted in Mumcu 1997), also uncovered the official court documents proving Turkish security collaboration with far-right paramilitary groups.

29. For the application of Kitson's strategies in Belfast, see Faligot 1983; Sluka 2000; and McGovern 2015.

30. The connections between *Aydınlık* and bureaucracy and military are now well established. See Jongerden and Akkaya 2018.

31. For the details of these maps see Aslan 2008.

2. "GAZAS OF ISTANBUL"

1. Çalışma ve Sosyal Güvenlik Bakanlığı, Çalışma Hayatı İstatistikleri, no. 31, Ankara, 2005, p. 27.

2. Çalışma ve Sosyal Güvenlik Bakanlığı, Çalışma Hayatı İstatistikleri, no. 23, Ankara, 1998, p. 65.

3. Çalışma ve Sosyal Güvenlik Bakanlığı, Çalışma Hayatı İstatistikleri, no. 23, Ankara, 1998, p. 65.

4. For the new forms of social mobilization in the 1990s in Turkey see Fiimfiek 2004.

5. For Alevi organizations in diaspora see Özyürek 2009; Sökefeld 2008. For feminist journals and this movement, see Arat 2002.

6. Established in 1996, the Özgürlük ve Dayanışma Partisi is an umbrella party, which included various socialist groups ranging from Stalinists to Trotskyites and from feminists and LGBTQ activists to libertarian socialists. Though the party is still active, it is now much smaller and is no longer an umbrella organization. Established in 1990, Halkın Emek Partisi is a leftist, pro-Kurdish party. Established in 1996, the Emek Partisi was inspired by the Party of Labor of Albania under the leadership of Enver Hoxha. Established in 1993, the Sosyalist İktidar Partisi was a Soviet-style Stalinist Party.

7. Established in 1978, the Revolutionary Left Party (Dev-Sol), was a splinter group of the Marxist-Leninist People's Liberation Party-Front of Turkey (Türkiye Halk Kurtulus Partisi-Cephe; THKP-C) which after the 1980 military coup and state of emergency became active again in the late 1980s. It embraced urban guerrilla warfare methods. In 1994, the party was renamed the Revolutionary People's Liberation Party-Front (Devrimci Halk Kurtuluş Partisi-Cephesi; DHPK-C) (Bargu 2014, 234). The PKK also emerged from within the THKP-C. The Marxist Leninist Communist Party (MLKP), established in 1995, adopted urban guerrilla warfare methods; it promotes a "unique blend of Maoist, workerist, and vanguardist warfare" (234). The Workers and Peasant Liberation Army of Turkey Party (TİKKO) was established in 1972. It is a Maoist party that is engaged in armed struggle both in urban and rural areas (232).

8. This success was met with a harsh response from the ruling elites. Just two years later, in July 1993, the twenty-two People's Labor Party members of parliament were accused of supporting terror, and the party was shut down by the constitutional court (Güneş 2013, 161).

9. Mahsun Korkmaz was the commander of the Eruh attack and joint commander of the Şemdinli attack, the PKK's first two armed attacks against the Turkish army. Both were conducted on August 15, 1984. I would like to thank Delal Aydın for attracting my attention to this elegy.

10. For British counterinsurgency's displacement policies in Malaya see Khalili 2010.

11. However, that does not mean that the relationship between Kurdish and Turkish leftists has been free of problems. Although there is a colonial relationship between Turkey and Northern Kurdistan, as Barış Ünlü (2016) demonstrates in his article on the Turkish leftists' positionality vis-à-vis the Kurdish liberation movement, a significant percent of Turkish leftists have failed to address it and have instead contributed to the reproduction of colonial power relations and racialized hierarchies between Turks and Kurds.

12. In 1996, political prisoners started a hunger strike in Turkey. Twelve prisoners died due to starvation, and an additional fourteen prisoners, four of whom were beaten to death, were killed by the state's security operations. For hunger strikes and "necroresistance" in Turkey see Bargu 2014.

13. BEKSAV, the Science Education Aesthetic Culture Art Research Foundation (Bilim Eğitim Estetik Kültür Sanat Araştırmaları Vakfı) is a MLKP-affiliated cultural center. It was established in 1995.

14. Çayan's strategy also inspired radical Islamist organizations. Established in 1984, İslami Büyük Doğu Akıncıları Cephesi (The Great East Islamic Raiders Front; IBDA-C), also conducted a series of armed actions against the representatives of the state in the 1990s.

15. "Intikam," *Milliyet*, January 31, 1990.

16. "Emekli Binbaşı Kurşunlandı," *Milliyet*, August 27, 1990.

17. "Son Hedef MIT," *Milliyet*, September 27, 1990.

18. "Savcı Öldürüldü," *Milliyet*, November 13, 1990.

19. "Mitçiyi Tamer'e Suikast," *Milliyet*, December 19, 1999.

20. "Asayiş Müdürüne 14 Kurşun," *Milliyet*, December 5, 1991; "Emekli Yarbay Ata Burcu Pendik'te uğradığı silahlı saldırı sonucu öldürüldü," *Cumhuriyet*, January 10, 1991; "Aynı Silahla 5'inci Suikast," *Milliyet*, April 8, 1991; "Kayacan'a Evinde Suikast," *Milliyet*, July 30, 1992. The DHKP-C's final targeting of a major figure during the 1990s was on June 9, 1996, when its militants killed two businessmen, Özdemir Sabancı and Haluk Görgün, as well as Sabancı's secretary, Nilgün Hasefe. "Şok," *Hürriyet*, January 10, 1996. Almost two decades later, the DHKP-C once again targeted a public figure. On March 31, 2015, the DHKP-C took Mehmet Selim Kiraz hostage. Kiraz had served as a public prosecutor in the murder case of Berkin Elvan, an Alevi teenager who was killed by the police during the Gezi protests in his home neighborhood of Okmeydanı. Kiraz lost his life in his office in an Istanbul courthouse in an armed clash between state security officers and DHKP-C militants that ended the hostage taking. "Savcı Mehmet Selim Kiraz Şehit Oldu," *Sabah*, April 1, 2015.

21. Human Rights Foundation of Turkey Annual Report 1995 (Türkiye İnsan Hakları Raporu), p. 75; "Gergin Cenaze," *Milliyet*, June 17, 1995.

22. Göral, Işık, and Kaya (2013) claim there were 1,283 disappearances between 1991 and 1999. This trend reached its peak in the period from 1993 to 1998, with the year 1994 recording 518 persons as "missing." Illegal detentions were of two kinds: the kidnapping, interrogation, and torture of activists in places such as empty buildings and forests and the undocumented detention, interrogation, and torture by police forces at police offices, always denied because no arrest report had been filed. The village guard system was introduced to divide Kurdish society from within and rule indirectly through local paramilitary groups. Subcontracting with local armed groups or forcing local groups to fight against the PKK, this system was inspired by the British-implemented "home guard" system in Malaya (Kışlalı 1996, 57). This system in Malaya was also designed to divide the population from within and control it through the co-optation and armament of local collaborators. For home guards and emergency rule in British Malaya, see Gurman 2013; Nonini 2015.

23. The story of *Gündem*, a pro-Kurdish newspaper, exemplifies the control exerted over and pressure placed on the Kurdish press in the 1990s. The emergency governor banned the distribution of the paper in the region. More than seventy-five employees were killed between 1992 to 1994. Newspaper sellers and distributors joined reporters on the list of those murdered for carrying out their jobs. In 1993, Turkey had the highest number of journalists killed of any country. For control over the Turkish mainstream media on the Kurdish issue, see Cemal 2003.

24. Diyarbakır is the unofficial capital of Northern Kurdistan.

25. Responsible for widespread human rights abuses both in the Kurdish region and in Western Turkey, Kozakçıoğlu was found dead in his home on May 22, 2013, soon after the negotiation process between the PKK and the Turkish government began. Accord-

ing to the autopsy, the cause of his death was suicide. "Kozakçıoğlu Evinde Intihar Etti," *Cumhuriyet*, December 31, 2013.

26. "Kozakçıoğlu Istanbul Valisi," *Cumhuriyet*, August 5, 1991.

27. *Hürriyet*, October 17, 1991.

28. "Terörün Arkasında Para Var," *Cumhuriyet*, February 12, 1992.

29. "Terörün Arkasında Para Var."

30. In her analysis of encounters between the police and the Kurdish and Alevi urban poor, Anna Secor (2007) argues that they are interpellated as guilty subjects.

31. *Armutlu'nun karakolmuş okulları / bahçesinde bir panzer yatarmı. / Panzerin gölgesinde büyürmüş çocuklar. / Panzer çocuğun topunu çalmış, / çocuk koşmuş topunu almaya. / Panzer yürümüş, / çocuk yedi yaşında kalmış.*

3. PROVOCATIVE COUNTERORGANIZATION

1. Only two policemen were found guilty of shooting into the crowd. Initially sentenced to four years' imprisonment, their sentence was commuted (Tüleylioğlu 2011). For TV coverage of the events, see Devrimozgurluk, "Gazi Ayaklanması—Katliamı," video, 19:33, March 12, 1995, accessed May 11, 2018, https://www.youtube.com/watch?v=A0e8ins S8N8&t=1s.

2. "Halka Ateş Açıldı," *Cumhuriyet*, March 18, 1995.

3. After the publication of his book on the Gülen movement and its infiltration of the Turkish police, Avcı spent four years in prison as part of the OdaTV case. His case was dismissed in 2015. See "Turkish Court Dismisses Charges against Former Police Chief Hanefi Avcı," *Daily Sabah*, May 6, 2015, accessed August 5, 2018, https://www.dailysabah.com/investigations/2015/05/06/turkish-court-dismisses-charges-against-former-police-chief-hanefi-avci.

4. "Alevilere Saldırı," *Cumhuriyet*, March 13, 1995.

5. "Alevi Gruplar Polisle Çatıştı," *Yeni Yüzyıl*, March 14, 1995.

6. "Provokasyon," *Milliyet*, March 13, 1995.

7. Ilhan Selçuk, "Bir Kibrit Çakımı," *Cumhuriyet*, March 15, 1995; Ataol Behramoğlu, "Yaralarım Tuz İçinde Kanıyor . . . ," *Cumhuriyet*, March 18, 1995, "Yüzyılların Mirasını Tüketmeyin," *Cumhuriyet*, March 17, 1995.

8. Fikret Bila, "Rejim ve Aleviler," *Milliyet*, March 16, 1995; Emin Pazarcı, "Rezil bir Provokasyon," *Akşam*, March 14, 1995; Behiç Kılıç, "Oyunun Yeni Yüzü," *Akşam*, March 16, 1995; Behiç Kılıç, "Provokasyonun Anatomisi I," *Akşam*, March 17, 1995; Behiç Kılıç, "Provokasyonun Anatomisi II," *Akşam*, March 18, 1995; Altan Öymen, "Hesap Belli," *Milliyet*, March 14, 1995.

9. Rıza Zelyut, "Teşekkürler Yenibosna . . . ," *Akşam*, March 16, 1995.

10. Rıza Zelyut, "Olayların İçindeydim . . . Sakin Olalım," *Akşam*, March 14, 1995.

11. Some segments of Kurdish-speaking Alevi communities do not identify as Kurds.

12. Hasan Ocak was a socialist teacher and alleged member of the Marxist-Leninist Communist Party. He was taken into custody on March 21, 1995, during the operations that followed the Gazi incidents. Fifty-eight days later, his body was found in a forest with clear signs of torture (Jongerden 2003).

13. The massacres that occurred in Maraş (1978), Çorum (1980), and Sivas (1993) in which hundreds of Alevis were killed have had a significant impact on the Alevi collective memory.

14. Martin Sökefeld (2008) notes that, even though the Gazi incidents were mainly associated with the Alevi community in the media, the Sivas massacre was represented primarily as an Islamist assault against Aziz Nesin, a self-proclaimed atheist who had translated Salman Rushdie's *Satanic Verses* into Turkish. In those media representations, Alevis "figure only as victims by chance as marginal to the event, not as the targets of

the attack" (121). Yet, as Sökefeld emphasizes, Alevi activists considered the Sivas massacre to be an event that targeted the Alevi community.

15. The Battle of Karbala was waged against the tyrant Yazid, who became synonymous with "persecutor" in the Alevi imaginary. "Yazid" is also used in a pejorative way to refer to Sunnis.

16. *Kurtuluş*, no. 4, August 24, 1996.

17. Here, I do not suggest that these organizations stopped working together with the PKK as a result of the Gazi events. Instead, I draw attention to the concurrence of these events. For an analysis of Turkish (nationalist) leftist critique of the Kurdish liberation movement, see Yegen 2016.

18. According to one newspaper study, the number of *hemşehri* associations in Istanbul grew from 416 in 1989 to 3,325 in 2004. See Ayda Kaya, "En baskın milliyetçilik hemşericilik," *Hürriyet*, February 28, 2004, accessed August 6, 2018, http://www.hurriyet.com.tr/kelebek/en-baskin-milliyetcilik-hemsericilik-205911. Among the ten districts with the most associations, five were Alevi-populated districts of Sivas, followed by two Alevi-populated districts of Erzincan. The majority of these associations were in Ümraniye, where the neighborhood of Bir Mayıs is located; Gaziosmanpaşa, where Gazi is located; and Kağıthane, a mixed Alevi–Sunni district where the predominantly Alevi-populated Nurtepe neighborhood is located (Pérouse 2005).

19. For the application of Kitson's strategy in Belfast and sectarian paramilitary violence, see Sluka 2000.

20. Interview accessed April 23, 2020, http://www.siddethikayeleri.com/portfolio/her-kayip-yakini-sevdiginin-son-sozunu-bilmek-ister/#.XqFBq9MzZQI.

21. Because of his disappearance after being taken into custody following the Gazi incidents, Hasan Ocak alone is seen as the heroic figure of Gazi. Another heroic revolutionary figure who was also there, Süleyman Yeter, is not remembered in relation to Gazi but for his trade union activities. Before dying under police torture, he was an educational specialist in one of the large trade unions, the Confederation of Revolutionary Workers Trade Unions (Devrimci İşçi Sendikaları Konfederasyonu; DİSK).

22. "Gazi'de Barikatlarla Gürlesti Sesimiz," *Kurtuluş*, no. 4, August 24, 1996, 10–12.

23. "Mahalleler Kentlerin Yumusak Karnı" *Dev-Sol*, 1995, no. 8, 10–19.

24. "Cephe Vuruyor," *Dev-Sol*, 1995, No. 7, 55–58.

25. "Mahalleler Kentlerin Yumuşak Karnı."

26. "Halk Patlayıcıları" *Dev-Sol*, 1995, no. 8, 82–85. "Bomba ve Molotof Yapımı," *Dev-Sol*, 1995, no. 8, 67–78.

27. See the previous chapter for details.

28. For an ethnographic analysis of the youths' motivation for engaging in routinized forms of violence in a similar, more recent context, see chapter 5.

29. For an ethnographically informed and detailed discussion of this phenomenon, see chapters 4 and 6.

30. See Van Bruinessen (1996b, 20–23).

31. "Kitle Calışması," *Dev-Sol*, July 2000, no. 15, p. 62.

32. For the promotion of Islam as a colonial governmental technique in Northern Kurdistan, see Kurt 2019.

33. Perhaps not coincidentally, internal divisions within the major revolutionary organizations had begun already before the Gazi events. In 1993, Dev-Sol's two leading figures parted ways, and in that same year one of them was killed by state security forces, together with four other Dev-Sol members. This event gave rise to conspiracies of collusion, ending in violent clashes between the two wings of Dev-Sol (Aydın and Can 1999, 233).

34. At the time of the leak to the public in 1990, Akyol harshly criticized the "leakers." As discussed in a special meeting on coups convened in the Turkish National Assembly in 2012, the leak revealed how Turkish security officers had been trained in US military academies in the 1960s and had since that time been creating paramilitary groups. In another special meeting on coups convened in the Turkish National Assembly in 2012, Colonel Talat Turhan confirmed that Turkish security forces were applying Cihat Akyol's techniques on the ground.

4. GOOD VIGILANTISM, BAD VIGILANTISM

1. This chapter draws on a previously published article (Yonucu 2018b).

2. To ensure the anonymity of my interviewees, I do not share the actual name of the association with the reader.

3. The Fight against Terrorism Act no. 3713 was enacted in 1991 and was amended in 2006 by Law no. 5532.

4. For the effect of charity networks in preventing "absolute poverty," see Işık and Pınarcıoğlu 2008.

5. For the criminalization of working-class youth in Turkey, see Yonucu 2008; Gönen 2016.

6. For excellent analyses of vigilantism and informal justice in the Global South, see Caldeira 2002; Buur and Jensen 2004; Comaroff and Comaroff 2016b; Goldstein 2012; Scheper-Hughes 2015.

7. Neighborhood coffeehouses are an important part of urban working-class life, where local men spend their time together drinking nonalcoholic beverages, playing cards, or watching television. Before the coup of 1989, beer was also sold in these places.

8. Military generals and other security force suspects in the Ergenekon Trials of 2008–16 were tried and held in Silivri Prison outside Istanbul. Ergenekon is the name given to an alleged "'shadowy organization,' a state within the state of Turkey, often referred to as the deep state" (Balcı 2010, 76) whose purported members were accused of attempting to overthrow the ruling AKP.

9. Gazi and Okmeydanı are predominantly Alevi-populated working-class neighborhoods of Istanbul.

10. To ensure the anonymity of the neighborhood, I do not provide the links for these videos.

11. To ensure the anonymity of the neighborhood and my interlocutors, I do not provide the links to the newspaper interview.

12. After the rape and murder of Italian artist Pippa Bacca in March 2008 in Turkey, a group of men established an initiative called "We Are Not Men." They organized several demonstrations, events, and workshops. The initiative's activities continued until 2011.

13. The Witness Protection Law No. 5726 went into effect in December 2007 with the aim of protecting the identities of "counterterrorism" criminal procedure witnesses and their families. In effect, the law allows the state to offer those imprisoned or facing trial a reduced sentence or release in exchange for new information that would benefit the state prosecution. In the wake of sensational secret witness recants, the law has since come under close critical scrutiny from international law and human rights organizations (Okuyucu-Ergun 2009). It is also well-noted that the prosecutors extensively rely on secret witness testimony (Turgay 2011; Yonucu 2018a)

14. I heard similar words from Kurdish activists and acquaintances when I visited the Kurdish region on various occasions between 2011 and 2015.

15. Article 1 of the law defines terrorism as "any kind of act done by one or more persons belonging to an organization with the aim of changing the characteristics of

the Republic as specified in the constitution as well as its political, legal, social, secular and economic system, damaging the indivisible unity of the State with its territory and nation, endangering the existence of the Turkish State and Republic, weakening or destroying or seizing the authority of the State, eliminating fundamental rights and freedoms, or damaging the internal and external security of the State, public order or general health by means of pressure, force and violence, terror, intimidation, oppression or threats."

16. The law defines more than sixty crimes, including sexual harassment and prostitution, as terrorist acts if they are committed with the "intention" of terror. See Inanıcı 2011.

17. To ensure the anonymity of the relevant revolutionary organization, I do not provide the links to the relevant journal articles.

18. For the sake of anonymity, I do not share the links of these videos or any published material on these groups.

5. INSPIRATIONAL HAUNTINGS

1. A version of this chapter is published under the title" Inspirational Hauntings and a Fearless Spirit of Resistance: Negotiating the Undercover Police Surveillance of Racialized Spaces in Istanbul," at *Current Anthropology* (2022).

2. For a detailed analysis of their trial process and the role of the undercover police in anti-terror trials, see Yonucu 2018a.

3. For the professionalization of police work in Turkey, see Babül 2017b.

4. Here, Foucault refers to effect of the narrations of the Karbala' event as a heroic act of defiance against the tyrant Yazid in 680 AD. Foucault believed that the narrations of self-sacrificial fight against injustice were immanent in Shia Islam.

5. This is also the case for many other Indigenous populations living in oppressive and colonial contexts, ranging from Mexico to Palestine. As Lori Allen (2009, 175) observes, in Palestine, not just "combatants" but also "anyone who is deemed to have died as a result of the occupation, both Christian and Muslim" is considered a martyr. Likewise, in Lebanon, victims of state violence, too, are considered to be martyrs (Knudsen 2016). Claudio Lomnitz-Adler (2003, 24) shows that in Mexico, in addition to the self-sacrificial death, "the dead of the innocents" are also seen as a "sacrifice for the nation."

6. For the commemoration of these violent incidents see Mutluer 2016.

7. Many of these youth were members of the Federation of Socialist Youth Associations (Sosyalist Genclik Dernekleri Federasyonu).

8. For leftist practices of remembering in Turkey see Houston 2020.

9. "IHD: Çukurca'da bir vahşet yaşanmış," *Evrensel*, November 2, 2011.

10. For the feeling of indebtedness towards the Kurdish martyrs among Kurdish populations see Ozsoy 2010.

11. "Gökçek'in cenazesi kaçırıldı," *Yeni Özgür Politika*, May 9, 2020.

12. I showed *La Haine* in a movie screening event in the neighborhood in the winter of 2012.

13. The word *delikanlı* is used to refer to young men who easily get excited or agitated and who cannot easily be restrained by law, order, or norms. It is also indexes courageousness, honesty, and toughness.

6. GEZI UPRISINGS

1. During the week of December 19–26, 2000, the Turkish government launched an operation dubbed the Return to Life Operation (*Hayata Dönüş Operasyonu*) to end the death fasts then taking place in a number of prisons. During the operation "10,000 Turkish soldiers violently occupied 48 prisons to end two months of hunger strikes and 'death fasts' by hundreds of political prisoners. Operation 'Return to Life'—which left at

least 31 prisoners and two soldiers dead—lasted a few hours in most prisons, and up to three days at one prison. Eight prisoners are reportedly 'disappeared,' and at least 426 prisoners have been wounded" (Paker 2000).

2. There were no Gezi-related uprisings in Northern Kurdistan. Because of the region's distinct political history as a sort of internal colony, Kurds in the Kurdish provinces approached the uprising with hesitancy (Bozçalı and Yoltar 2013; Tambar 2016). Because of the ongoing peace negotiations between the Kurdish liberation movement and the Turkish state, the movement did not issue an official call for Kurds to participate in the uprising. Even so, many Kurds living in Istanbul and other western provinces participated in the demonstrations.

3. In their work on the Turkish counterinsurgency against the Kurdish liberation movement, Aysegul Aydın and Cem Emrence (2015) argue that the Turkish ruling elite has repeatedly blamed foreign sponsors for mobilizing dissent. The hand of foreign powers wishing to destroy Turkey has been conjured as far back as the Armenian and Macedonian revolutionary movements of the late Ottoman period and for the Kurdish movement in modern Turkey (94).

4. See chapter 3.

5. This scene appears in the documentary *Taksim Commune: Gezi Park and the Uprisings in Turkey*. The unidentified man said, "I realize now that the Turkish army and the police are not our friend, it is the PKK. I want to say bravo to my Kurdish sisters and brothers" (minute 32). Brandon Jourdan, "Taksim Commune: Gezi Park and the Uprisings in Turkey," video, 32:34, August 8, 2013, accessed August 30, 2018, https://www.youtube.com/watch?v=i8hbmA5LgZU.

6. Şeker TV, "Berkin Elvan'ın Katledilişinin İyileştirilmiş Görüntüleri (16.06.2013)," video, 5:58, June 16, 2013, accessed August 30, 2018, https://www.youtube.com/watch?v=b5LkAsJMzgM.

7. As an example of how a peaceful protest can became a clash between the youth and the police in Okmeydanı, see Fatih Pınar, "September 9, 2013: Okmeydanı/İstanbul. Justice Chain Protest for Berkin Elvan," video, 3:53, September 9, 2013, accessed July 25, 2017, https://vimeo.com/74134305.

8. "Okmeydanı: Berkin Elvan'a destek gösterisine sert müdahale," BBC News Türkçe, September 9, 2013, last accessed August 10, 2018, https://www.bbc.com/turkce/haberler/2013/09/130909_okmeydani_mudahale.

9. For a detailed report of the events, see the Human Rights Organization's (Insan Haklari Dernegi, IHD) Gülsuyu Observation Report, October 15, 2013, accessed June 12, 2018. https://www.ihd.org.tr/images/pdf/2013/GULSUYU.pdf

10. "Gülsuyu'nda kürtlere silâhlı saldırı," *Etha*, July 15, 2013, last accessed August 10, 2018, http://www.etha.com.tr/Haber/2013/07/15/guncel/gulsuyunda-kurtlere-silahli-saldiri/.

11. The attack is believed to have been perpetrated by the Islamic State. Earlier that year, Kobanê "played host to an intense battle for control between Kurdish forces and IS militants across the border in Syria." *Bianet English*, July 23, 2015, accessed August 10, 2018, https://m.bianet.org/bianet/politics/166239-how-culpable-is-turkey-for-the-suruc-massacre.

12. "'Gülsuyu Çetesi' ESP'ye silahlı saldırı düzenledi," *ANF News*, August 7, 2013, accessed August 10, 2018, https://anfturkce.net/guncel/gulsuyu-cetesi-esp-ye-silahli-saldiri-duzenledi-24058.

13. Jennifer Rubin, "Trump Cannot Even Commemorate Charlottesville Correctly," *Washington Post*, August 12, 2018, accessed August 10, 2018, https://www.washingtonpost.com/blogs/right-turn/wp/2018/08/12/trump-cannot-even-commemorate-charlottesville-correctly/?utm_term=.b9c2ddc52483.

14. "Örgüt-Torbacı Savaşı," *Akşam*, August 9, 2013; "Gülsuyun'da Çete Terörü" *Radikal*, August 9, 2013; "Mafya Istanbul'a Geri Döndü," *Time Turk*, August 9, 2013.

15. "Üçüncü Köprü'nün Adi Yavuz Sultan Selim," *Radikal*, May 30, 2013.

16. Etyen Mahçupyan, "Gezi Artık Bir Proje," *Zaman*, September 26 2013.

17. Müfit Yüksel, "Gezi Olayları Çerçevesinde Alevilik Sorunu," *Yeni Şafak*, June 22, 2013; Rasim Ozan Kütayalı "Aleviler Kışkıtılıyor," *Sabah*, July 16, 2013; Rasim Ozan Kütayalı, "15 Ağustos Kaos Planı ve Aleviler," *Sabah*, July 16, 2013; Hilal Kaplan, "Gezi ve Aleviler," *Sabah*, September 15, 2013; Özlem Albayrak, "Aleviler ve Suriye: Örnek mi Alalım, İbret mi Alalım? *Yeni Şafak*, September 26, 2013; Nagehan Alçı, "Aleviler ve Gezi," *Milliyet*, November 30, 2013.

18. At the height of the Gezi uprising, the pro-AKP journalist Rasim Ozan Kütahyalı argued that Alevis would start an armed uprising. See "Aleviler Kışkıtılıyor," *Sabah*, July 16, 2013; "15 Ağustos Kaos Planı ve Aleviler," *Sabah*, July 16, 2013.

19. Mehmet Ali Kışlalı, "Antiterör doktrinleri," *Radikal*, January 11, 2008.

20. David Patreaus, *The US Army/Marine Corps Counterinsurgency Field Manual*, 2006. Accessed June 25, 2019, http://www.freeinfosociety.com/media/pdf/3095.pdf.

21. Constanze Letsch, "Man Shot Dead at Funeral as Police and Protesters Clash in Istanbul," *Guardian*, May 22, 2014, accessed July 25, 2017, https://www.theguardian.com /world/2014/may/22/cleaner-shot-riot-police-istanbul-funeral. Commenting on the event, then-prime minister Erdoğan said that he did not understand how the police could be so patient, making his support of police violence in the neighborhood clear to his audience (Karakaya-Stump 2014).

22. "Armutlu Cemevi'ne Özel Harekat Baskini," *Sendikaorg*, October 18, 2015, accessed August 13, 2018, http://sendika63.org/2015/10/armutlu-cemevine-ozel-harekatci -baskini-302396/; "Cemevi'ne Düzenlenen Baskin Sonucunda 26 Kisi Tutuklandi," *Diken*, December 20, 2016, accessed August 13, 2018, http://www.diken.com.tr/cemevine -duzenlenen-baskin-sonucunda-26-kisi-tutuklandi/; "Polis Gazi Cemevine Baskin Düzenkledi *Evrensel*, July 27, 2015.

23. For an excellent analysis of some Gezi protesters' frustration that "Kurdish cities had not displayed the bold street politics for which they are often known," see Tambar (2016, 42).

24. The International Freedom Battalion is a unit of international socialists and anarchists in the Syria-based People's Protection Units (Yekîneyên Parastina Gel), the armed wing of the Kurdish Democratic Party (Partiya Yekîtiya Demokrat).

25. Here Ercan refers to the 1992 Turkish security force killings of Kurdish people while they were celebrating Newroz, the Kurdish spring feast, in Cizre and other Kurdish towns (Güneş 2013).

EPILOGUE

1. Giorgio Agamben, "From the State Control to a Praxis of Destituent Power," *ROAR*, February 4, 2014, https://roarmag.org/essays/agamben-destituent-power-democracy/.

References

Abrahams, Raphael Garvin. 1998. *Vigilant Citizens: Vigilantism and the State*. Cambridge: Polity Press.

Abrams, Philip. 1988. "Notes on the Difficulty of Studying the State." *Journal of Historical Sociology* 1, no. 1: 58–89.

Açıksöz, Salih Can. 2019. *Sacrificial Limbs: Masculinity, Disability, and Political Violence in Turkey*. Berkeley: University of California Press.

Adaman, Fikret, and Oya Pınar Ardıç. 2008. "Social Exclusion in the Slum Areas of Large Cities in Turkey." *New Perspectives on Turkey* 38: 29–60.

Afary, Janet. 2003. "Shi'i Narratives of Karbala and Christian Rites of Penance: Michel Foucault and the Culture of the Iranian Revolution, 1978–1979." *Radical History Review* 86, no. 1: 7–35.

Agamben, Giorgio. 1988. *Homo Sacer*. Stanford: Stanford University Press.

——. 2014. "From the State of Control to a Praxis of Destituent Power." *ROAR*, February 4.

Ahmad, Feroz. 1993. *The Making of Modern Turkey*. London: Routledge.

——. 2010. "Military and Politics in Turkey." In *Turkey's Engagement with Modernity*, edited by Celia Kerslake, Öktem Kerem, and Philip Robins, 92–116. Cham, Switzerland: Springer.

Ahmed, Sara. 2003. "The Politics of Fear in the Making of Worlds." *International Journal of Qualitative Studies in Education* 16, no. 3: 377–98.

——. 2013. *Strange Encounters: Embodied Others in Post-Coloniality*. London: Routledge.

Akıncı, Eylül Fidan. 2017. "Performativities of Necropolitics and Mourning in Neoliberal Turkey." In *Performance in a Militarized Culture*, edited by Sara Brady and Lindsey Mantoan. London: Routledge. 47–66.

Akyildiz, Kaya. Forthcoming. "The Affirmation of Sunni Supremacism in Erdoğan's 'New Turkey.'" In *The Politics of Culture in Contemporary Turkey*, edited by Pierre Hecker, Ivo Furman, and Kaya Akyıldız. Edinburgh: Edinburgh University Press.

Akyol, M. Cihat. 1971. "Gayri Nizami Kuvvetlere Karşı Hareket." *Silahli Kuvvetler Dergisi Eki*, March.

——. 1990. *Kontrgerilla*. Ankara: Şafak Matbaası.

Ali, Arshad Imitaz. 2016. "Citizens under Suspicion: Responsive Research with Community under Surveillance." *Anthropology & Education Quarterly* 47, no. 1: 78–95.

Ali, Nosheen. 2010. "Sectarian Imaginaries: The Micropolitics of Sectarianism and State-Making in Northern Pakistan." *Current Sociology* 58, no. 5: 738–54.

Allen, Lori. 2009. "Martyr Bodies in the Media: Human Rights, Aesthetics, and the Politics of Immediation in the Palestinian Intifada." *American Ethnologist* 36, no. 1: 161–80.

——. 2012. "The Scales of Occupation: 'Operation Cast Lead' and the Targeting of the Gaza Strip." *Critique of Anthropology* 32, no. 3: 261–84.

Altheide, David L. 2003. "Mass Media, Crime, and the Discourse of Fear." *Hedgehog Review* 5, no. 3: 9.

——. 2006. *Terrorism and the Politics of Fear*. New York: Rowman & Littlefield.

Althusser, Louis. 1976. *Essays on Ideology*. London: Verso.

Aras, Ramazan. 2013. *The Formation of Kurdishness in Turkey: Political Violence, Fear and Pain*. London: Routledge.

Arat, Yeşim. 2004. "Rethinking the Political: A Feminist Journal in Turkey, Pazartesi." *Women's Studies International Forum* 27, No. 3: 281–292.

Arendt, Hannah. 1958. "Totalitarian Imperialism: Reflections on the Hungarian Revolution." *Journal of Politics* 20, no. 1: 5–43.

———. 1972. *Crises of the Republic: Lying in Politics, Civil Disobedience on Violence, Thoughts on Politics, and Revolution*, Vol. 219. Boston: Houghton Mifflin Harcourt.

———. 2007. *The Origins of Totalitarianism*. Durham: Duke University Press.

———. 2013. *The Human Condition*. Chicago: University of Chicago Press.

Arendt, Hannah, and Günter Gaus. 1964. "VIDEO. Hannah Arendt 'Zur Person [Im Gespräch with Günter Gaus],' 1964." Hannah Arendt Center for Political Studies. October 28. http://www.arendtcenter.it/en/2016/12/11/hannah-arendt-zur-person-im-gesprach-with-gunter-gaus/.

Aretxaga, Begoña. 1995. "Dirty Protest: Symbolic Overdetermination and Gender in Northern Ireland Ethnic Violence." *Ethos* 23, no. 2: 123–48.

———. 2000. "Playing Terrorist: Ghastly Plots and the Ghostly State." *Journal of Spanish Cultural Studies* 1, no. 1: 43–58.

Aslan, Şükrü. 2008. *1 Mayıs Mahallesi: 1980 Öncesi Toplumsal Mücadeleler ve Kent*. Istanbul: İletişim Yayınları.

Auyero, Javier. 2006. "The Political Makings of the 2001 Lootings in Argentina." *Journal of Latin American Studies* 38, no. 2: 241–65.

Auyero, Javier, Philippe Bourgois, and Nancy Scheper-Hughes. 2015. *Violence at the Urban Margins*. Oxford: Oxford University Press.

Ayata, Bilgin, and Deniz Yükseker. 2005. "A Belated Awakening: National and International Responses to the Internal Displacement of Kurds in Turkey." *New Perspectives on Turkey* 32: 5–42.

Aydın, Aysegul, and Cem Emrence. 2015. *Zones of Rebellion: Kurdish Insurgents and the Turkish State*. Ithaca, NY: Cornell University Press.

Aydın, Delal. 2005. *Mobilising the Kurds in Turkey: Newroz as a Myth*. Ankara: MA thesis, Graduate School of Social Sciences, Middle East Technical University, Ankara, Turkey.

Aydın, Derya. 2017. "Cemeteries and Memorials: Violence, Death and Mourning in Kurdish Society." Master's thesis, Sabancı University, Istanbul.

Aydın, Sinan, and Serhat Can. 1999. *Sol İçi Şiddet*. Istanbul: Devrimci Çözüm Yayınları.

Babül, Elif. 2017a. *Bureaucratic Intimacies: Translating Human Rights in Turkey*. Stanford: Stanford University Press.

———. 2017b. "Morality: Understanding Police Training on Human Rights (Turkey)." In *Writing the World of Policing: The Difference Ethnography Makes*, edited by Didier Fassin, 139. Chicago: University of Chicago Press.

Balci, Ali. 2010. "A Trajectory of Competing Narratives: The Turkish Media Debate Ergenekon." *Mediterranean Quarterly* 21, no. 1: 76–100.

Bali, Rıfat. 2008. "The 1934 Thrace Events: Continuity and Change within Turkish State Policies regarding Non-Muslim Minorities. An Interview with Rıfat Bali." *European Journal of Turkish Studies: Social Sciences on Contemporary Turkey*, no. 7.

———. 2012. *Model Citizens of the State: The Jews of Turkey during the Multi-Party Period*. Lanham, MD: Lexington Books.

Barber, Willard Foster, and C. Neale Ronning 1966. *Internal Security and Military Power: Counterinsurgency and Civic Action in Latin America*. Columbus: The Ohio State University Press.

Bargu, Banu. 2014. *Starve and Immolate: The Politics of Human Weapons*. New York: Columbia University Press.

Bayat, Asef. 2015. "Plebeians of the Arab Spring." *Current Anthropology* 56, no. S11: S33–43.

Bayır, Derya. 2014. "The Role of the Judicial System in the Politicide of the Kurdish Opposition: | The Kurdish Question in Turkey." In *the Kurdish Question in Turkey*, edited by Cengiz Güneş and Welat Zeydanlıoğlu, 37–62. London: Routledge.

Beaufre, André. 1965. *An Introduction to Strategy: With Particular Reference to Problems of Defense, Politics, Economics, and Diplomacy in the Nuclear Age*. New York: Praeger.

——. 1969. *Hareket Stratejisi*. Ankara: Genel Kurmay Başkanlığı Basımevi.

Benjamin, Walter. 1996. "Critique of Violence." In *Selected Writings*, Vol. 1: *1913–1926*, 236–52. London: Belknap Press.

Berksoy, Biriz G. 2007. "The Policing of Social Discontent and the Construction of the Social Body: Mapping the Expansion and Militarization of the Police Organization in Turkey in the Post-1980 Period." PhD. diss., Institute for Graduate Studies in the Social Sciences, Boğaziçi University, İstanbul.

Beşikçi, İsmail. 2004. *International Colony Kurdistan*. London: Taderon Press.

Bora, Tanıl. 2019. "State and Civilian Violence against 'Dangerous' Others." In *Authoritarianism and Resistance in Turkey*, edited by Esra Özyürek, Gaye Özpınar, and Emrah Altındiş, 229–35. Cham: Springer.

Borneman, John. 2009. "Fieldwork Experience, Collaboration, and Interlocution." In *Being There: The Fieldwork Encounter and the Making of Truth*, edited by John Borneman and Abdellah Hammoudi, 237–58. Berkeley: University of California Press.

Bourgois, Philippe. 2003. *In Search of Respect: Selling Crack in El Barrio*, Vol. 10. Cambridge: Cambridge University Press.

Bozarslan, Hamit. 2001. "Human Rights and the Kurdish Issue in Turkey: 1984–1999." *Human Rights Review* 3, no. 1: 45–54.

——. 2008. "Kurds and the Turkish State." In *The Cambridge History of Turkey*, Vol. 4: *Turkey in the Modern World*, edited by Reşat Kasaba, 333–56. Cambridge: Cambridge University Press.

Bozçalı, Firat, and Çagri Yoltar. 2013. "A Look at Gezi Park from Turkey's Kurdistan: Fieldsights—Hot Spots." *Cultural Anthropology Online* 31.

Brownlow, Alec. 2005. "A Geography of Men's Fear." *Geoforum* 36, no. 5: 581–92.

Bruce, Steve. 1992. *The Red Hand: Protestant Paramilitaries in Northern Ireland*. Oxford: Oxford University Press.

Bozarslan, Hamit, 2003. "Alevism and the Myths of Research." In *Turkey's Alevi Enigma: A Comprehensive Overview*, edited by Paul J. White and Joost Jongerden. Leiden: Brill.

Buğra, Ayşe. 2002. "Labour, Capital, and Religion: Harmony and Conflict among the Constituency of Political Islam in Turkey." *Middle Eastern Studies* 38, no. 2: 187–204.

Buğra, Ayşe, and Çağlar Keyder. 2003. *New Poverty and the Changing Welfare Regime of Turkey*. Ankara: United Nations Development Programme.

Butler, Judith. 1997. "Gender Is Burning: Questions of Appropriation and Subversion." *Cultural Politics* 11: 381–95.

——. 2013. *Excitable Speech: A Politics of the Performative*. London: Routledge.

Buur, Lars, and Steffen Jensen. 2004. "Introduction: Vigilantism and the Policing of Everyday Life in South Africa." *African Studies* 63, no. 2: 139–52.

Caldeira, Teresa PR. 2002. "The Paradox of Police Violence in Democratic Brazil." *Ethnography* 3, no. 3: 235–63.

Casier, Marlies, Joost Jongerden, and Nic Walker. 2013. "Turkey's Kurdish Movement and the AKP's Kurdish Opening: Kurdish Spring or Fall?" In *The Kurdish Spring: Geopolitical Changes and the Kurds*, edited by Michael Gunther and Mohammed M. A. Ahmed, 12:135–62. Costa Mesa, CA: Mazda Publishers.

Çayan, Mahir. 1992. *Bütün Yazılar*. Istanbul: Atılım Yayınları.

Çaylı, Eray. 2014. "Architectural Memorialization at Turkey's Witness Sites: The Case of the Madimak Hotel." *Contemporary Turkey at a Glance*, edited by Kamp, Kristina, Ayhan Kaya, E. Fuat Keyman, and Ozge Onursal Besgul, 13–24. Wiesbaden: Springer.

Çaylı, Eray. 2018. "Conspiracy Theory as Spatial Practice: The Case of the Sivas Arson Attack, Turkey." *Environment and Planning D: Society and Space* 36, no. 2: 255–72.

Çelik, Aziz. 1996. "Bahar Eylemleri 1989." *Türkiye Sendikacılık Ansiklopedisi* 1: 103–4.

Cemal, Hasan. 2003. *Kürtler*. Istanbul: Doğan Kitap.

Césaire, Aimé. 2001. *Discourse on Colonialism*. New York: New York University Press.

Cetin, Umit. 2016. "Durkheim, Ethnography and Suicide: Researching Young Male Suicide in the Transnational London Alevi-Kurdish Community." *Ethnography* 17, no. 2: 250–77.

———. 2017. "Cosmopolitanism and the Relevance of 'Zombie Concepts': The Case of Anomic Suicide amongst Alevi Kurd Youth." *The British Journal of Sociology* 68, no. 2: 145–166.

Chong Ho Shon, Phillip. 2000. "'Hey You C'me Here!': Subjectivization, Resistance, and the Interpellative Violence of Self-Generated Police-Citizen Encounters." *International Journal for the Semiotics of Law* 13, no. 2: 159–79.

Cizre-Sakallıoğlu, Umit. 1997. "The Anatomy of the Turkish Military's Autonomy." *Comparative Politics* 29, no. 2: 151–56.

Comaroff, Jean, and John Comaroff. 2006. "Law and Disorder in the Postcolony: An Introduction." In *Law and Disorder in the Postcolony*, edited by Jean Comaroff and John Comaroff, 1. Chicago: University of Chicago Press.

———. 2016a. "Reflections on the Anthropology of Law, Governance and Sovereignty." In *Rules of Law and Laws of Ruling*, edited by Franz von Benda-Beckmann and Keebet von Benda-Beckmann, 31–60. London: Routledge.

———. 2016b. *The Truth about Crime: Sovereignty, Knowledge, Social Order*. Chicago: University of Chicago Press.

Coşan-Eke, Deniz. 2019. "The Changing Leadership Role of Dedes in the Alevi Movement from the 1990s to the Present." PhD diss., Ludwig-Maximillians University, Munich.

Cunningham, David. 2004. *There's Something Happening Here: The New Left, the Klan, and FBI Counterintelligence*. Berkeley: University of California Press.

Das, Veena. 1995. *Critical Events: An Anthropological Perspective on Contemporary India*, Vol. 7. Delhi: Oxford University Press.

Della Porta, Donatella. 2006. *Social Movements, Political Violence, and the State: A Comparative Analysis of Italy and Germany*. Cambridge: Cambridge University Press.

Demirsu, Ipek. 2017. *Counter-Terrorism and the Prospects of Human Rights*. Cham: Palgrave.

Deniz, Dilşa. 2020. "Re-Assessing the Genocide of Kurdish Alevis in Dersim, 1937–38." *Genocide Studies and Prevention: An International Journal* 14, no. 2: 5.

Derrida, Jacques. 1992. "Force of Law: The 'Mystical Foundation of Authority.'" In *Deconstruction and the Possibility of Justice*, edited by Drucilla Cornell, Michael Rosenfeld, and David Carlson, 3–67. London: Routledge.

Dikeç, Mustafa. 2006. "Two Decades of French Urban Policy: From Social Development of Neighbourhoods to the Republican Penal State." *Antipode* 38, no. 1: 59–81.

———. 2011. *Badlands of the Republic: Space, Politics and Urban Policy*, Vol. 78. New York: John Wiley & Sons.

———. 2013. "Beginners and Equals: Political Subjectivity in Arendt and Rancière." *Transactions of the Institute of British Geographers* 38, no. 1: 78–90.

Diken, Bülent. 2015. "Political Spirituality: The Devils, Possession, and Truth-Telling." *Cultural Politics* 11, no. 1: 18–35.

Dölek, Caglar. 2015. "Privatization of Security as a State-Led and Class-Driven Process: The Case of Turkey." *Science & Society* 79, no. 3: 414–41.

Douglas, Mary. 1992. *Risk and Blame: Essays in Cultural Theory.* London: Routledge.

Elicin, Yeseren. 2011. "Social Capital, Leadership and Democracy: Rethinking Fatsa." *International Journal of Social Sciences and Humanity Studies* 3, no. 2: 509–18.

Ercan, Harun. 2013. "Talking to the Ontological Other: Armed Struggle and the Negotiations between the Turkish State and the PKK." *Dialectical Anthropology* 37, no. 1: 113–22.

Ertan, Mehmet. 2015. "Politikleşmeden Kimlik Siyasetine: Aleviliğin Politikleşmesi ve Sosyalist Sol." *Birikim* 309/310: 43–56.

——. 2019. "The Latent Politicization of Alevism: The Affiliation between Alevis and Leftist Politics (1960–1980)." *Middle Eastern Studies* 55, no. 6: 932–44.

Ertür, Başak. 2016. "The Conspiracy Archive: Turkey's 'Deep State' on Trial." In *Law, Memory, Violence*, edited by Stewart Motha and Honni van Rijswijk, 187–204. London: Routledge.

Faligot, Roger. 1983. *Britain's Military Strategy in Ireland: The Kitson Experiment.* London: Zed Books.

Fassin, Didier. 2013. *Enforcing Order: An Ethnography of Urban Policing.* Cambridge: Polity.

Feldman, Allen. 1991. *Formations of Violence: The Narrative of the Body and Political Terror in Northern Ireland.* Chicago: University of Chicago Press.

Feldman, Ilana. 2007. "Observing the Everyday: Policing and the Conditions of Possibility in Gaza (1948–1967)." *Interventions* 9, no. 3: 414–33.

——. 2015. *Police Encounters: Security and Surveillance in Gaza under Egyptian Rule.* Stanford: Stanford University Press.

Fernandes, Desmond, and İ Özden. 2001. "United States and NATO Inspired 'Psychological Warfare Operations' against the 'Kurdish Communist Threat' in Turkey." *Variant* 2, no. 12: 10–16.

Fiimfiek, Sefa. 2004. "New Social Movements in Turkey since 1980: Turkish Studies." *Turkish Studies* 5 (2). https://www.tandfonline.com/doi/abs/10.1080/1468384042000228611.

Fletcher, Laurel E., and Harvey M. Weinstein. 2002. "Violence and Social Repair: Rethinking the Contribution of Justice to Reconciliation." *Human Rights Quarterly* 24, no. 3: 573–639.

Foucault, Michel. 1988. *Technologies of the Self: A Seminar with Michel Foucault.* Amherst; University of Massachusetts Press.

——. 1990. *The History of Sexuality: An Introduction*, Vol. I, translated by Robert Harley. New York: Vintage.

——. 1997. "The Ethics of the Concern of the Self as a Practice of Freedom." In *Michel Foucault: Ethics, Subjectivity and Truth: The Essential Works of Michel Foucault 1954–1984*, edited by Paul Rabinow. 281–303. London: Penguin Books.

——. 2005 [1978]. *The Hermeneutics of the Subject: Lectures at the Collège de France 1981–1982.* New York: Macmillan.

——. 2007. *Security, Territory, Population: Lectures at the Collège de France, 1977–78.* New York: Springer.

——. 2012. *Discipline and Punish: The Birth of the Prison.* New York: Vintage.

——. 2013. *Society Must Be Defended: Lectures at the Collège de France, 1975–1976.* Vol. 1. New York: Macmillan.

Fraser, Nancy. 1990. "Rethinking the Public Sphere: A Contribution to the Critique of Actually Existing Democracy." *Social Text* 25/26: 56–80.

Frosh, Stephen. 2013. *Hauntings: Psychoanalysis and Ghostly Transmissions.* London: Palgrave Macmillan.

Galula, David. 1964. *Counterinsurgency Warfare: Theory and Practice*. Westport, CT: Greenwood.

———. 1965. *Ayaklanma Bastırma Hareketleri: Teori ve Tatbikatı*. Ankara: Genel Kurmay Başkanlığı Basımevi.

———. 2002. *Pacification in Algeria, 1956–1958*. Santa Monica, CA: RAND.

Gambetti, Zeynep. 2014. "Occupy Gezi as Politics of the Body." In *The Making of a Protest Movement in Turkey: # Occupygezi*, edited by Umut Özkırımlı, 89–102. Cham: Springer.

Gambetti, Zeynep, and Joost Jongerden. 2015. *The Kurdish Issue in Turkey: A Spatial Perspective*. London: Routledge.

Gans, Herbert J. 2017. "Racialization and Racialization Research." *Ethnic and Racial Studies* 40, no. 3: 341–352.

Ganser, Daniele. 2005. *NATO's Secret Armies: Operation Gladio and Terrorism in Western Europe*. London: Routledge.

Garriott, William. 2013a. "Introduction: Police in Practice: Policing and the Project of Contemporary Governance." In *Policing and Contemporary Governance: The Anthropology of Police in Practice*, 1–30. London: Springer.

———. 2013b. "Policing Methamphetamine: Police Power and the War on Drugs in a Rural US Community." In *Policing and Contemporary Governance*, 53–76. London: Springer.

Gill, Lesley. 2004. *The School of the Americas: Military Training and Political Violence in the Americas*. Durham, NC: Duke University Press.

Girard, René. 1988. *To Double Business Bound: Essays on Literature, Mimesis and Anthropology*. Baltimore: Johns Hopkins University Press.

———. 1996. *Mimesis and Violence*, edited by James G. Williams. New York: Crossroads.

Gledhill, John. 2015. *The New War on the Poor: The Production of Insecurity in Latin America*. London: Zed Books.

Glück, Zoltán, and Setha Low. 2017. "A Sociospatial Framework for the Anthropology of Security." *Anthropological Theory* 17, no. 3: 281–96.

Godoy, Angelina Snodgrass. 2006. *Popular Injustice: Violence, Community, and Law in Latin America*. Stanford: Stanford University Press.

Goldstein, Daniel M. 2012. *Outlawed*. Durham, NC: Duke University Press.

Goldstein, Donna M. 2013. *Laughter out of Place: Race, Class, Violence, and Sexuality in a Rio Shantytown*. Berkeley: University of California Press.

Göner, Özlem. 2005. "The transformation of the Alevi collective identity." *Cultural Dynamics* 17, no. 2: 107–134.

Gönen, Zeynep. 2016. *The Politics of Crime in Turkey: Neoliberalism, Police and the Urban Poor*. London: Bloomsbury.

Göral, Özgür Sevgi, Ayhan Işik, and Özlem Kaya. 2013. *The Unspoken Truth: Enforced Disappearances*. Istanbul: Truth Justice Memory Center (Hafıza Merkezi).

Gordon, Avery. 2008. *Ghostly Matters: Haunting and the Sociological Imagination*. Minneapolis: University of Minnesota Press.

———. 2011. "Some Thoughts on Haunting and Futurity." *Borderlands* 10, no. 2: 1–21.

Gordon, Paul. 1987. "The Killing Machine: Britain and the International Repression Trade." *Race & Class* 29, no. 2: 31–52.

Graham, Stephen. 2009. "Cities as battlespace: The new military urbanism." *City* 13, no. 4: 383–402.

Green, Linda. 1999. *Fear as a Way of Life: Mayan Widows in Rural Guatemala*. New York: Columbia University Press.

Gregory, Derek. 2008. "The Rush to the Intimate: Counterinsurgency and the Cultural Turn in Late Modern War." *Radical Philosophy* 150: 8–23.

Güneş, Cengiz. 2013. *The Kurdish National Movement in Turkey: From Protest to Resistance*. London: Routledge.

Gurman, Hannah. 2013. *Hearts and Minds: A People's History of Counterinsurgency*. London: New Press.

Hage, Ghassan. 2010. "The Affective Politics of Racial Mis-Interpellation." *Theory, Culture & Society* 27, no. 7–8: 112–29.

Han, Clara. 2017. "Experience: Being Policed as a Condition of Life (Chile)." In *Writing the World of Policing: The Difference Ethnography Makes*, edited by Didier Fassin, 162. Chicago: University of Chicago Press.

Harcourt, Bernard E. 2018. *The Counterrevolution: How Our Government Went to War against Its Own Citizens*. New York: Basic Books.

Hashimato and Bezici 2016. "Do the Kurds Have 'No Friends but the Mountains'? Turkey's Secret War against Communists, Soviets and the Kurds." *Middle Eastern Studies* 52, no. 4: 640–655.

Haysom, Nicholas. 1989. *Vigilantes: A Contemporary Form of Repression*. Johannesberg: University of the Witwatersrand Centre for the Study of Violence and Reconciliation.

——. 1990. "Vigilantism and the Policing of African Townships: Manufacturing Violent Stability." In *Towards Justice? Crime and State Control in South Africa*, edited by Desiree Hansson and Dirk Van Zyl Smit, 63–84. Cape Town: Oxford University Press.

Hertz, Robert. 1969. *Death and the Right Hand*, Vol. 4. London: Routledge.

Hirschon, Renée. 2003. *Crossing the Aegean: An Appraisal of the 1923 Compulsory Population Exchange between Greece and Turkey*, Vol. 12. Oxford: Berghahn Books.

Houston, Christopher. 2017. "Revolutionary Ethics." In *the Politics of Culture in Turkey, Greece & Cyprus: Performing the Left Since the Sixties*, edited by Leonidas Karakatsanis and Nikolaos Papadogiannis, 4: 231. London: Routledge.

——. 2020. *Istanbul, City of the Fearless: Urban Activism, Coup D'état, and Memory in Turkey*. Los Angeles: University of California Press.

Huggins, Martha K. 1987. "US-Supported State Terror: A History of Police Training in Latin America." *Crime and Social Justice*, 27/28: 149–71.

Human Rights Foundation of Turkey. 1995. *Annual Report*.

İçduygu, Ahmet, Şule Toktas, and B. Ali Soner. 2008. "The Politics of Population in a Nation-Building Process: Emigration of Non-Muslims from Turkey." *Ethnic and Racial Studies* 31, no. 2: 358–89.

İnancı, Haluk. 2011. "İddianameler ve İddianamelerin Kabulünde Savunma Hakkı." In *Parçalanmış Adalet: Türkiye'de Özel Ceza Yargısı*, edited by Haluk İnancı. Istanbul: İletişim.

Insel, Ahmet. 2012. *Bir Iktidar Aracı Olarak Teror Kavrami*. Istanbul: Birikim.

Isbell, Billie Jean. 2009. "Written on My Body." In *Violence: Ethnographic Encounters*, edited by Parvis Ghassem-Fachandi. 15–34. Oxford: Berg.

İşeri, Gülşen. 2010. *Metropol Sürgünleri: Denize Ekmek Banıp Yiyenlerin Hikayesi*. Istanbul: Su Yayınevi.

——. 2014. *Ateşin ve Sürgünün Gölgesinde: Kentsel Dönüşüm*. Istanbul: Notabene Yayınları.

Işık, Ayhan. 2019. "The Emergence of Paramilitary Groups in Turkey in the 1980s."*Kurds in Turkey: Ethnographies of Heterogeneous Experiences*, edited by Lucie Drechselová and Adnan Çelik, 59–80. London: Lexington Books..

Işık, Oğuz, and M. Melih Pınarcıoğlu. 2012. *Nöbetleşe Yoksulluk: Gecekondulaşma ve Kent Yoksulları, Sultanbeyli Örneği*. Ankara: İletişim Yayınları.

Jacoby, Tim. 2010. "Political Violence, the 'War on Terror' and the Turkish Military." *Critical Studies on Terrorism* 3, no. 1: 99–118.

Jeganathan, Pradeep. 2004. "Checkpoint: Anthropology, Identity, and the State." In *Anthropology in the Margins of the State*, edited by Veena Das and Deborah Poole, 67–80. Santa Fe, NM: School of American Research Press.

Jongerden, Joost. 2003. "Violation of Human Rights and the Alevis in Turkey." In *Turkey's Alevi Enigma: A Comprehensive Overview*, edited by Paul J. White and Joost Jongerden, 71–92. Leiden: Brill.

——. 2007. *The Settlement Issue in Turkey and the Kurds: An analysis of Spatial Policies, Modernity and War*. Leiden: Brill.

——. 2010. "Village Evacuation and Reconstruction in Kurdistan (1993–2002)." *Études Rurales* no. 186: 77–100.

Jongerden, Joost, and Ahmet Hamdi Akkaya. 2018. "The Kurdistan Workers Party (PKK) and Kurdish Political Parties in the 1970s." In *Routledge Handbook of the Kurds*, edited by Michael Gunther, 270–82. London: Routledge.

Jongerden, Joost, Hugo de Vos, and Jacob van Etten. 2007. "Forest Burning as Counter-Insurgency in Turkish Kurdistan: An Analysis from Space." *International Journal of Kurdish Studies* 21, no. 1–2: 1–15.

Karakaya-Stump, Ayfer. 2014. "Alevizing Gezi." *Jadaliyya*.

——. 2018. "The AKP, Sectarianism, and the Alevis' Struggle for Equal Rights in Turkey." *National Identities* 20, no. 1: 53–67.

Karandinos, George, Laurie Kain Hart, Fernando Montero Castrillo, and Philippe Bourgois. 2014. "The Moral Economy of Violence in the US Inner City." *Current Anthropology* 55, no. 1: 1–22.

Karasulu, Ahu. 2016. "We May Be Lessees, but the Neighbourhood Is Ours." In *Everywhere Taksim*, edited by Isabel David and Kumru Toktamıs, 201. Amsterdam: Amsterdam University Press.

Karpiak, Kevin G. 2010. "Of Heroes and Polemics: 'The Policeman' in Urban Ethnography." *PoLAR: Political and Legal Anthropology Review* 33, no. 1: 7–31.

Karpiak, Kevin G., and William Garriott. 2018. *The Anthropology of Police*. London: Routledge.

Kazmaz, Remzi. 2016. *Gereği Düşünüldü: Gazi Davası*. Istanbul: Çiviyazilari.

Kelly, John D., Beatrice Jauregui, Sean T. Mitchell, and Jeremy Walton, eds. 2010. *Anthropology and Global Counterinsurgency*. University of Chicago Press, 2019.

Kelly, Tobias. 2010 "In a Treacherous State: The Fear of Collaboration Among West Bank Palestinians." *Traitors*, edited by Thiranagama, Sharika, and Tobias Kelly, 169–187. Philadelphia: University of Pennsylvania Press.

Kennedy, Liam. 2013. *Race and Urban Space in American Culture*. London: Routledge.

Khalili, Laleh. 2010. "The New (and Old) Classics of Counterinsurgency." *Middle East Report*, no. 255.

——. 2012. *Time in the Shadows: Confinement in Counterinsurgencies*. Stanford: Stanford University Press.

——. 2014. "The Utility of Proxy Detentions in Counterinsurgencies." *War, Police and Assemblages of Intervention*, edited by Bachmann, Jan, Colleen Bell, and Caroline Holmqvist, 92–108. Abingdon, VA: Routledge.

Kieser, Hans-Lukas. 2003. "Alevis, Armenians and Kurds in Unionist/Kemalist Turkey (1908–1938)." In *Turkey's Alevi Enigma: A Comprehensive Overview*, edited by Paul Joseph White and Joost Jongerden, 177–96. Leiden: Brill.

Kilcullen, David. 2006a. "Counter-Insurgency Redux." *Survival* 48, no. 4: 111–30.

——. 2006b. "Twenty-Eight Articles Fundamentals of Company-Level Counterinsurgency." *Marine Corps Gazette* 90, no. 7: 29–50.

——. 2007. "Religion and Insurgency." *Small Wars Journal* 12.

Kışlalı, M. Ali. 1996. *Güneydoğu, Düşük Yoğunluklu Çatışma*. Istanbul: Ümit Yayıncılık.

Kitson, Frank. 1971. *Low-Intensity Operations: Subversion, Insurgency and Peacekeeping*. London: Faber and Faber.

Knudsen, Are John. 2016. "Death of a Statesman—Birth of a Martyr: Martyrdom and Memorials in Post-Civil War Lebanon." *Anthropology of the Middle East* 11, no. 2: 1–17.

Koc, Ismet, Attila Hancioglu, and Alanur Cavlin. 2008. "Demographic Differentials and Demographic Integration of Turkish and Kurdish Populations in Turkey." *Population Research and Policy Review* 27, no. 4: 447–57.

Koskela, Hille. 1997. "'Bold Walk and Breakings': Women's Spatial Confidence versus Fear of Violence." *Gender, Place and Culture: A Journal of Feminist Geography* 4, no. 3: 301–20.

Kumral Şefika 2017. "Ballots with Bullets: Elections, Violence, and the Rise of the Extreme Right in Turkey." *Journal of Labor and Society* 20, no. 2: 231–261.

Kurt, Mehmet. 2017. *Kurdish Hizbullah in Turkey: Islamism, Violence and the State*. London: Pluto Press.

———. 2019. "'My Muslim Kurdish Brother': Colonial Rule and Islamist Governmentality in the Kurdish Region of Turkey." *Journal of Balkan and Near Eastern Studies* 21, no. 3: 350–65.

Kurt, Umit. 2010. "The Doctrine of 'Turkish-Islamic Synthesis' as Official Ideology of the September 12 and the "Intellectuals' Hearth—Aydınlar Ocağı'" as the Ideological Apparatus of the State." *European Journal of Economic and Political Studies*, 111.

Kwon, Heonik. 2013. "The Social and Political Theory of the Soul." *A Companion to the Anthropology of Religion*, edited by Boddy, Janice Patricia, and Michael Lambek. London: Wiley Blackwell.

Laçiner, Ömer. 1996. *1 Mayıs 1996: Yol Ayrımı*. Istanbul: Birikim.

Larkins, Erika Robb. 2015. *The Spectacular Favela: Violence in Modern Brazil*. Los Angeles: University of California Press.

LeBrón, Marisol. 2019. *Policing Life and Death: Race, Violence, and Resistance in Puerto Rico*. Berkeley: University of California Press.

Lomnitz-Adler, Claudio. 2003. "Times of Crisis: Historicity, Sacrifice, and the Spectacle of Debacle in Mexico City." *Public Culture* 15, no. 1: 127–47.

Lord, Ceren. 2017. "Rethinking the Justice and Development Party's 'Alevi Openings.'" *Turkish Studies* 18, no. 2: 278–96.

Maksudyan, Nazan. 2005. "The Turkish Review of Anthropology and the Racist Face of Turkish Nationalism." *Cultural Dynamics* 17, no. 3: 291–322.

Mamdani, Mahmood. 2002. "Good Muslim, Bad Muslim: A Political Perspective on Culture and Terrorism." *American Anthropologist* 104, no. 3: 766–75.

———. 2018. *Citizen and subject: Contemporary Africa and the Legacy of late Colonialism*. New Jersey: Princeton University Press.

Manning, Peter K. 2018. "An Anthropology of Policing." In *The Anthropology of Police*, edited by Kevin G. Karpiak and William Garriott, 23–33. New York: Routledge.

Marcus, Aliza. 1996. "'Should I Shoot You?': An Eyewitness Account of an Alevi Uprising in Gazi." *Middle East Report*, no. 199: 24–26.

Markussen, Hege Irene. 2012. *Teaching History, Learning Piety: An Alevi Foundation in Contemporary Turkey*. Lund: Sekel Bokförlag.

Marx, Gary T. 1974. "Thoughts on a Neglected Category of Social Movement Participant: The Agent Provocateur and the Informant." *American Journal of Sociology* 80, no. 2: 402–42.

———. 1989. *Undercover: Police Surveillance in America*. Berkeley: University of California Press.

Marx, Karl. 1975 [1844]. "On the Jewish Question." In *Collected Works*, edited by Karl Marx and Fredrich Engels, Vol. III. London: Lawrence and Wishart.

Masco, Joseph. 2014. *The Theater of Operations: National Security Affect from the Cold War to the War on Terror*. Durham, NC: Duke University Press.

Massicard, Elise. 2003. "Alevism as a Productive Misunderstanding: The Hacıbektaş Festival." In *Turkey's Alevi Enigma: A Comprehensive Overview*, edited by Paul J. White and Joost Jongerden,125–40. Leiden: Brill.

——. 2013. *The Alevis in Turkey and Europe: Identity and Managing Territorial Diversity*. London: Routledge.

Mbembe, J.-A. 2003. "Necropolitics." *Public Culture* 15, no. 1: 11–40.

——. "The society of enmity." *Radical Philosophy* 200, no. 1: 23–35.

McCuen, John J. 1966. *The Art of Counter-Revolutionary War: The Strategy of Counter-Insurgency*. Mechanicsburg: Stackpole Books

McFate, Montgomery. 2005. "Anthropology and Counterinsurgency: The Strange Story of their Curious Relationship." *Military Review* 85, no. 2: 24.

McFate, Montgomery, and Andrea V. Jackson. 2006. "The Object beyond War: Counterinsurgency and the Four Tools of Political Competition." *Military Review*, February.

McGovern, Mark. 2011. "The Dilemma of Democracy: Collusion and the State of Exception." *Studies in Social Justice* 5, no. 2: 213–30.

——. 2013. "Inquiring into Collusion? Collusion, the State and the Management of Truth Recovery in Northern Ireland." *State Crime Journal* 2, no. 1: 4–29.

——. 2015. "State Violence and the Colonial Roots of Collusion in Northern Ireland." *Race & Class* 57, no. 2: 3–23.

Meclis Araştırması Komisyonu. 2012. "Darbe Arastirmalari Komisyonu Tutanagi, Dördüncü Oturum." Ankara. https://www.tbmm.gov.tr/arastirma_komisyonlari /darbe_muhtira/docs/tutanak_son/27_may%C4%B1s_alt_komisyonu/27 _may%C4%B1s_alt_komisyonu/26.06.2012/Talat%20Turhan-26-06-2012.pdf.

Mills, Charles W. 2014. *The Racial Contract*. Ithaca, NY: Cornell University Press.

Moffat, Chris. 2018. "Politics and the Work of the Dead in Modern India." *Comparative Studies in Society and History* 60, no. 1: 178–211.

Mumcu, Uğur.1997 [1990]. *Saklı Devletin Güncesi: "Çatlı Vs. . . ."* Ankara: Uğur Mumcu Araştırmacı Gazetecilik Vakfı Yayınları.

Mutluer, Nil. 2016. "The Looming Shadow of Violence and Loss: Alevi Responses to Persecution and Discrimination." *Journal of Balkan and Near Eastern Studies* 18, no 2: 145–156.

Navaro-Yashin, Yael. 2012. *The Make-Believe Space: Affective Geography in a Postwar Polity*. Durham, NC: Duke University Press.

Neocleous, Mark. 2011. "'A Brighter and Nicer New Life': Security as Pacification." *Social & Legal Studies* 20, no. 2: 191–208.

Nonini, Donald M. 2015. "'At That Time We Were Intimidated on All Sides': Residues of the Malayan Emergency as a Conjunctural Episode of Dispossession." *Critical Asian Studies* 47, no. 3: 337–58.

Öcalan, Abdullah. 2017. *The Political Thought of Abdullah Öcalan: Kurdistan, Woman's Revolution and Democratic Confederalism*. London: Pluto Press.

Oğuz, Öznur, Ercüment Akdeniz, and Iskender Bayhan. 2012. *Gençliğin Mücadelesi ve Örgütlenmesi Üzerine*. Istanbul: Evrensel Basim Yayin.

Okuyucu-Ergun, Gunes. 2009. "Witness Anonymity in Turkish Criminal Law: Some Comparative Observations." *Journal of Comparative Law* 4: 170.

Özdağ, Ümit. 2005. *Türkiye'de Düşük Yoğunluklu Çatışma ve PKK*. Istanbul: 3ok Yayıncılık.

Ozsoy, Hisyar. 2010. "Between Gift and Taboo: Death and the Negotiation of National Identity and Sovereignty in the Kurdish Conflict in Turkey." PhD diss., University of Texas at Austin.

Özyürek, Esra. 2009. "'The Light of the Alevi Fire Was Lit in Germany and Then Spread to Turkey': A Transnational Debate on the Boundaries of Islam." *Turkish Studies* 10, no. 2: 233–53.

Paker, Murat. 2000. "Turkey's Operation 'Return to Life.'" *Middle East Report Online,* December 29.

Parenti, Christian. 2000. *Lockdown America: Police and Prisons in the Age of Crisis.* London: Verso.

Patreaus, David, et al. 2010. *The US Army/Marine Corps Counterinsurgency Field Manual.* Brattleboro, VT: Echo Point Books.

Pérouse, Jean-François. 2005. "Phénomène Migratoire, Formation et Différenciation Des Associations de Hemşehri à Istanbul: Chronologies et Géographies Croisées." *European Journal of Turkish Studies: Social Sciences on Contemporary Turkey,* no. 2.

Perugini, Nicola. 2008. "Anthropologists at War: Ethnographic Intelligence and Counter-Insurgency in Iraq and Afghanistan." *International Political Anthropology* 1, no. 2: 213–27.

Pile, Steve. 2005. *Real Cities: Modernity, Space and the Phantasmagorias of City Life.* London: SAGE.

Pratten, David, and Atreyee Sen. 2007. *Global Vigilantes: Perspectives on Justice and Violence.* London: Hurst.

Price, David H. 2002. "Lessons from Second World War Anthropology: Peripheral, Persuasive and Ignored Contributions." *Anthropology Today* 18, no. 3: 14–20.

———. 2011. *Weaponizing Anthropology: Social Science in Service of the Militarized State.* Oakland, CA: AK Press.

———. 2016. *Cold War Anthropology: The CIA, the Pentagon, and the Growth of Dual Use Anthropology.* Durham, NC: Duke University Press.

Puar, Jasbir K. 2015. "The 'Right' to Maim: Disablement and in Humanist Biopolitics in Palestine." *Borderlands* 14, no 1: 1–27.

Rabinow, Paul. 2009. "Foucault's Untimely Struggle: Toward a Form of Spirituality." *Theory, Culture & Society* 26, no. 6: 25–44.

Ralph, Laurence. 2014. *Renegade Dreams: Living through Injury in Gangland Chicago.* Chicago: University of Chicago Press.

———. 2015. "The Limitations of a 'Dirty' World." *Du Bois Review: Social Science Research on Race* 12, no. 2: 441–51.

———. 2020. *The Torture Letters: Reckoning with Police Violence.* Chicago: University of Chicago Press.

Rancière, Jacques. 1995. "Politics, Identification, and Subjectivization." In *The Identity in Question,* edited by John Rajchman, 63–70. New York: Routledge.

———. 1999. *Disagreement: Politics and Philosophy.* Minneapolis: University of Minnesota Press.

———. 2001. "Ten Theses on Politics." *Theory & Event* 5 (3).

———. 2012. *Proletarian Nights: The Workers' Dream in Nineteenth-Century France.* London: Verso.

———. 2015. *Dissensus: On Politics and Aesthetics.* London: Bloomsbury.

Rancière, Jacques, and Davide Panagia. 2000. "Dissenting Words: A Conversation with Jacques Rancière." *Diacritics* 113–26.

Ratele, Kopano. 2013. "Subordinate Black South African Men without Fear." *Cahiers d'études Africaines* 53, no. 209–210: 247–68.

Rios, Victor M. 2011. *Punished: Policing the Lives of Black and Latino Boys.* New York: New York University Press.

Rose, Gillian. 1993. *Feminism & Geography: The Limits of Geographical Knowledge.* Minneapolis: University of Minnesota Press.

Selod, Saher, and David G. Embrick. 2013. "Racialization and Muslims: Situating the Muslim Experience in Race Scholarship." *Sociology Compass* 7, no. 8: 644–655.

Saglam, Erol. 2021. "Taking the Matter into Your Own Hands: Ethnographic Insights into Societal Violence and the Reconfigurations of the State in Contemporary Turkey." *Southeast European and Black Sea Studies* 21, no. 2: 213–230.

Salem, Sara. 2019. "Haunted Histories: Nasserism and the Promises of the Past." *Middle East Critique* 28, no. 3: 261–77.

Samet, Robert. 2019. *Deadline: Populism and the Press in Venezuela.* Chicago: University of Chicago Press.

Sayari, Sabri, and Bruce Hoffman. 1991. "Urbanization and Insurgency: The Turkish Case, 1976–1980." RAND Note N-3228-USDP. Santa Monica, CA: RAND.

——. 1994. "Urbanisation and Insurgency: The Turkish Case, 1976–1980." *Small Wars & Insurgencies* 5, no. 2: 162–79.

Scheper-Hughes, Nancy. 2015. "Death Squads and Vigilante Politics in Democratic Northeast Brazil." In *Violence at the Urban Margins*, edited by Javier Auyero, Philippe Bourgois, and Nancy Scheper-Hughes, 266–304. Oxford: Oxford University Press.

Schmitt, Carl. 2007. *The Concept of the Political.* Chicago: University of Chicago Press.

Schrader, Stuart. 2019. *Badges without Borders: How Global Counterinsurgency Transformed American Policing*, Vol. 56. Berkeley: University of California Press.

Secor, Anna J. 2007. "Between Longing and Despair: State, Space, and Subjectivity in Turkey." *Environment and Planning D: Society and Space* 25, no. 1: 33–52.

Shalhoub-Kevorkian, Nadera. 2015. *Security Theology, Surveillance and the Politics of Fear.* Cambridge: Cambridge University Press.

Shirlow, Peter. 2003. "'Who Fears to Speak': Fear, Mobility, and Ethno-Sectarianism in the Two 'ardoynes." *Global Review of Ethnopolitics* 3, no. 1: 76–91.

Silverstein, Paul, and Chantal Tetreault. 2005. "Urban Violence in France." *Middle East Report Online.*

Simpson, Audra. 2007. "On Ethnographic Refusal: Indigeneity, 'Voice' and Colonial Citizenship." *Junctures: The Journal for Thematic Dialogue*, no. 9: 67–80.

Skidmore, Monique. 2012. *Karaoke Fascism: Burma and the Politics of Fear.* Philadelphia: University of Pennsylvania Press.

Sluka, Jeffrey. 1995. "Cultures of Terror and Resistance in Northern Ireland." *PoLAR: Political and Legal Anthropology Review* 18, no. 1: 97–106.

——. 2010. "'For God and Ulster.'" In *Death Squad: The Anthropology of State Terror*, edited by Sluka, Jeffrey, 127–157. University of Pennsylvania Press.

——. 2012. "Reflections on Managing Danger in Fieldwork: Dangerous Anthropology in Belfast." *Ethnographic Fieldwork: An Anthropological Reader*, edited by Robben, Antonius CGM, and Sluka, Jeffrey, 283–295, Sussex: John Wiley & Sons.

Smith, Rupert. 2008. *The Utility of Force: The Art of War in the Modern World.* New York: Vintage.

Sökefeld, Martin. 2004. "Religion or Culture? Concepts of Identity in the Alevi Diaspora." In *Diaspora, Identity and Religion: New Directions in Theory and Research*, edited by Waltraud Kokot, Khachig Tölölyan, and Caroline Alfonso, 133–55. London: Routledge.

——. 2008. *Struggling for Recognition: The Alevi Movement in Germany and in Transnational Space.* Oxford: Berghahn Books.

Söyler, Mehtap. 2013. "Informal Institutions, Forms of State and Democracy: The Turkish Deep State." *Democratization* 20, no. 2: 310–34.

Sparks, Richard, Evi Girling, and Ian Loader. 2001. "Fear and Everyday Urban Lives." *Urban Studies* 38, no. 5–6: 885–98.

Stanko, Steve, and Kahy Hobdell. 1993. "Assault on Men: Masculinity and Male Victimization." *British Journal of Criminology* 33, no. 3: 400–15.

Steenkamp, Chrissie. 2005. "The Legacy of War: Conceptualizing a 'Culture of Violence' to Explain Violence after Peace Accords." *Round Table* 94, no. 379: 253–67.

Stewart, Charles. 2017. "Uncanny History: Temporal Topology in the Post-Ottoman World." *Social Analysis* 61, no. 1: 129–142.

Swyngedouw, Erik. 2009. "The Antinomies of the Postpolitical City: In Search of a Democratic Politics of Environmental Production." *International Journal of Urban and Regional Research* 33, no. 3: 601–20.

Tambar, Kabir. 2010. "The Aesthetics of Public Visibility: Alevi Semah and the Paradoxes of Pluralism in Turkey." *Comparative Studies in Society and History* 52, no. 3: 652–79.

———. 2014. *The Reckoning of Pluralism: Political Belonging and the Demands of History in Turkey.* Stanford: Stanford University Press.

———. 2016. "Brotherhood in Dispossession: State Violence and the Ethics of Expectation in Turkey." *Cultural Anthropology* 31, no. 1: 30–55.

Taussig, Michael. 1984. 1992. *The Nervous System.* New York: Psychology Press.

———. 1993. *Mimesis and Alterity: A Particular History of the Senses.* London: Routledge.

———. 1999. *Defacement: Public Secrecy and the Labor of the Negative.* Stanford: Stanford University Press.

Trouillot, Michel-Rolph. 2001. "The Anthropology of the State: Close Encounters of a Deceptive Kind. Forum on Theory in Anthropology." *Current Anthropology* 42, no. 1: 125–38.

Tuğal, Cihan. 2009. *Passive Revolution: Absorbing the Islamic Challenge to Capitalism.* Stanford: Stanford University Press.

Tullis, Tracy. *A Vietnam at Home: Policing the Ghettos in the Counterinsurgency Era.* PhD diss., New York University, 1999.

Tüleylioğlu, Orhan. 2011. *Namlunun Ucundaki Mahalle: Gazi Mahallesi Olayları, 12–13 Mart 1995.* Istanbul: Uğur Mumcu Araştırmacı Gazetecilik Vakfı.

Turgay, D. 2011. "Gizli Tanık." In *Parçalanmış Adalet,* edited by Haluk Inanıcı, 243–50. Istanbul: Iletişim.

Ünal, Mehmet Burak. 2014. "The Possibility of Arendtian Action: Founding New Public Spaces in Fatsa 1979–80 and the Occupy Wall Street Movement." PhD diss., Middle East Technical University, Ankara.

Ünlü, Barış. 2016. "The Kurdish Struggle and the Crisis of the Turkishness Contract." *Philosophy & Social Criticism* 42, no. 4–5: 397–405.

———. 2018. *Türklük Sözleşmesi: Oluşumu, Işleyişi ve Krizi.* Ankara: Dipnot Yayınları.

Van Bruinessen, Martin. 1994. "Genocide of the Kurds." *The Widening Circle of Genocide* 3: 165–92.

———. 1996a. "Kurds, Turks and the Alevi Revival in Turkey." *Middle East Report,* no. 200: 7–10.

———. 1996b. "Turkey's Death Squads." *Middle East Report* 199: 20–23.

Verdery, Katherine. 2014. *Secrets and Truth: Ethnography in the Archive of Romania's Secret Police,* Vol. 7. Budapest: Central European University Press.

———. 2018. *My Life as a Spy: Investigations in a Secret Police File.* Durham, NC: Duke University Press.

Wacquant, Loïc. 2009. *Punishing the Poor: The Neoliberal Government of Social Insecurity.* Durham, NC: Duke University Press.

Weizman, Eyal. 2012. *Hollow Land: Israel's Architecture of Occupation*. London: Verso.

Weld, Kirsten. 2014. *Paper Cadavers: The Archives of Dictatorship in Guatemala*. Durham, NC: Duke University Press.

White, Jenny. 1997. "Pragmatists or Ideologues? Turkey's Welfare Party in Power." *Current History* 96, no. 606: 25.

——. 2004. *Money Makes Us Relatives: Women's Labor in Urban Turkey*. London: Routledge.

——. 2011. *Islamist Mobilization in Turkey: A Study in Vernacular Politics*. Seattle: University of Washington Press.

Willis, Graham Denyer. 2015. *The Killing Consensus: Police, Organized Crime, and the Regulation of Life and Death in Urban Brazil*. Berkeley: University of California Press.

Wilson, Richard A., John Borneman, Anne Griffiths, Deborah A. James, Sally Engle Merry, Laura Nader, Fiona Ross, Owen B. Sichone, and Richard A. Wilson. 2000. "Reconciliation and Revenge in Post-Apartheid South Africa: Rethinking Legal Pluralism and Human Rights." *Current Anthropology* 41, no. 1: 75–98.

Yassin, Nasser. 2010. *Violent Urbanization and Homogenization of Space and Place: Reconstructing the Story of Sectarian Violence in Beirut*. Helsinki: World Institute for Development Economics Research.

Yegen, Mesut. 2016. "The Turkish left and the Kurdish Question." *Journal of Balkan and Near Eastern Studies* 18, no. 2: 157–176.

Yıldız, Ali Aslan, and Maykel Verkuyten. 2011. "Inclusive Victimhood: Social Identity and the Politicization of Collective Trauma among Turkey's Alevis in Western Europe." *Peace and Conflict: Journal of Peace Psychology* 17, no. 3: 243–69.

Yılmaz, Birgül. 2020. "Language Attitudes and Religion: Kurdish Alevis in the UK." *Kurdish Studies*, 8 no: 133–161.

Yonucu, Deniz. 2008. "A Story of a Squatter Neighborhood: From the Place of the 'Dangerous Classes' to the 'Place of Danger.'" *Berkeley Journal of Sociology* 52: 50–72.

——. 2013. "European Istanbul and Its Enemies: Istanbul's Working Class as the Constitutive outside of the Modern/European Istanbul." In *The Economies of Urban Diversity*, edited by Darja Reuschke et al., 217–33. Cham: Springer.

——. 2014. "Türkiye'de Bir Yönetim Biçimi Olarak Mekansal Ayrıştırma: Tehlikeli Mahalleler, Olağanüstü Hal ve Militarist Sınır Çizimi' [Spatial Segregation as a Technology of Governance in Turkey: Dangerous Neighbourhoods, State of Emergency and the Drawing of Militarized Boundaries]." *Yeni Istanbul Çalışmaları [New Istanbul Studies]* Istanbul: Metis.

——. 2018a. "The Absent Present Law: An Ethnographic Study of Legal Violence in Turkey." *Social & Legal Studies* 27, 6: 716–33.

——. 2018b. "Urban Vigilantism: A Study of Anti-Terror Law, Politics and Policing in Istanbul." *International Journal of Urban and Regional Research* 42, no. 3 (2018): 408–422.

——. 2022. "Inspirational Hauntings and a Fearless Spirit of Resistance: Negotiating the Undercover Police Surveillance of Racialized Spaces in Istanbul," *Current Anthropology*.

Zerilli, Linda M. G. 2005. *Feminism and the Abyss of Freedom*. Chicago: University of Chicago Press.

Zeydanlıoğlu, Welat. 2009. "Torture and Turkification in the Diyarbakır Military Prison." In *Rights, Citizenship & Torture: Perspectives on Evil, Law and the State*, edited by Welat Zeydanlıoğlu and John Parry, 73–92. London: Inter-Disciplinary Press.

Zilberg, Elana. 2007. "Gangster in Guerilla Face: A Transnational Mirror of Production between the USA and El Salvador." *Anthropological Theory* 7, no. 1: 37–57.

Index

Abdal, Pir Sultan, 32, 32f
Abrams, Philip, 35
active minority of insurgents, 7, 8
Adalet ve Kalkinma Partisi. *See* Justice and
  Development Party
affect, 12, 74, 77, 93, 110
affect-and-emotion-generating security
  strategies, 13, 25, 73–74, 77, 93, 146
affective security strategies, 18, 26
Agamben, Giorgio, 148, 158
agents provocateurs, 12, 39, 50, 75, 79–80;
  Black Panthers infiltrated by, 136; politics
  and, 85–88; revolutionary groups infiltrated
  by, 136
Ahmed, Sara, 70
Alevi cultural archive of oppression and
  resistance, 25, 28, 30–33, 124
Alevi opening (*Alevi açılımı*), 20
Alevi rebellions, Ottoman-era, 32
Alevis, 1, 3, 8, 12, 16–18, 28, 75–76;
  discrimination of Kurds and, 22, 133–34;
  double racialization of Kurdish Alevis, 4;
  ethnic heterogeneity of, 4; Gezi uprising
  blame on, 146; identity of, 30, 79–82;
  insecurity resurrected by sectarian
  imaginary, 147–50; Kurds and, 84–85, 93,
  149–50; marginalization of, 156–57; media
  representation of, 3, 147–48; negative
  interpellation in racialization of, 84;
  people's courts and historical practice of,
  40–42; racialization of, 3, 26, 76–78, 81–82,
  95, 135–36, 160; as revolutionaries, 30–33;
  ruling elites framing, in Gazi incidents of
  1995, 86–87; shootings in community of,
  72–73; state-backed Islamist violence
  against, 64; Sunni-Turkish polarizing, 76; as
  threat, 147; vigilantism among working-
  class, 100–102; working-class, 27, 64, 97,
  129, 139–40, 143f
Alevism: definitions of, 30–31, 82
Alevi-Sunni conflict, 150
Algeria, 26
Algerian War, 94
Ali, Arshas Imitaz, 118, 129–30
Ali, Nosheen, 82, 140

Ali and the twelve imams, 32f
Alibeyköy Cemevi, 60
Allen, Lori, 95
Allied Joint Doctrine of Counterinsurgency
  (COIN), 6, 10, 13, 24, 74–75, 92, 118–19, 130
Altheide, David, 88, 147
Althusser, Louis, 77–78
amendment no. 5532, 108
anarchists, 49
anti-Alevi, 27, 84, 126, 140, 146–47
anti-Alevi pogroms, 8, 164n16
anti-apartheid struggle, of South Africa, 94
anticolonial, 5, 7, 93, 156, 164n8
antiterror law, 26, 131, 154, 159; crime,
  community justice, mimetic policing and,
  96–115; expansion of, 108–9, 111–12;
  no. 3713, 108; provocative counterorganization strategies' use of, 97
antiterror operation, 107, 114, 116, 143, 152–53
Apê Musa, 56
Arendt, Hannah, 44, 49, 54, 78, 81, 112; on
  politics, 33–34; on the proletariat, 33–34, 47
Aretxaga, Begoña, 35
armed propaganda, 58
Armenian Genocide (1915), 7–8
Armutlu, 4, 68–69
artificial balance theory, 58
asayiş group, 38–40
assassinations, 59–60
Aydınlık (newspaper), 51

banlieus, 81, 134
Barış ve Demokrasi Partisi. *See* Peace and
  Democracy Party
Batman, 29
Beaufre, André, 94–95
Bedreddin (Sheikh), 32, 122
Bekaa Valley, 56
BEKSAV, 57–58
Belfast, 35, 50, 85, 93, 146
Benjamin, Walter, 123–24, 127, 130
Bir Mayıs, 4, 16–17, 29, 35, 49
Black Panthers, 94, 136
Borneman, John, 118
Bosporus Strait, 146

Bozkurt, Mahmut Esat, 8
Brazil, 41, 99, 100
Brecht, Bertolt, 45, 168n22
Burma, 118
Butler, Judith, 77–78

Çayan, Mahir, 17f, 58–59, 122
Çayan Mahallesi, 4
cem ceremonies, 30, 31, 41–42
cemevi (cem house), 30, 32f, 130
cemevleri, 124
central governance, 33
Central Intelligence Agency (CIA), 6
Césaire, Aimé, 54
çeteci (gangsters), 100–102
charity networks, 98
checkpoints, ix, 53, 65–71, 81, 91
children of laborers (emekçi çocukları), 45–46
Chong Ho Shon, Phillip, 78
CIA. See Central Intelligence Agency
Cigerxwîn, 56
Çiller, Tansu, 75
COIN. See Allied Joint Doctrine of Counterinsurgency
Cold War, 4, 10, 113, 154, 158; counterinsurgency strategies of, 5, 25, 27; Romania in era of, 118; War on Terror linked to, 12
colonial "boomerang effect," 25, 54
colonialism, 13, 124, 155–56; policing and, 91; violence and, 54
colonialist fascist police state (sömürgeci faşist polis devleti), 130
colonial school of warfare, 5, 27
Communist Party of Turkey / Marxist-Leninist (TKP/ML), 128–29
Comraroffs, 5
Confederation of Public Employees' Trade Union (KESK), 55
conservatism, in post-coup Turkey, 63
consumerism, 98
corruption, of police, 99
Çorum, 49
counterguerrilla, 10, 22, 39, 66, 93, 166n32, 168n20
counterinsurgency: in Algeria, 26; ethnography and, 19; framing as, 74–77; in Malaya, 56, 146, 165n22, 170n22; of 1990s, 159; in Northern Ireland, 26, 85; against PKK, 110; as policing, 7; politics and, 13–15, 158–59, 161; psychological warfare of, 12, 39; in South Africa, 94; Turkish Left and, 9; Turkish military officers, training in the US,

39–40; of Turkish state, 61; as war on politics, 13–15, 161
counterinsurgency strategies, 6, 12–13, 50, 145–47; of AKP, 113–14; in Cold War, 5, 25, 27; Northern Kurdistan exporting, 65–66; provocation of fear as, 147
Counterinsurgency Warfare (Galula), 10, 94–95
counterrevolution, 13
counterviolence: defensive, 88–89; in Gaza, 95; moral dilemma and, 151–54; security agents provoking, 10; of state security apparatus, 5; state violence and, 155–56
coup attempt, Turkey (2016), 20, 130
coup d'état, Turkey (1980), 8–9, 40, 51, 54–58, 71; Devrimova post-, 52; injustice in post-, 60–64; revolutionary organization in, 53; state violence post-, 62–63
crime: community justice, mimetic policing, and the antiterror laws, 96–115; criminalization and, 97–100; petty, 97, 98, 104; sociopolitical roots of, 103–8; state security apparatus connected to, 99–100; working-class youth involvement in, 103–4
criminalization, 22–23; crime and, 97–100; of the racialized Alevi and Kurdish working-class, 24; of urban poor, 103–4; of working-class youth, 18, 173f; of youths, 15; in Zeytinburnu, 98
culture-centric warfare, 24

the dead, 127–30
decolonial era, 5–6, 10, 18
dede, 41, 63–64, 72
deep state, of Turkey, 39
defamation, of dissident groups, 48–49
defensive counterviolence, 88–89
Della Porta, Donatella, 62
Demirtaş, Selahattin, 159
Devrimci Halk Kurtuluş Partisi Cephesi. See Revolutionary People's Liberation Party Front
Devrimci Sol. See Revolutionary Left
Devrimova, 5, 12, 26, 41, 42–44, 56–57, 90, 122–25, 142; displacement of Kurds in, 99; in early 2000s, 100–102; ethnography in, 19–22; Kurds and Alevis in, 84–85, 93; in late 2000s, 117; mob violence in, 50; nationalism in, 38; in 1980s, 53; in 1990s, 53, 57–58, 61–63, 66–71; people's courts in, 29, 36, 40, 41, 44–46; police checkpoints in, 65, 67–71; police raidings of houses in, 49; as revolutionary neighborhood, 36–37; revolutionary

organization in, 16–18; as sanctuary space, 34–36; socialist workers in, 24; as state of emergency zone in 1990s, 66

Devrimovans, 41, 136; as political actors, 29–30; stigmatization of, 47–48

Dikeç, Mustafa, 33–34, 81

dirty alliance (*kirli ittifak*), 109, 161

disappearances, 8, 20, 61–62, 113

Discipline and Punish (Foucault), 118

discrimination, 22, 104, 133–34

disorder (*kargaşa*), 145, 158–61

dissensus, 28–52, 156

dissent, 60–61, 146, 151; against AKP, 138–39, 140; policing as management of, 5, 27; ruling elites intervening in political, 156–57; sectarian, 81

dissident groups, 10, 113; defamation of, 48–49; ruling elites of Turkey compared with violence of, 94; stigmatization of, 39, 159

dissident neighborhoods (*muhalif mahalleler*), 4

dissociation, of population within politics, 160

distribution of the sensible, 15, 22, 25, 47, 52–53, 58, 110, 112, 129, 156–57

docility, 11–12, 129, 158–59; refusal of, 26, 120, 130

Doğru Yol Partisi. *See* True Path Party

Douglas, Mary, 98–99

drug dealing, 22, 26, 97–99, 102, 103; gangs and, 144

Duran, Bayram, 75

Durkheim, Émile, 121

Elvan, Berkin, 142

endocolonization, 4, 65

Erbay, Yeliz, 31f, 87f

Erdoğan, Recep Tayyip, 20, 146

Ergenekon Trials, 19–20

ethnography, 41; culture-centric warfare and, 24; in Devrimova, 19–22; of policing compared with politics, 15

ethnosectarian enclaves, 25–26, 71, 73, 82, 85, 112–13, 149–50, 154, 156; of Gazi, 76–77; racialization and, 158–59; violent interpellation strengthening, 88

extended battlefield techniques, 94–95

fascism, 49, 122–23

Fassin, Didier, 78–79

Fatsa, 29, 44

fatwas, 148–49

FBI. *See* Federal Bureau of Investigation

fear, 131; defensive counterviolence and, 88–89; of persecution, 160–61;

provocation of, as counterinsurgency strategy, 147

fearlessness, 91, 125, 131, 134–35

Federal Bureau of Investigation (FBI), 39, 94

Feldman, Allen, 19, 50–51

Feldman, Ilana, 7, 91

foreign forces (*dış mihraklar*), 139–40

Foucault, Michel, 7, 11, 54, 118, 135–36; on ethical self-formation, 120; on Iran, 119–20; on permanent obligation of justice, 120; on political spirituality, 137; on spirituality, 121

framing, 74–77

Freedom and Solidarity Party (ÖDP), 55

Galula, David, 7, 10, 92

gangs, 48; counter, 50, 85, 92; drug dealing and, 144; masculinity in vigilantism and, 106; police in mimetic relationship to, 110–11; violence, 103, 143–44, 147, 151–52; youth and, 104

Gangs and Counter-Gangs (Kitson), 50

Garner, Steve, 163n3

Garriot, William, 99

Gaza: counterviolence in, 95; as "hostile entity," 65; of Istanbul, 53–71

Gazi, 1, 4, 16–17, 64; ethnosectarian enclaves of, 76–77; Gezi uprising of 2013 and, 138–57; Kurds and Alevis in, 84–85, 93

Gazi Cemevi, 32f, 130

Gazi incidents of 1995, 25, 72–73, 74–75, 85, 87f, 121–22; aftermath of, 82–84, 86–88; ruling elites framing Alevis in, 86–87; self-defense needs of Gazi residents post-, 88; violence post-, 88–89; violent and negative interpellation in, 79–80

Gazi Investigation Committee, 76

gecekondu, 28, 29, 34, 35, 67, 135

Gedik, Hasan Ferit, 1–2, 17, 122, 144

gendered distribution of roles, 18, 37, 43, 106, 137

gender relations, within NA, 105–6

Gezi Commune, 138–39

Gezi Park, 138, 139, 140

Gezi uprising of 2013, 1, 23, 27, 69, 74, 76, 115, 142, 147–50; Alevis blamed for, 146; gang violence in Gülsuyu, 143–44; Gazi and, 138–57; Kurdish liberation movement in, 149; police and, 2–3; police violence in Okmeydanı, 141–45, 148; revolutionaries brought together by, 151–52; solidarity during, 155–56

Gezmiş, Deniz, 31

ghost, 16, 120–21, 127

Girard, René, 109–10
Girling, Evi, 98–99
Gladio, 6
Gökçek, İbrahim, 130
Göktepe, Metin, 138
Goldstein, Donna, 99
Gordon, Avery, 16, 120, 122
Graham, Stephen, 54
The Gray Wolves (Bozkurtlar), 49
Grup Özgürlük Türküsü (band), 69
Grup Yorum (band), 56, 130
guerrillas, 10–11, 59–60, 128–29
Gülsuyu, 1, 4, 151–54; gang violence in, 143–44; police violence in, 142–45
Gündem (newspaper), 170n23
Güreş, Doğan, 73–74, 93

Hage, Ghassan, 78
La Haine (movie), 133–34
Halkın Emek Partisi. See People's Labor Party
Han, Clara, 135–36
Harcourt, Bernard, 13
Hasan Ferit Gedik Rehabilitation Center, 16–17
haunting, 26, 33, 120–22, 135, 137, 149
hemşehri (hometown) associations, 84–85
How the Steel Was Tempered, And Quiet Flows the Don (Ostrovsky), 23, 104
Huggins, Martha, 164n13
Human Rights Association (IHD, İnsan Hakları Derneği), 66
Human Rights Foundation of Turkey (Türkiye İnsan Hakları Vakfı), 18, 69
hunger strikes, 57, 130
Hüseyin, Inan, 31
Huseyn, Imam, 31

immortals (ölümsüzler), 121–22, 152
imperious interpellation, 78–79
imprisonment, 107, 149–50
informants, 39–40, 92, 118–19, 129, 136
injustice, 60–64
Inönü, Erdal, 56
Inönü, Ismet, 56
Insan Hakları Derneği. See Human Rights Association
inspirational hauntings, 26, 116–37
internal enemies, counterinsurgency strategies and, 6
International Freedom Battalion, 152
interpellation, 84; imperious, 78–79; negative, 78–79, 84; violent, 77–82, 86–87, 88
Introduction to Strategy (Beaufre), 94–95

IRA. See Irish Republican Army
Iran, Foucault on, 119–20
Iranian Revolution, 119–20
Irish Republican Army (IRA), 48, 91–92, 95
The Iron Heel (London), 23
Isbell, Billie Jean, 21
Islam, 8–9, 30
Islamist groups, 38, 75–76, 83–84
Islamist Hezbollah, 93
Israel, 11–12, 65

justice: community, 96–115; extralegal, 96; Foucault on permanent obligation of, 120; outsourcing, 112
Justice and Development Party (AKP), 1, 19–20, 27, 102, 155; counterinsurgency strategies of, 113–14; dissent against, 138–39, 140; loss of power of, 141; transformation of working-class neighborhoods, 142–43

Kadıköy, 57, 151
kahvehane (coffeehouses for men), 83, 84–85, 100–102
Karandinos, George, 103
Karbala massacre, 30–31
Kavak, Gülay, 134
Kaymaz, Uğur, 127
Kaypakkaya, Ibrahim, 128–29
Kazan, PKK guerrillas in, 128–29
KESK. See Confederation of Public Employees' Trade Union
Khalili, Laleh, 13
Kilcullen, David, 146
Kitson, Frank, 3, 50, 85, 91–92
Kizilbash, 163n2
Kobanê, 122, 144, 175n11
Kocadağ, Hasan, 75
Koma Civakên Kurdistan. See Kurdistan Communities Union (KCK)
Kontrgerilla (Akyol), 168n18, 168n28
Kozakçıoğlu, Hayri, 66–67, 75
Küçük Armutlu, 1
Kurdish and Alevi "openings" (Kürt ve Alevi açılımı), 113
Kurdish liberation movement, 5–6, 9, 20, 52, 54, 56, 71, 84, 108, 144, 149, 159, 165n21, 169n7, 175n2; and anticolonial struggle, 5, 164n8; in Gezi uprising of 2013, 149
Kurdish opening (Kürt açılımı), 20
Kurdistan Communities Union (KCK), trials of, 108–9

Kurdistan Workers' Party (PKK), 5–6, 9, 11,
    55, 58, 60–61, 76, 95, 141, 149; blamed for
    Gazi incidents of 1995, 86; counterinsur-
    gency against, 110; growth of, 71; guerrillas
    in Kazan, 128–29; psychological warfare
    against, 92
Kurds, 8, 16–18; accused of dividing class
    struggle, 110–11; Alevis and, 84–85, 93,
    149–50; Alevis and, in Devrimova, 84–85, 93;
    colonial power relations between Turks and
    Kurds, 169n11; in Devrimova, 56–57;
    discrimination of Alevis and, 22, 133–34;
    displacement of, 99; marginalization of,
    156–57; massacres of, 164n16; racialization
    of, 4, 26, 95, 135–36, 160; racialized
    hierarchies between Turks and Kurds, 165n21
Kurtuluş (newspaper), 84
Kwon, Heonik, 121

Laurence, Ralph, 24, 167n41
lawfare, 20, 108–9
leftist revival, 25, 54–58, 66, 71
left-wing groups, 39, 70–71
liberated zones, 48–51
Liebknecht, Karl, 122–23
Loader, Ian, 98–99
Lomnitz-Adler, Claudio, 174n5
low-intensity conflict, 91–95, 97, 113, 158
low-intensity conflict doctrine, 71, 73, 91,
    156–57
Low-Intensity Conflict in Turkey and the PKK
    (Özdağ), 71
Low-Intensity Operations (Kitson), 50
"Low-Intensity Warfare in the Year 2000,"
    73–74
Luxemburg, Rosa, 122–23

mahalle derneği. See Neighborhood
    Association
mahalleli (Devrimova residents), 38, 52,
    79–80, 90, 133–34
Malatya, 49
Malaya, 56, 146, 170n22
Maraş, 49
Mardin, xi, 130
marginalization: of Alevis and Kurds, 156–57;
    of Dev-Sol, 91; masculinity and, 132–33
martyrs, 26, 125, 133, 135, 142; affective power
    of, 17–18, 26; memorials of, 130; as spirit,
    16–18, 120–22; working-class and, 131
martyrs of revolution (*devrim şehitleri*),
    121–22
Marx, Gary, 39, 94, 136

Marxism, 28, 112
Marxist, 55, 126, 128, 169n7, 171n7; move-
    ment, 28; PKK's, 93, 164n8; principle, 38
Marxist-Leninist Communist Party (MLKP),
    2f, 58
Masco, Joseph, 12
masculinity, 104; in gangs and vigilantism,
    106; marginalization and, 132–33; rage,
    revenge, and, 130–37; in revolutionary
    groups, 90–91; in working-class, 93–94
May Day, 35, 43, 57, 88, 91, 95; demonstrations
    of 1980s, 59; demonstrations of 1990s, 60,
    61, 64
Mbembé, Achille, 11, 65
media-driven political interference, 3, 145–48
Mehmed I (Sultan), 122
militarization, 51–52, 53–71, 54
militarized spatial control, 4, 53, 67, 69, 75
military vehicles, ix, 3, 21, 35, 53, 61, 65–71,
    89–91, 107, 111
Milliyetçi Hareket Partisi. See National Action
    Party
mimesis, 96–115, 155–56
mimetic policing, 96, 110
missing persons, 170n22
MLKP. *See* Marxist-Leninist Communist
    Party
mobilization, left-wing, 8, 28, 53, 70–71
Molotov cocktail, 2–3, 90, 131, 132f
muhtar (neighborhood head), 52, 83
Mumcu, Uğur, 165n18, 168n22
music, left-wing bands, 56, 69, 130

NA. *See* Neighborhood Association
National Action Party (MHP), 165n18
nationalism, 7–8, 38, 63, 82
Nationalist Action Party (*Milliyetçi Hareket
    Partisi*), 49
Nationalist Movement Party, 51–52
National Security Council, 51
NATO. *See* North Atlantic Treaty
    Organization
Navaro-Yashin, Yael, 17–18, 125
negative interpellation, 78, 84
Neighborhood Association (NA), 96, 100–102,
    103, 104, 116, 127; drug dealing within,
    106–7; gender relations within, 105–6;
    imprisonment of members of, 107, 149–50;
    solidarity created by, 112–13; vigilantism
    and, 109, 112
neoliberalism, 54, 97–98, 142–43
1970s, 42–44, 90
1980s, 8–9, 40, 51, 53, 54–58, 59, 60–64, 98

1989 Spring Actions (*Bahar Eylemleri*), 54
1990s, 56, 90, 98; counterinsurgency of, 159; Devrimova in, 53, 57–58, 61–63, 66–71; Dev-Sol assassinations in, 59–60; left-wing revival in Turkey of, 57–58; May Day demonstrations of, 64
North Atlantic Treaty Organization (NATO), 10, 13, 24, 74–75, 92, 118–19, 130; stay-behind forces of, 8; in Turkey, 6
Northern Ireland, 19, 48, 95; British counterinsurgency in, 26, 85; working-class of, 92
Northern Kurdistan, 56, 61, 75, 90–91, 122, 141; counterinsurgency techniques exported from, 65–66; as an internal colony, 54, 165n21, 175n2; Istanbul compared to, 54; low-intensity conflict in, 93

Ocak, Hasan, 79–80, 85–87, 87f, 90–91, 121, 134, 149–50
Ocak, Maside, 85–86
OHAL emergency region, 65–67, 71
Okmeydanı, 4, 16–17, 60, 141–45
Okmeydanı Cemevi, 148
Ördekci, Mahmut Murat, 138
Örentepe, 67–68
Ostrovskiy, Nikolay, 23, 104
Öter, Şirin, 2f, 31f, 87f
Ottoman Empire, 3, 32, 148–49
Özarslan, Günay, 132f
Özel Harp Dairesi. *See* Special Warfare Department
Özgürlük ve Dayanışma Partisi. *See* Freedom and Solidarity Party

PAGAD. *See* People against Gangsterism and Drugs
Palestine, 57, 95, 118, 174n5
paramilitary groups, 10–11, 49, 60, 165n18, 168n28; Islamist, 50; in Northern Ireland, 50, 85, 92; in Northern Kurdistan, 56, 93
Paris, 81, 134
partitioning, 14, 27, 29, 85
Partiya Karkerên Kurdistan. *See* Kurdistan Workers' Party
Peace and Democracy Party (BDP), 108, 144
People against Gangsterism and Drugs (PAGAD), 48
People's committees (*halk komiteleri*), 86; Feminist politics and, 42–44; sanctuary spaces, dissensus, and, 28–52; self-governance and, 36–40; vigilantism and legacy of, 100–102

people's courts (*halk mahkemesi*), 29–30; of Alevis, 40–42; in Devrimova, 44–46; Feminist politics and, 42–44
People's Democracy Party (Halkın Demokrasi Partisi, HDP), 9, 60, 156, 159
People's Labor Party (HEP), 55, 56
People's Liberation Party-Front of Turkey, 17f
Pir Sultan Abdal Culture Association (Pir Sultan Abdal Kültür Derneği, 63–64
Pir Sultan Abdal Festival, 122
pogroms, 49, 164n16
police, 3f, 24, 78, 99, 141; in Devrimova, 49, 65–66, 67–71, 101, 105, 129; gang violence and, 110–11, 147; Gezi uprising and, 2–3; militarization of, in Turkey, 51–52; operation against NA, 127; politics compared with, 13–15, 29–30; revolutionaries targeted by, 69–70; undercover, 26, 114–15, 128; vigilante as, 100; violence of, 139, 142–45
policing, 7, 14, 29, 78, 135–36, 158–61; of Alevis, 12, 139; colonialism and, 91; community-oriented, 117–18; ethnography and, 15, 19; as management of dissent, 5, 27; Rancière on, 108, 112
political actors, 29–30, 34
political Islam, 8, 63
political spirituality, 135–36, 137
politics, 158–59, 160; agents provocateurs and, 85–88; counterinsurgency as war on, 13–15, 161; Feminist, 42–44; police compared with, 13–15, 29–30; possibility of, 28–52
population, 3–4, 6–9, 158–59, 160
poverty, 98, 104, 135–36. *See also* urban poor
Proletarian Nights (Rancière), 34, 46
the proletariat, 124; Arendt on, 33–34, 47; Rancière on, 33–34, 46–48
provocative counterorganization strategies, 10–11, 12–13, 25, 71–73, 75–76, 78–92, 94–95, 156; affect- and emotion-generating, 74, 77, 93, 110; ruling elites using, 158; use of antiterror laws, 97
psychological warfare, 12, 39, 40, 71, 92

racialization, 7, 12, 22, 41, 84, 113; of Alevis, 3–4, 26, 76–77, 81–82, 95, 135–36, 160; ethnosectarian enclaves and, 158–59; of Kurds, 4, 26, 95, 135–36, 160; subjectivation and, 78–79; of urban poor, 24, 145; of working-class, 14–15, 134
racism, 7–8, 135–36, 139–40
Rancière, Jacques, 13–15, 25, 29–30, 46–47, 49, 85, 114, 137, 157; on dissensus, 34; on

policing, 108, 112; on the proletariat, 33–34; on state security apparatus, 160

RAND Corporation, 18, 48, 73

Rapid Action Forces, 51–52

refusal, 22, 68, 126, 134; of docility and complicity, 26, 120, 130; ethnographic, 24; of fear, 126, 136

resistance, 16–18; solidarity and, 136, 138–57; spirits of, 116–37; within subjectivity, 134–35. *See also* Alevi cultural archive of oppression and resistance

revolutionaries, 29, 114, 134, 149; Alevis as, 30–33; Gezi uprising of 2013 bringing together, 151–52; in Istanbul, 56–57; masculinity and, 90–91; privileged compared with proletariat, 46–47; student, 37–38; violence of, 110–11; working-class women as, 42–44

Revolutionary Left (Dev-Sol), 55, 56, 84; appeal of, 58–60; assassinations of, 59–60; cortege in May Day demonstrations of 1996, 61; marginalization of, 91; popularity of, among urban poor, 64; on revolutionary violence, 88–89

revolutionary militia, 152, 155f

revolutionary neighborhoods (*devrimci mahalleler*), 4

revolutionary organizations, 16–18, 53, 59–60, 88

Revolutionary People's Liberation Party Front (DHKP-C), 17f, 48

revolutionary violence, 88–91, 151, 153–54

Rojava, 129, 152, 163n1

Salem, Sara, 121

sanctuary space, 28–52

Schmitt, Carl, 11

School of Americas, 168n19

sectarian imaginary, 147–50, 156–57

self-defense, 88, 151, 152–54

self-formation, ethical, 17–18, 26, 120, 135–36, 137

self-governance: people's committees and, 36–40; revolutionaries of Turkey using, 29; terrorism compared with, 48

Selim, Yavuz Sultan, 146

Selod, Saher, 163n3

senses of governance, 17–18

shootings, in Alevi community, 72–73

Sibel Yalçın Park, 16–17

Silivri Prison, 102

Singh, Bhagat, 129

Sivas massacre, 64, 80, 122

Skidmore, Monique, 118

Sluka, Jeff, 22

Social Democratic Populist Party (SHP), 56

Socialist Party of the Oppressed (Ezilenlerin Sosyalist Partisi), 159

Socialist Power Party (SİP), 55

Socialist Youth Associations Federation (SGDF), 144

Sökefeld, Martin, 81

solidarity, 98, 104; disruption of, 115; during Gezi uprising of 2013, 155–56; NA creating, 112–13; resistance, the Great Divide, and, 138–57; resistance and, in Devrimovans, 136; spirits of resistance and, 125–27; undercover police, resistance, and spirits of, 116–37

Solmaz, Edip, 29

Sönmez, Fikri, 29

Sosyal Demokrat Halkçı Parti. *See* Social Democratic Populist Party

Sosyalist Gençlik Dernekleri Federasyonu. *See* Socialist Youth Associations Federation

Sosyalist İktidar Partisi. *See* Socialist Party of the Oppressed

South Africa, 48, 94, 100, 131

Soviet-style council, 41

space and security, 11–13, 65

spaces of intervention, 9, 26–27

Sparks, Richard, 98–99

spatial counterinsurgency techniques, 25, 53–54, 65

spatialization of conflict, 50

Special Air Service, 51–52

Special Operations Unit, 51–52

Special Warfare Department (ÖHD), 10–11, 39, 94

speech, action, 154–57

spirit: spirit of solidarity, resistance, and, 116–37

the state, 35–36; Alevi-Sunni conflict provoked by, 150; Althusser on subjectivation and, 77–78; violence initiated and backed by, 151, 159–60

state security apparatus, 5, 24, 35, 65, 93, 95; antiterror sting operations of, 114; crime connected to, 99–100; Rancière on, 160; spatial control of neighborhood by, 105

state-subject, 35–36

Steenkamp, Chrissie, 151

stigmatization: of Alevis and Kurds in Cold War, 4; of Devrimovans, 47–48; of dissident groups, 39, 113, 159; of the racialized urban poor, 24; of working-class youth, 98

strikes: in the 1970s, 54; in the 1990s, 54
Student Coordination (Öğrenci Koordinasyonu), 54–55
student movement, 59–60
subaltern counterpublics, 14–15, 47
subjectivation, 134–35; Althusser on the state
and, 77–78; racialization and, 78–79
Sunni-Turkish, 7–8, 20, 28, 44; Alevis
polarizing, 76; working-class, 58, 63
Suruç bombing, 122, 123, 144
surveillance: Foucault on panoptic, 118; police
and, in Devrimova, 105; in Syria, 118;
undercover, 21, 105, 112, 114, 117–19, 125; in
the US, 118
Syria, 118, 144

Taksim Square, 57, 138, 140–41, 145
Tercüman (newspaper), 48–49
terrorism, 129–30; accusations of, 67, 73, 96,
107–9, 116, 118; punishment for convicted,
108–9; self-governance compared with, 48
TKP/ML. See Communist Party of Turkey /
Marxist-Leninist
trade unions, 59–60
the Troubles, 50
Trouillet, Michel-Rolph, 19
True Path Party (DYP), 60, 61–62
Trump, Donald, 144
Tuğal, Cihan, 163
Turhan, Talat, 39–40
Türkeş, Alparslan, 49
Turkey, 1, 3–4, 22, 25, 39, 94; counterinsurgency of Turkish state, 61; extralegal
right-wing groups in, 114; fascism in, 49;
within global drug trade, 98; left-wing
mobilization in, 8, 28, 53; militarization of
police in, 51–52; NATO in, 6; neoliberalism
in, 97–98; 1990s left-wing revival in, 57–58;
racism in, 7–8; revolutionaries in, 53, 114;
state security apparatus of, 93; supremacism
and nationalism in, 7–8
Turkish National Assembly, 18, 39–40, 159
Turkish National Assembly's Gazi Investigation Committee, 76
Turkish National Intelligence Agency, 59
Turkish National Police, 117–18
Turkishness contract, 165n21
Türkiye İşçi Köylü Kurtuluş Ordusu. See
Workers and Peasant Liberation Army of
Turkey
2000s: Devrimova in, 100–102, 117; revolutionary working-class youth of Turkey
in, 114

undercover police, 26, 105, 112, 114–15,
117–19, 125. See also police
United States, 39–40, 100
University Students' Platform (Üniversite
Öğrenciler Platformu), 54–55
urban margins, 29, 54, 64, 71
urban poor, 70–71; criminalization of, 103–4;
lack of police security for, 99; racialization
of, 24, 145; Revolutionary Left popularity
among, 64
US Army/Marine Corps Counterinsurgency
Field Manual, 146

Veli, Haci Bektashi, 32f
vigilante, 5, 100, 114; revolutionary groups,
4, 88
vigilantism, 26, 56; armed, 111–12; good and
bad, 96–115; legacy of people's committees
and, 100–102; masked and armed, 109–12;
NA withdrawing from, 109; women
approach to, 106; among working-class
Alevis, 100–102; of youth, 96–97, 109,
110–12
village guard system, 61, 165, 170n22
violence, 2–3, 24, 50, 54, 74, 109–11, 131;
Feldman, A., on contained and permitted,
50–51; gang, 103, 143–44, 147, 151–52;
post-Gazi incidents of 1995, 88–89;
revolutionary, 88–91, 151, 153–54; ruling
elites of Turkey compared with dissident,
94; sectarian imaginary and fear of past,
82–85; state, 60–64, 91, 151, 155–56,
159–60; in working-class neighborhoods,
142–45
violent interpellations, 77–82, 86–87; Arendt
on, 148; ethnosectarian enclaves strengthened by, 88
violent stability, 114–15

War on Politics, 13, 108, 114, 158, 161
War on Terror, 12, 158
We Are Not Men Initiative, 106
Weizman, Eyal, 11–12, 65
Western Kurdistan, 152
Workers and Peasant Liberation Army of
Turkey, Party (TİKKO), 56
working-class, 22–23, 28, 48–51, 88; Alevis, 27,
64, 129, 139–40; communist politics among
Alevi, 25; intensification of violence in,
neighborhoods, 142–45; masculinity in,
93–94; of Northern Ireland, 92; in Paris,
134; racialization of, 14–15, 134; revolution-
ary youth of Turkey in late 2000s, 114;

Sunni-Turkish, 58, 63; upper-middle-class compared with, 1–2; vigilantism among Alevis of, 100–102; youth and drugs, 98
world-building practice, 25, 33, 112

Yalçın, Sibel, 60, 64
Yazid (Caliph), 30–31, 83, 84
Yeter, Süleyman, 86
youth, 3f, 15; gangs and, 104; imprisonment of activist, 107–9; involvement in crime, 103–4; Kurdish, 20, 107, 111, 113, 117, 154; revolutionary, 4, 13, 46, 89–91, 94, 110, 114, 119, 135, 154–56, 161; revolutionary violence and, 89–91; vigilantism of, 96–97, 109, 110–12; working-class, 98, 114
Yüksekdağ, Figen, 9, 159

Zapatista National Liberation Army, 17f
Zeytinburnu, 98
Zilberg, Elena, 109–10

CPSIA information can be obtained
at www.ICGtesting.com
Printed in the USA
LVHW031540280222
712222LV00008B/1412